THE LETTERS OF ABELARD AND HELOISE

PETER ABELARD was a French scholastic philosopher and the greatest logician of the twelfth century. He taught mainly in Paris where his fame attracted students from all over Europe and laid the foundations of the University of Paris. Heloise was his pupil, and after the tragic end of their love affair and marriage she became a nun, and Abelard a monk in the Abbey of St Denis. He continued to teach theology, but his unorthodoxy led to open conflict with St Bernard of Clairvaux and his condemnation by the Church. His last months were spent under the protection of Peter the Venerable, and he died in a Cluniac priory. Heloise became abbess of the convent of the Paraclete which Abelard founded, and was acclaimed for her learning and administrative capability.

BETTY RADICE read classics at Oxford, then married and, in the intervals of bringing up a family, tutored in classics, philosophy and English. She became joint editor of the Penguin Classics in 1964. As well as editing the translation of Livy's *The War with Hannibal* she translated Livy's *Rome and Italy*, the Latin comedies of Terence, Pliny's *Letters* and Erasmus's *Praise of Folly*, and has also written the Introduction to Horace's *The Complete Odes and Epodes* and *Propertius: The Poems*, all for the Penguin Classics. She has also edited and introduced Edward Gibbon's *Memoirs of My Life* for the Penguin English Library. She has edited and annotated her translation of the younger Pliny's works for the Loeb Library of Classics, and translated from Italian, Renaissance Latin and Greek for the Officina Bodoni of Verona. She was collaborating as a translator in the Collected Works of Erasmus in preparation by the University of Toronto, editing an eight-volume production of Gibbon's *Decline and Fall of the Roman Empire* for the Folio Society, and was the author of the Penguin reference book *Who's Who in the Ancient World*. Betty Radice was an honorary fellow of St Hilda's College, Oxford, and a Vice-President of the Classical Association. She died in 1985.

The Letters of Abelard and Heloise

. . . .

TRANSLATED

WITH AN INTRODUCTION

BY BETTY RADICE

PENGUIN BOOKS

PENGUIN BOOKS

Published by the Penguin Group
Penguin Books Ltd, 27 Wrights Lane, London W8 5TZ, England
Penguin Books USA Inc., 375 Hudson Street, New York, New York 10014, USA
Penguin Books Australia Ltd, Ringwood, Victoria, Australia
Penguin Books Canada Ltd, 10 Alcorn Avenue, Toronto, Ontario, Canada M4V 3B2
Penguin Books (NZ) Ltd, 182–190 Wairau Road, Auckland 10, New Zealand

Penguin Books Ltd, Registered Offices: Harmondsworth, Middlesex, England

Published in Penguin Books 1974
19 20 18

Printed in England by Clays Ltd, St Ives plc
Set in Monotype Garamond

Contents

TWO HYMNS BY ABELARD

MAPS

Acknowledgements

My grateful thanks are due to the many scholars, past and present, whose published works I have made use of and listed in the bibliography, and to the Librarian and staff of the London Library who let me keep these books on loan for so long; to the late E. V. Rieu for entrusting me with the translation some years ago, and to friends and members of my family who have taken an interest in it, amongst them Elizabeth Stephenson for deftly typing much of the script and helping with proofs; and above all to those who have given me generous expert advice, Professor Lewis Thorpe, Professor David Luscombe, and Sister Benedicta Ward, S.L.G., whose experience and enthusiasm have given me necessary encouragement as her acute practical criticism has been a pleasure to receive. The remaining mistakes must lie where I did not ask for the further help I needed.

Highgate
February 1973

BETTY RADICE

Introduction

Most people have heard of Abelard and Heloise as a pair of lovers as famous as Dante and Beatrice or Romeo and Juliet, and many know that their story is told in the letters they exchanged. If we are interested in what is generally called the Twelfth-Century Renaissance we soon find that Abelard is a key figure, one of the most original minds of his day, that the medieval university of Paris arose out of his fame as a teacher, and that his theological views brought him into conflict with St Bernard of Clairvaux. Heloise too was more than a girl deeply in love and a pupil avid for learning; she was the widely respected abbess of a famous convent and its daughter foundations. The two are representative of the best of their time in their classical knowledge and the way they express themselves, in their passionate interest in problems of faith and morality, and in their devotion to the Christian Church which ruled their lives. At the same time their dilemma is of timeless interest, created less by circumstances than by the relations between two highly complex personalities.

Peter Abelard was born into the minor Breton nobility in 1079, and his career to the age of about fifty-four is set out in a remarkable piece of autobiographical writing, the *Historia calamitatum* or *Story of His Misfortunes*. His father served the Count of Brittany and wished his sons to have some education before following the same career. Abelard soon decided to renounce his rights as the eldest son and to become a real scholar. 'I preferred the weapons of dialectic to all the other teachings of philosophy, and armed with these I chose the conflicts of disputation instead of the trophies of war. I began to travel about in several provinces, disputing like a true peripatetic philosopher wherever I had heard there was keen interest in the art of dialectic.' (p. 58)

Abelard is writing rather formally in Latin and using semi-technical expressions which would be more readily understood by his contemporaries than they are today, but these two sentences take us straight into the intellectual ferment of the early twelfth century and the revolution in teaching in which Abelard played a leading part. The accepted course for higher education at this time (and for a long time to come) was that of the seven liberal arts: the *trivium*, consisting of grammar and rhetoric, which were the study of classical (Latin) language and literature, and logic, or dialectic as it was called, followed by the *quadrivium*, the sciences of geometry, arithmetic, astronomy and music. Beyond these lay the highest studies of theology, canon law and medicine. Abelard never shows much interest in science, and his knowledge of mathematics was elementary. He evidently decided at the start to concentrate on the *trivium* and, in particular, on logic (dialectic). The Greeks had been masters of logic, but at this time there was very little knowledge of their work. Abelard is not thought to have known any Greek, and what he knew of Aristotle was mainly from Porphyry's Introduction to Aristotle's *Categories* and Aristotle's *De Interpretatione*, both in a Latin translation by the sixth-century Roman scholar Boethius. Logic covered both linguistic logic, or theory of meaning of words and sentences, and formal logic, the theory of the correct manner to systemize known facts and to draw conclusions. It was 'an instrument of order in a chaotic world',[1] and in Abelard's hands it could provide a genuine intellectual education for his students. His unwavering determination to apply the rules of logic to all fields of thought was to dominate his life.

Secondly, Abelard speaks of himself as moving from place to place wherever he heard that there was the teaching he wanted. This is the period of the 'wandering scholars'. All teaching was in the hands of the Church, in some form, but the Cathedral schools were becoming more prominent and beginning to replace the monastic schools such as those of Bec and Cluny; out of them would develop the medieval universities. Abelard's movements and his own career show

1. R. W. Southern, *The Making of the Middle Ages*, p. 172. See further his chapter 'The Tradition of Thought'.

that in these early days a teacher could set up a school of his own wherever he knew he could muster sufficient pupils, and the success or failure of a school rested on the teacher's popularity and skill. His own pupils sought him out wherever he settled, and were even prepared to camp out in the remote countryside to be near him. One tends today to think of logic as something dry and scholastic, perhaps by contrast with renaissance humanism, but Abelard can make it sound new and invigorating, the opening of a door on to wider horizons.

Abelard also speaks of himself as 'disputing', and here again he shows himself in the vanguard of a new movement. By *disputatio* is meant a new technique to replace the traditional *lectio*, a lecture by a teacher on a selected passage of Scripture which was read aloud sentence by sentence and then expounded by glosses on the grammar and commentaries on the meaning drawn from the writings of the early Fathers of the Church. Disputation adopted a more conversational method, posing a problem and discussing it by means of question and answer, by setting out the difficulties and attempting to resolve conflicts. One method of teaching should not exclude the other, but Abelard was never anything but impatient with the orthodox lecture – witness his unjustified attack on Anselm of Laon (p. 62). He must have been a thorn in his teachers' flesh, conscious as he was of his own intellectual superiority, no respecter of persons and revelling in the cut-and-thrust of debate. So William of Champeaux found when Abelard arrived in Paris about 1100 and joined the Cloister School of Notre Dame. Tension increased until Abelard set up his own school, first at Melun, then at Corbeil, with the intention of destroying William's reputation. There was a respite when his health broke down through overwork, and he spent about six years in Brittany. How he spent the time he does not say, but he returned to the fray to find that William had joined the Order of Canons Regular, but was still teaching at the Abbey of St Victor. Abelard started to attend his lectures again, this time on the subject of rhetoric, and soon made his position impossible.

The *Historia calamitatum* then raises the question of universals, or general and abstract terms. It had been discussed by Plato and Aristotle, and mentioned though not fully examined by Porphyry, and it was now hotly debated. If you and I and all of us are human, i.e. we belong to the human species, does anything exist which is humanity independent of the individuals who belong to the species? Abelard never says which teachers he sought out when he was a wandering scholar, but he must surely have stopped at Loches on his way to Paris to hear Jean Roscelin, the chief exponent of Nominalism. Roscelin held that universals or abstract terms were no more than names given to the individuals which alone existed. This was seen by the Church as endangering the doctrine of Unity in the Trinity, because Roscelin was thought to postulate three individual Gods and not one God. He had been tried for heresy and banished, but later allowed to return to France and resume his teaching. William of Champeaux headed the opposite faction, that known as Realism. Following Plato and the Neoplatonist Porphyry, the Realists believed in the actual existence outside awareness of abstract ideas – Plato's Forms or Ideas. Abelard is brief to the point of obscurity about what happened, but he seems to have forced William to modify his view by pointing out the absurdities of its logical development. William had taught that the essence of humanity was totally and essentially present in all human beings who are differentiated only by 'accidents' or local modifications outside their common nature. If this is so, it is hard to see how you and I can be genuinely different individuals. Under pressure from Abelard William modified 'essentially' to 'indifferently', meaning that you and I are united in the human species by non-difference or absence of difference. But William's lectures then fell into disrepute 'as if the whole subject rested solely on the question of universals'.

For Abelard logic meant more than the nature of universals and also something rather different. He distinguished clearly (as William and many of his contemporaries did not) between logic and physic or metaphysic, the one concerned with *words* and how we express concepts in words, the other with *things* (physic) or the ultimate reality (metaphysic). Logic for him was linguistic logic, an essential discipline for understanding, and the problem of universals was only one element in it. His was a critical approach to the meaning of words and concepts as the basis of rational understanding. He was not trying to develop a philosophy of nature nor a system of theology. But the Realists did not draw the same distinction between things which exist outside our awareness and the expression in words of our understanding of them, so that for them the nature of universals was crucial.

Abelard's triumph over William greatly increased his reputation, and a good many of William's pupils joined the rival school he set up on Mont Ste Geneviève, from which the university of Paris was to grow. There was continued friction between the students as William did his best to prevent Abelard from succeeding him as head of the Cloister School. Once again Abelard was summoned to Brittany, this time to see his mother, who was preparing to take vows and follow her husband into the religious life – a normal procedure at this time. He was not away long, and returned to find that William was now installed as bishop of Châlons and there was no rival for the headship of the Cloister School. Yet Abelard says that he returned to France for the express purpose of studying theology – *maxime ut de divinitate addiscerem* – and left Paris at once for Laon, where he could hear Anselm, who had long been established there as the greatest teacher. He gives no reason; some have wondered if it was his mother's request that her brilliant eldest son should turn to more constructive thoughts of salvation. But in a *Story of His Misfortunes* this was a decision which was to have lasting and serious consequences.

Anselm's reputation was deserved, both as a lecturer and part-compiler of the *Glossa ordinaria* or *Ordinary Gloss* on the Bible, a standard work for theological students for a long time. His teaching was conservative, dogma was discussed entirely within the biblical framework, and he made no use of disputation; his wonderful eloquence was confined to lecture and exposition. As a trained dialectician and one who valued ability more highly than seniority, Abelard had little use for him, and soon made this clear. He fell out with the other students and was easily provoked into offering to produce an exposition himself by the light of his natural intelligence and a close study of the text. He soon showed that he could beat Anselm at his own game and, to the indignation of the students, Anselm was incited by his two leading pupils to forbid Abelard to teach in Laon. Abelard then returned to Paris to be head of the Cloister School, presumably taking many of the students from Laon with him. To his fame for dialectic and rhetoric he could now add a growing reputation for theology, and Anselm's death soon afterwards left him supreme. Paris gained students from all over the civilized world.

Abelard was then in his mid thirties, at the peak of his powers. All accounts agree that he was a wonderful teacher, with a rare gift for kindling enthusiasm in his pupils and inspiring their devotion. He tells us himself that he had 'exceptional good looks', and Heloise adds that he had a talent for verse and song, though there is no mention of his enjoying the lighter side of student life as a young man but rather the suggestion that he kept himself aloof (p. 66). He had established himself as a logician by offering his own solution to the problem of universals, the middle way which was to be known as Conceptualism: universals were neither realities nor mere names but the concepts formed by the intellect when abstracting the similarities between perceived individual things. It is remarkable that Abelard arrived independently at a solution much like that of Aristotle, in which we have perception of the particular and we know the universal, but we know it through the particular and perceive the particular in the universal. But he was already running personal risks as a professional dialectician who was now concerning himself with theology. The two pupils of Anselm, Alberic of Rheims and Lotulf of Lombardy, were his enemies from now on, and led the prosecution of Abelard for heresy at the Council of Soissons in 1121. This was not forgotten, and the final fateful clash between Abelard and St Bernard arose largely out of Abelard's application of dialectic to questions of theology.

By temperament Abelard was stimulated by controversy and one can imagine him bored by finding himself at the top without a rival. As he says (p. 65), 'But success always puffs up fools with pride, and worldly security weakens the spirit's resolution and easily destroys it through carnal temptations. I began to think myself the only philosopher in the world, with nothing to fear from anyone, and so I yielded to the lusts of the flesh ... There was in Paris at the time a young girl named Heloise, the niece of one of the canons ...'

Abelard relates the opening stages of the story as a calculated seduction on his part, confident as he was of easy success, and there is never anything romantic or idealistic about his attitude to sexual love. To do him justice, he may have chosen this cool tone deliberately because the *Historia calamitatum* was written as a letter addressed to a third party, and omitted the painfully intimate details which emerge in his subsequent letters to Heloise (p. 146 and p. 147). But however the relationship started, he was soon totally involved. Many years later Heloise accused him of feeling only lust for her, not love, and he admitted this. Several of her modern champions have emphasized that he could never attain the heights of her selfless devotion. But in the modern idiom, they were passionately in love, their lovemaking was uninhibited and ecstatic, and Abelard was completely carried away and consequently quite reckless in his general behaviour. He neglected his pupils, abandoned all pretence of serious teaching, paid no attention to gossip, and allowed his love songs which mentioned Heloise's name to be sung in public. When her uncle accepted the truth of what was common knowledge and tried to separate them, they took even greater risks and were found in bed together. Soon after, Heloise found she was pregnant and Abelard removed her to his people in Brittany where a son was born.[1] From a later letter

1. A lingering recollection of Heloise in Brittany has possibly left its trace in Breton folk-lore. *Barzaz-Breiz, Chants populaires de la Bretagne,*

(p. 146) we know that he disguised her as a nun. Abelard returned to Paris and offered amends to Fulbert: he would marry Heloise so long as the marriage was kept secret so that his reputation did not suffer. Fulbert agreed, and Abelard returned to Brittany to fetch Heloise. It is at this point that she reveals her personality in an unexpected way.

Nothing at all is known of Heloise's parentage, though much has been conjectured.[1] She is thought to have been about seventeen at this time and born in 1100 or 1101. Fulbert's possessiveness has suggested to some that she was really his daughter, but taken with his brutal treatment of Abelard it would seem to have a strong sexual element, probably subconscious. Every credit is due to the nuns at Argenteuil for her early education, and to Fulbert for his encouragement of her remarkable gifts at a time when women were rarely educated at all. During the short time she was studying with Abelard they probably worked on philosophy; it was certainly a trained logical mind which argued so cogently against the marriage he proposed.

Heloise saw clearly, as Abelard would not, that a *secret* marriage was not going to satisfy Fulbert for a public scandal and, indeed, 'that no satisfaction could ever appease her uncle'. She therefore opposed any form of marriage, first because of the risk to Abelard, secondly because it would disgrace them both. Both have a low view of marriage, derived from St Paul and St Jerome; they see it from the Christian monastic standpoint as no more than legalization

---

recueillis et publiés aveo une traduction française by Th. Hersart de la Villemarque (1839) is often quoted. In this Heloise says she followed 'mon clerc, mon bien cher Abailard' to Nantes at the age of twelve, knowing only Breton, but now she knows Latin and French as well and has magical powers, so that she and Abelard between them could turn the world upside down. Some of the French text is printed in M. Jouhandeau, *Lettres d'Héloïse et Abélard*, pp. 244–5, and is translated in Enid McLeod, *Héloïse*, pp. 55–6. De la Villemarque said that he found twenty versions in four Breton dialects and believed that the poem incorporated earlier Druidical magical songs, but the authenticity of its details has often been questioned.

1. McLeod, op. cit., p. 8 ff. and notes.

of the weakness of the flesh. As a scholar Abelard was a clerk (*clericus*), and as *magister scholarum* of Notre Dame he would be a member of the Chapter and a canon. Neither was a legal bar to marriage; though a married *magister* might be unusual, one feels that his personality could have made the situation acceptable. It is not known whether he was a priest in orders at this time: probably not. In any case, the Church forbade marriage only to the higher orders of the clergy. It is important to remember that there was no career open to an educated man at this time except in the Church, and that Abelard was prepared to sacrifice his ambitions for high office in order to secure Heloise for himself. He admits in a later letter (p. 149) that 'I desired to keep you whom I loved beyond measure for myself alone.' Any marriage, open or secret, would be an effective bar. An open marriage would damage his reputation but might, just possibly, appease Fulbert, though Heloise who knew him well thought not. A secret marriage would not be damaging but would be dangerous in its effects on Fulbert.

All the authorities are now agreed that the question of reputation is crucial to Heloise's arguments and refers to something much deeper than self-interest on Abelard's part. If her arguments are read closely it is clear that she was much less concerned with the possible loss of Abelard's services to the Church than with the betrayal of the ideal which they both admired, that of the philosopher as a man who is set apart and above human ties. She argues from a classical rather than a Christian viewpoint, and she takes her illustrations from Theophrastus, Cicero, Seneca, and Socrates as recorded by St Jerome. 'The great philosophers of the past have despised the world, not renouncing it so much as escaping from it, and have denied themselves every pleasure so as to find peace in the arms of philosophy alone.' (p. 72) She points out the distractions and petty hindrances of domestic life which are inimical to philosophic contemplation, and compares the philosophers with 'those who truly deserve the name of monks', that is, the dedicated solitaries such as John the Baptist or the ascetic sects of Jewish history. She concludes

(Abelard says) that 'the name of mistress instead of wife would be dearer to her and more honourable for me', because then they would both be free from a permanent legal tie and Abelard would not incur the disgrace of renouncing the realization of his true self as a philosopher. They should be bound only by *gratia* – love freely given; marriage can add nothing of significance to an ideal relationship which is also classical in concept: that described in Cicero's *De amicitia*, a work they both knew, which sets the standard for true friendship in 'disinterested love' where physical love would be sublimated.

Heloise amplifies this point in her first letter (p. 114), in the well-known passage where she says that if the Emperor Augustus offered marriage she would still choose to be Abelard's whore; she says this in the context of preferring 'love to wedlock and freedom to chains'. She has loved Abelard only for himself, not for anything he could give her, and indeed, in her view, marriage for what either party could get from the other was no better than prostitution. By contrast, a lasting relationship should rest on the complete devotion of two persons; this is true disinterested love, based on what she calls 'chastity of spirit'. To such an ideal union a legal marriage could add nothing, and the presence or absence of an erotic element is, in a sense, irrelevant. The intention towards the ideal relationship is all-important. This is the 'ethic of pure intention' in which both Abelard and Heloise believed and to which she often returns. 'Wholly guilty though I am, I am also, as you know, wholly innocent. It is not the deed but the intention of the doer which makes the crime, and justice should weigh not what was done but the spirit in which it is done. What my intention towards you has always been, you alone who have known it can judge.' (p. 115–16)

For Heloise the issue was clear and unequivocal, however difficult it is for us to follow her. Conventional morality would speak of a young woman who is willing to 'live in sin' with a man, so as not to stand in his path, as sacrificing herself, but for her living wholly for Abelard is self-realization.

Abelard was torn by an impossible conflict between his desire for Heloise and all the jealous possessiveness which went with it, and his belief that his duty was to realize himself as a philosopher and to preserve his intention towards that ideal. It has been pointed out[1] that the quotations used by Heloise all appear in a work of his own (Book II of his *Theologia Christiana*) written after they parted but several years before the *Historia*. It certainly seems likely that he filled in the outlines of her arguments with references to chapter and verse when he wrote his account for circulation. But there is no suggestion that he did not accept their validity; he simply refused to be persuaded. Perhaps it was too much to expect of an ardent lover and a proud and hypersensitive man. 'But at last she saw that her attempts to persuade or dissuade me were making no impression on my foolish obstinacy, and she could not bear to offend me; so amidst deep sighs and tears she ended in these words: "We shall both be destroyed. All that is left us is suffering as great as our love has been." In this, as the whole world knows, she showed herself a true prophet.' (p. 74)

Heloise never reproaches Abelard for the *secrecy* of the marriage, which to her must have seemed an act of hypocrisy and another betrayal of the ideal. She was even ready to lie on Abelard's behalf and deny it when Fulbert broke his promise and spread the news. Years later, however, in a bitter moment she pointed out the irony of the fact that they had been spared when guilty of fornication but punished 'through a marriage which you believed had made amends for all previous wrong-doing' (p. 130). There were furtive meetings followed by scenes with Fulbert, which made Abelard decide to remove her from her uncle's house. The convent at Argenteuil where she had spent her childhood was the obvious place to take her, and it was near enough Paris for further meetings to be fairly easy. We know that Abelard could not keep away; he argues in one of his letters (p. 146) that they were more justly punished for their conduct when married than for anything they did before, because of their sacrilege

1. J. T. Muckle, *Mediaeval Studies*, Vol. XII, pp. 173–4.

in making love in a corner of the convent refectory, the only place where they could snatch a moment together alone. What he had in mind when he made her wear a postulant's habit no one can know, unless it was to give greater protection from Fulbert, but it was a disastrous thing to do. She could have stayed indefinitely with the nuns without it, and Fulbert very naturally assumed that Abelard was trying to get rid of her by making her a nun. This was the immediate cause of his horrible revenge: his servants broke into Abelard's room at night and castrated him.

Long afterwards Abelard could write of this to Heloise with hindsight as an act of God's mercy which rid him of his personal dilemma along with the torments of the flesh. But in the *Historia* what he vividly recalls is the pain and horror, his urge to escape and hide from the noisy sympathy of the crowds outside and the outcry of his pupils pushing into his room, his feelings of humiliation and disgust at being a eunuch, the unclean beast of Jewish law. He admits that 'it was shame and confusion in my remorse and misery rather than any devout wish for conversion which brought me to seek shelter in a monastery cloister' (p. 76).

His entry into the Abbey of St Denis must have been hurried on quickly (and the period of novitiate entirely waived), for Abelard says that his wound was scarcely healed when the clerks were clamouring for him to continue his teaching from the cloister. He accepted the challenge, by far the best thing he could have done, for teaching took him out of the retirement which was unsuited to his temperament and enabled him to get back into the company where he was happiest – that of eager, questioning young minds. He emerged from the crisis still the perfectionist, the uncompromising challenger of beliefs and practices which he judged to fall short of truth and honesty, and now single-minded in his purpose. And whatever his original motives were for entering the religious life, there is no reason to doubt that his subsequent conversion was completely sincere. In his way Abelard was as firm an upholder of the faith and the purity of monastic life as St Bernard, and to the end of his days he spoke out against the shortcomings of the Church wherever he detected them. He remained a dedicated humanist and scholar, seeing that he could use his knowledge of Greek philosophy to lead his pupils on to the 'true philosophy', as the great Origen had done (p. 77). There was a general interest amongst twelfth-century scholars in Origen's works through Latin translations, and Abelard had a close personal feeling for Origen, also a eunuch, though self-inflicted. He draws the comparison explicitly in a letter to Heloise (p. 148). Abelard's continued interest in Greek philosophy was one of the charges against him by St Bernard, who said that Abelard proved himself a pagan by attempting to turn Plato into a Christian.

The *Historia calamitatum* is a faithful record of his life between his entry into St Denis in 1119 and its circulation sometime after 1132. It is not necessary here to recapitulate in detail all his tribulations: quarrels with the unreformed monks of St Denis, persecution by his old rivals and enemies leading to his condemnation at the Council of Soissons in 1121, further trouble at St Denis and his flight to Champagne, retirement to a hermitage near Troyes to which his students followed him and built the oratory he named the Paraclete. He was certainly greatly helped and sustained by the devotion of these young people, and by the knowledge that his gifts as a teacher were unimpaired by calamity and what he saw as the jealousy of his contemporaries, but he is so vague when writing about his continued dangers and apprehensions of further charges of heresy that one wonders if he was developing a persecution complex. There must have been some foundation for his fears; at one point he seriously considered abandoning Christendom to seek refuge among the Saracens (p. 94). Instead he accepted an invitation in 1126 to be abbot of the remote monastery of St Gildas de Rhuys on the west coast of Brittany.

This time he could hardly have made a worse decision. The monks were not only idle and dissolute but murderous in intent when he tried to reform them, and he felt himself isolated amongst illiterate savages. 'I used to weep as I thought what a useless life I led, as profitless to myself as to others; I had once done so much for the clerks, and now all I did for them and for the monks was equally fruitless. I had proved ineffective in all my attempts and undertakings, so that now above all men I justly merited the reproach "There is the man who started to build and could not finish".' (p. 96) He was tormented especially by the thought that the oratory of the Paraclete was deserted and neglected. It was not until 1128 that he heard that Adam Suger, who had become abbot of St Denis in 1122 and was engaged in active and necessary reforms, had found documents establishing the abbey's claim to the convent of Argenteuil, and had expelled the nuns. Heloise was already prioress, and this is the first mention of her since she took her vows some nine years before.

She had taken them at his command and with no sense of vocation, as Abelard very well knew. She had had about eighteen months with him, and was nineteen when she renounced any hope of further life outside the convent walls. Abelard says that she had refused to listen to those 'who in pity for her youth had tried to dissuade her from submitting to the yoke of monastic rule as a penance too hard to bear'; she had wept, and quoted from Lucan, a Stoic Roman poet whose works they both knew, Cornelia's last words before her suicide after the death of her husband Pompey. 'So saying she hurried (*properat*) to the altar, quickly took up (*confestim tulit* – almost 'snatched') the veil blessed by the bishop and publicly bound herself to the religious life.' (p. 76) Her mood was not one of Christian hope but of tragic despair. Abelard says nothing about her admission being as hurried and irregular as his own, and records only the bare fact that she took her vows before he did. From her letters we learn that this hurt and offended her more than anything, and the memory still rankled for years. Had he been afraid that she would turn back, like Lot's wife? She saw it as a sign of mistrust, though he knew that she would have followed him to the gates of Hell (p. 117). She may have guessed – and rightly – that jealous possessiveness prompted Abelard in this as in the secret marriage.

It is only from references in her letters that we know anything at all about her life as a nun at Argenteuil, and these are painful reading. Abelard was a changed man, physically and spiritually; she was not changed, she felt no vocation for convent life, and was tormented by frustrated sexual love. 'The pleasures of lovers which we shared have been too sweet – they can never displease me, and scarcely be banished from my thoughts. Wherever I turn they are always there before my eyes, bringing with them awakened longings and fantasies which will not even let me sleep ...' (p. 133) Any meetings they had had after his mutilation to arrange her hurried reception into the convent had been impersonal, and very probably in the presence of the nuns. In her first letter she reproaches him for giving her no sympathy nor support in person or by letter. Yet though she evidently did not pretend to herself that love of God had supplanted love of Abelard, her good brains and strong character must have saved her from going to pieces. She would have social standing as the niece of a canon, but she would not have been chosen to be prioress of the convent unless her outward behaviour had been scrupulously correct. The prioress stood second to the abbess and had many responsibilities, one being the education of the nuns, novices, and children brought up in the convent as Heloise had been herself.

Abelard writes defensively, in answer to her reproach, that he had not thought it necessary to write a letter of advice or sympathy, knowing her good sense (*prudentia*): 'God's grace has bestowed on you all essentials to enable you to instruct the erring, comfort the weak and encourage the fainthearted, both by word and example, as, indeed, you have been doing since you first held the office of prioress under your abbess.' (p. 119) It is arguable that Heloise was already prioress as early as 1123, though this is no more than a supposition based on a contemporary document, the obituary roll of the Blessed Vital, abbot and founder of the monastery of Savigny in the diocese of Avranches, who died in 1122. It was a monastic custom when a Church dignitary or benefactor died to inscribe the news of his death and a eulogy of his life on a parchment roll which a monk would then take round the monastic houses. Each of these would inscribe its full title and promises to pray for the departed, often with a request for similar prayers for members of its own community. The roll of the Blessed Vital contains the names of two hundred and seven religious houses in France and England, that of Ste Marie of Argenteuil being the fortieth. Beneath the title on the left is a Latin poem, while the conventional formulae for prayers are rather squeezed in on the right. There are other poems on the roll, four of them by convents of nuns, but this is written in correct Latin elegiacs (though the sentiments are not original in any way), and the handwriting is clear and well formed. It has therefore been supposed that this is the work and the writing of Heloise herself, and she would not have been entrusted with it had she not already been prioress.[1]

Abelard travelled from St Gildas to make arrangements to hand over the Paraclete to Heloise and some of the dispossessed nuns who stayed together, and there they met after a separation of ten years. Abbot Suger had made no provision at all for the nuns, and the *Historia* records briefly that at first they suffered great hardship. The buildings could not have been more than the small church of wood or stone which the students had built to replace Abelard's original chapel and the primitive cells they had occupied, and the women were dependent on what they could get out of the stream and the fields, helped out by gifts from the neighbourhood, which were generous when their plight was known. In 1131 Pope Innocent the Second visited Auxerre and granted a charter to the abbess Heloise confirming the nuns' possession of the gifts they had received and any subsequent gifts in perpetuity.[2] There were further meetings, all on an impersonal basis as the letters show, for the *Historia* records that at first

1. See further McLeod, op. cit., pp. 86 ff., and frontispiece to *Héloïse*.
2. The original document is in the Bibliothèque of Châlons-sur-Marne; the text is printed in Cousin, *Petri Abaelardi Opera*, Vol. I, pp. 719–20.

local opinion criticized Abelard for not doing enough for the nuns, and then when he visited them more often, there was malicious gossip about his former relations with Heloise and the fact that he still seemed unable to keep away from her. It seems likely that he was absent from St Gildas for some time, for he had installed them in the Paraclete in 1129 and we know that on 20 January 1131, during Innocent the Second's progress through France, Abelard was present at a large gathering in the Benedictine abbey of Morigny, near Etampes, where the pope consecrated the high altar. He had gone to ask for a papal legate to be sent to St Gildas for its reform (p. 104); there for the first time he met St Bernard. The journey between St Gildas and the Paraclete was some 360 miles and would take ten to fourteen days, so he would hardly have travelled to and fro. He had indeed cherished hopes of finding a haven of peace with the sisters, but the last pages of the *Historia* show that he is back at St Gildas, feeling himself an outcast and a wanderer like Cain, that he is recovering from a painful fracture after a fall from his horse, and has narrowly escaped from attempts to murder him by poison and ambush, and sees no prospect of any improvement in his position.

The *Historia calamitatum* was evidently written in 1132 or soon after, and Heloise says in her first letter that by chance someone brought it to her. If it was a genuine, personal letter of consolation to an unnamed friend and fellow-monk, as Abelard says, one wonders why it went further than him. It seems more probable that Abelard intended it for circulation (there may have been more than one copy) in order to win sympathy for his predicament and to pave the way for release from St Gildas so that he could return to his true vocation of teaching. He was still remembered for this; in the account of his meeting with Bernard he is described as 'monk and abbot and so himself of the monastic order, the most distinguished master of the school to which flocked the scholars of almost all the Latin world'.[1] It is known that he left St Gildas with his bishop's consent and the right to retain his rank of abbot, and that he was teaching in Paris in 1136 at Mont Ste Gene-

1. The Chronicle of Morigny; P.L. 212, 1035.

viève when John of Salisbury heard him lecture on dialectic, though he left Paris before John did.[1] Perhaps this was only temporary; there are no other dates or indications of his whereabouts until 1140 (the Council of Sens), but it is probable that most of the time he was in or near Paris and teaching, for this is the period of his greatest mental activity and output.

A first impression of the *Historia* can be that it is written by a self-centred though not insensitive man, whose youthful years were ruled by self-assertion, pride and ambition. On reflection one sees it more as an attempt to put on record, from a detached standpoint, the facts of a life which the writer believed had often been misjudged and was now at risk. It has also been said that 'the writing of this letter became the act of catharsis that turned what might have been merely an apology into a true self-revelation'. In this sense the *Historia* is a search for identity and a personal autobiography comparable with those of St Augustine, Cellini, St Teresa and Rousseau.[2]

Heloise's reactions in her first letter are dismay at the recital of his misfortunes, the details of which are unlikely to have reached her before, and horror at the idea of his life being in danger at St Gildas. She then points out that if he can write a long letter of consolation to a 'friend', he can also write to advise and encourage the community at the Paraclete, as is his duty as their founder. He is wasting himself on monks such as he describes, but would find her nuns receptive. He can also write to *her*, to whom he has a personal obligation. For twelve years or more she has brooded over his apparent indifference in never giving her a word of recognition for the sacrifice she made in entering monastic life. He knows very well that she did it only for love of him, but his neglect has

1. John of Salisbury, *Metalogicon*, 2.10; P.L. 199, 867. The date is precisely given as the year after the death of King Henry I of England. John of Salisbury had learned all he could from Abelard and was disappointed by Abelard's premature departure; he then had to move on to Alberic of Rheims.

2. Mary M. McLaughlin, 'Abelard as Autobiographer: the Motives and Meaning of his *Story of Calamities*', *Speculum*, Vol. XLII (1967), pp. 463–88.

forced her to the conclusion that what he had felt for her was no more than lust and, when physical desire had gone, any warmth of affection had gone with it. She virtually demands a letter of explanation from him as her right.

Abelard defends himself on the charge of negligence: he had not supposed that after their joint conversion Heloise had need of him. Could he really have thought that? No one can be sure, but it cannot be dismissed as simple wishful thinking. Disgust with his mutilated person may have made him want to shut the past out of his mind; he was changed, and knowing she was prioress and now abbess he may have been all too ready to believe that she was changed too. And his own conversion had, at some point, been sincere and permanent, so that he was now dedicated to God. The tone of his letter is set by the superscription: he writes as abbot to abbess. If the community is anxious for his safety, he says, they should remember the power of prayer, and she must know that the sacrament of marriage which binds them as well as 'the integrity of our faith ... and our profession of the same religious life' increases the effectiveness of her own prayers. I think one should not see this as a selfish refusal to be drawn on Abelard's part, but more as an attempt to put their relationship on a different basis because he knew this was in her best interests. But he certainly does not allow himself to enter imaginatively into Heloise's plight, and this prompts her to be more explicit.

She now writes urgently of her sexual frustration and inability to forget their happiness as lovers. She puts her dilemma clearly: she took vows not for love of God but for love of Abelard. Taking vows meant that she ought to be a nun in the true sense, and that her life should be ruled by love of God, but how was that possible when she loved him alone? She is perpetually conscious of being a hypocrite, for when the world admires her piety it sees only her outward behaviour and this means nothing to her; the intention is all, and her intention is lacking. She looks for reward only from Abelard, and he has denied it to her. She can hope for nothing from God for she has denied him, and she cannot repent. 'How can it be called repentance for sins, however great the mortification of the flesh, if the mind still retains the will to sin and is on fire with its old desires?' She implores his help in resolving an intolerable situation.

This is a terrible picture of a soul in agony and of total human love which has brought only suffering. It is painful to contemplate how such intensity of feeling had been stoically concealed from the outside world for years of a young woman's life. It is characteristic of Heloise that she never compromises, and never wavers from the moral view she shared with Abelard, that of the ethic of intention.[1] Her keen intellect can analyse herself and her problem clearly, but the feeling behind the words is passionate and painful. This letter jolts Abelard out of any suspected complacency. He replies at length, especially on the point of 'your old perpetual complaint against God concerning the manner of our entry into religious life and the cruelty of the act of treachery performed on me' (p. 137). The epithets (repeated later) imply that he had heard it before; the only time could have been when they met between his mutilation and her taking the veil. He sounds irritated by her raking it all up again, but perhaps that is reading too much into his words. He will not recall the past with nostalgia, as she does, but at least he shows he has not forgotten. He reminds her of certain events – their mockery of God when she dressed as a nun to go to Brittany, their overwhelming desire which led them to make love during the season of the Passion or in the refectory at Argenteuil – but he tries to make her see them as episodes which called for just punishment from God or, rather, for an act of God's mercy which freed them both from the flesh which can be only a barrier to divine love. He begs her to make a supreme effort to shake off bitterness and resentment and to think only of the love of Christ. 'It was he who truly loved you, not I. My love, which brought us both to sin, should be called lust, not love ... You say I suffered for you ... but he suffered truly for your salvation, on your behalf of his own free will ...' She must see herself as chosen to be the bride of Christ, and

1. Letter I, note 2, p. 115.

know that by surmounting her bodily suffering she can win the martyr's crown which can never be his, for where there is no battle there is no victory. All the time he is trying to make her see the whole story of their relationship from its start until their entry into religion from the Christian monastic point of view, knowing that they were at least agreed in believing that chastity was something higher than wedlock. The letter ends with a prayer that though parted on earth they may be forever united in heaven.

Heloise replies with great dignity, and the first paragraph of her letter marks the turning point of the correspondence. She will not argue nor trouble him further with heart-searchings; she now asks only for his help in occupying her mind with more constructive thoughts. We are never to know if she was able to achieve a change of heart and reorientation of herself towards God. Time the healer would make the physical severance from Abelard less acutely felt, and one hopes that she found compensation in her service to the Paraclete. Perhaps later on she came to feel that this was a true form of devotion to God and more than outward works under a cloak of hypocritical piety – as everyone who has written about her has wanted to think. Meanwhile she asks on behalf of her community for information about the origin of the order of nuns and for advice on a Rule suitable for women.

Remembering what has gone before we can only admire Heloise's resolute self-control, and equally her intellectual and practical ability. She has lived under the Benedictine Rule for at least fourteen years, observing it, in a sense, from the outside. With her intelligence and erudition she is well equipped to offer criticism of what seems to her unsuitable if the Rule is to apply to women. She can appreciate that St Benedict was willing to temper his Rule to meet men's capacity to observe it, and suggests that women should not have too great demands made upon their physique. She also argues cogently that many details of observance can be categorized as outward 'works' and are unimportant in comparison with faith and spiritual intent. Accordingly she asks for guidance on questions such as manual labour, fasting, clothing and diet, as well as for suitable arrangements for the Divine Office and for the reading of the Gospel at night. The emphasis throughout is on reasonable demands, avoidance of extremes, and sincerity of intent; it is better to promise what one is capable of doing and then do more than to break down under impossible demands. She would have a longer novitiate, a deeper personal commitment, and a truly spiritual training; she wants a poorer and a simpler life – different perhaps from the one she had known at Argenteuil – for she sees that 'those who are true Christians are wholly occupied with the inner man ... but they have little or no concern for the outer man' (p. 174).

Abelard replies with two long treatises, one (summarized here on p. 180 ff.) to answer Heloise's question about the origin of religious communities of women, the other a detailed Rule for observance at the Paraclete. There is so little written about women's Orders that this is a document of intrinsic interest for convent life at this time, though it is not very well expressed nor logical in its arrangement, and despite its elaborate formal opening it breaks off with curious abruptness. It combines long passages of sermonizing and erudition with a down-to-earth approach to practical details; the nuns are to be sensibly dressed in underwear and habit which hangs clear of the dust, with a full change of clothing and necessary sanitary protection, to wear proper stockings and shoes and to have adequate bedding. Dirty hands and knives are not to be wiped on bread intended for the poor, to spare the tablecloths. There is to be no self-imposed fasting, no undue mortification of the flesh, and no cutting down of hours of sleep or the nuns will not be mentally alert for their prayers or studies. There is a characteristic emphasis on education; routine practical tasks are to be assigned to nuns with no aptitude for letters, but any nun with the ability to learn must be taught to read and write. As far as possible we should worship God with understanding, a statement which Abelard amplifies into an attack on current illiteracy in monasteries (p. 260 ff.).

This letter seems to be the basis for a later set of rules[1] which were preserved in a manuscript at the Paraclete and were intended for the use of a mother-foundation and its daughter houses; six of the latter were set up in Heloise's lifetime, and this rather later Rule has been thought to be by her, but it cannot be firmly dated. It differs from Abelard's recommendations in certain essentials and in a few less important points. There is no provision for the male superior ruling a double monastery such as he advocates (p. 210), but the abbess is to have authority over the monks and lay monks serving the convent, and the nuns are not strictly cloistered but may go outside the convent for necessary business. The blankets and pillows he specifies are not mentioned, and the nuns appear to sleep fully clothed instead of in their shifts as he wants; they may also eat pure wheat bread whereas he makes a point of one third of the flour being of coarse grain. These are minor modifications, but a great deal has been read into the words *in refectorio nostro cibi sine carnibus sunt legumina*... If they are translated as 'in our refectory our meals are vegetables without meat ...' this would accord with stricter monastic practice but directly contravene the founder's ruling (p. 246) that meat may be eaten three times a week and his expressed view that nothing except excess is forbidden. But if the words mean 'the meatless meals consist of vegetables' there is simply a reference to what Abelard goes on to say about the days when no meat is to be taken.

These long 'Letters of Direction', as they are often called, written in the rather stiff, formal style of contemporary scholarship, are also vital for an understanding of Abelard and Heloise. They provide the necessary depth of background to their relationship and show how this developed in the only way possible to them. In a sense Heloise has won her point; she has forced Abelard to look at her problem honestly and to renew contact with her, though not in the way she first hoped. Abelard has sincerely tried to show her that the only

1. The text of these is in P.L. 178, 313–26 and Cousin, Vol. I, pp. 213–24.

love which can now unite them is love of God, and that God has acted mercifully towards them, but he has had to learn something of what human love such as hers really means. She has agreed to try to put the past behind her, and from now on she has only to ask and Abelard will put all his learning and practical wisdom at the service of the Paraclete.

The texts are preserved of a good deal which subsequently passed between them. Abelard writes a long letter addressed to the nuns on the importance of study and even urges them to apply themselves to Hebrew. In this he twice refers to Heloise as having knowledge of Greek and Hebrew as well as Latin[1] – a surprising statement, as Abelard himself shows no knowledge of Hebrew apart from an occasional word and had little or no Greek, and though Peter the Venerable had admired her learning and gift for logic when he was a young man (p. 277), no one else has said she knew any Hebrew except the monk William Godel, writing in 1173 (p. 46). She probably had enough Greek for liturgical purposes. Heloise writes a short letter in which she addresses him as 'loved by many but most dearly loved by us' to accompany what are known as the 'Problems of Heloise': forty-two difficulties of interpretation in the Scriptures, to each of which Abelard gives carefully reasoned answers.[2] Her request for hymns for the use of the nuns is lost, but his answer accompanying the first batch he wrote gives the gist of it and shows how they now wrote to each other:[3]

At your urgent request, my sister Heloise, once dear to me in the world, now dearest in Christ, I have written what are called 'hymns' in Greek, 'tehillim' in Hebrew. When you and the sisters of your holy profession kept begging me to write these, I asked your purpose in doing so, for I thought it superfluous for me to compose new hymns when you had plenty of existing ones, and it seemed almost sacrilegious for new hymns by sinners to rank as

1. P.L. 178, 325–36; Cousin, Vol. I, pp. 225–36. With rhetorical understatement Abelard describes Heloise as 'not unfamiliar' (*non expers*) with Greek and Hebrew.

2. P.L. 178, 677–730; Cousin, Vol. I pp. 237–94.

3. P.L. 178, 1771–4; Cousin, Vol. I, pp. 296–8.

high or higher than the ancient hymns of the saints. I received several different answers, among them this reasoned argument of your own: We know, you said, that the Latin Church in general and the French Church in particular follows customary usage rather than authority as regards both psalms and hymns. We still do not know for certain who was the author of the translation of the Psalter which our own French Church uses. If we want to reach a decision on the basis of the words of the variant translations, we shall still be a long way from a universally accepted interpretation and, in my opinion, this will carry no weight of authority. Customary practice has so long prevailed that although we have St Jerome's corrected text for the rest of the Scriptures, the translation of the Psalter, which we use so much, is of doubtful authority. Moreover, the hymns we use now are in considerable confusion; they are never or rarely distinguished by titles or names of the authors, and even when they appear to have definite authors, of whom Hilary and Ambrose are considered the best, and next to them Prudentius and several others, the words are often so irregular in scansion that it is hardly possible to fit them to the music: and without this there is no hymn at all, according to the definition that it is 'praise of God with song'. You went on to say that several of the feasts had no hymns of their own, those of the Innocents and the Evangelists, for example, or those for saintly women who had been neither virgins nor martyrs, and there were also some feasts during which those who sang the hymns could not be truthful, either because these did not fit the occasion or because false material has been inserted ...

The letter continues with a detailed discussion of certain hymns, and ends: 'And so as you beg this of me, brides or handmaids of Christ, in my turn I beg you through your prayers to relieve my shoulders of the burden you laid on them, so that the sower and the reaper of this harvest may rejoice in their work together.'

There are 133 extant Latin hymns by Abelard, evidently sent to the Paraclete in three batches, the second two with short accompanying letters addressed to the whole community, as well as some fine verse Laments. The most famous of these are the Hymn for Saturday Vespers (*O quanta qualia sunt illa sabbata* – 'How mighty are the Sabbaths') and the Hymn for the Third Nocturn of Good Friday (*Solus ad victimam procedis, Domine* – 'Alone to sacrifice thou goest, Lord').[1]

Abelard also wrote thirty-four short sermons for the Paraclete, which were evidently sent with the following accompanying letter:[2]

I recently completed at your request a little book of hymns or sequences, Heloise my sister whom I love and revere in Christ, and then, as you asked me, hastened to write as best I could (for it is not the kind of writing I am used to) several short sermons for you and your spiritual daughters gathered together in our oratory. As I was concerned with the written rather than the spoken word, I concentrated on clarity of exposition, not eloquence of style, literal sense rather than elaborate rhetoric. And it may be that plain wording instead of rhetorical speech will be easier for simple minds to understand as being more direct; moreover, for the type of person who will be listening, the simplicity of ordinary speech will seem like elegant refinement and will have a pleasant taste suitable for girls of limited understanding. In writing or rather, arranging these, I have kept to the order of the feasts of the Church, beginning with the start of our redemption. Farewell in the Lord, you who are his handmaid, once dear to me in the world, now dearest in Christ, and in the profession of the religious life, my companion.

This shows a side of Abelard we have not seen before: considerate, self-effacing and patient with the young. What he offers the nuns here seems decidedly more practical than advice to study Hebrew and Greek.

It was also at Heloise's request that he wrote the *Hexameron*, a commentary on the six days of the Creation, and this too is now generally thought to have been written during the 1130s.

Whether Abelard ever visited the Paraclete again is not known, but as all his writings for the nuns are introduced by letters to Heloise, it seems probable that they did not meet again. Apart from the bare fact that John of Salisbury heard

1. No. 44 in G. M. Drèves, *Petri Abaelardi Peripatetici Palatini Hymnaris Paraclitensis*, Paris, 1891, p. 109; not in P.L. or Cousin. See p. 295 for Helen Waddell's translation (*Mediaeval Latin Lyrics*, pp. 175–9). For J. M. Neale's version of *O quanta qualia* see *The English Hymnal*, No. 465.

2. P. L. 178, 379–80; Cousin, Vol. I, p. 350. But at least one of the extant sermons (No. 11, on the Passion) is addressed to *fratres*.

him lecture in Paris in 1136, nothing is recorded of his movements until his confrontation with Bernard in 1140, but as he was attacked then mainly for the corrupting influence of his theological teaching, it sounds as though he was mainly with his students in Paris.

Bernard was born in 1090 and entered the Cistercian foundation of Cîteaux in 1112. In 1115 he was chosen to be abbot of the new foundation at Clairvaux, which by the end of his life in 1153 was famous throughout Europe, with sixty-eight daughter houses. Most monastic foundations hitherto had been based on the Rule of St Benedict of about 530, and the Cistercians preached 'The Rule to the last dot' (*Regula ad apicem literae*). But they also looked to the asceticism of the early Fathers of the Egyptian desert. Their return to the past was prompted by the desire to free themselves from the fetters of customary practice and an increasingly elaborate liturgy, in order to live a simpler life and thereby gain true spiritual freedom for meditation on the love of God. Many of the Benedictine houses at this time belonged to the congregation of Cluny, and from 1122 Cluny had its own outstanding leader in the person of Peter the Venerable. One of his most famous letters is addressed to Bernard[1] and is a reasoned defence of the Cluniac way of life and its interpretation of the Rule according to the spirit rather than the letter. But as Bernard permitted nothing either to the individual or to the community which could distract from the exacting demands of the Cistercian life, it follows that he was opposed to knowledge for its own sake and to any disinterested pursuit of learning, as a hindrance to the quest for perfection. Teaching in a Cistercian monastery was confined to its members, starting from the novitiate, and its purpose was salvation.

The clash between Abelard and Bernard was a *cause célèbre* of the twelfth century[2] and is in part an instance of the rivalry

1. No. 28 in Giles Constable, *The Letters of Peter the Venerable*. It was written about 1127.

2. For the issue between Abelard and Bernard, see chapters 6, 7 and 8 in Leif Grane's *Peter Abelard*; chapter 4 in D. E. Luscombe's *The School of Peter Abelard*; and A. V. Murray's *Abelard and St Bernard*.

between two opposing systems of teaching, the traditional monastic instruction in the cloister and the greater freedom of the Cathedral schools. It rests still more on the conflicting temperaments of the two men, and the tragedy is that they had certain things in common. Abelard no less than Bernard criticizes insincerity, corruption and worldliness in the Church. He is as uncompromising with the licence and prejudice he found at St Denis as with the flagrant immorality at St Gildas; he and Heloise exchange letters on precipitate entry into monastic life without proper preparation (p. 167), elaborate monastic building and luxurious living (p. 195), abbots who boast of the numbers in their care without being able to provide for them (p. 252), monks who leave their monasteries (p. 254), ignorance and illiteracy (p. 260), 'the empty chatter of idleness, to which we see present-day monastic cloisters much addicted' (p. 266), and the prevalence of works instead of faith: 'They clean the outside of the pot or dish but pay little heed to cleanliness inside ...' (p. 240) But as a logician he believed in the importance of clear thinking, and as a Benedictine he taught that knowledge and understanding served faith, not hindered it.

For Bernard the mystery of faith transcends human knowledge and can be gained only through mystic contemplation. He sees himself as a preacher with a sacred duty to proclaim revealed truth and to defend it and, for all his reforming zeal, he stands against Abelard as a champion of tradition. He sees Abelard as a danger to the faith of young people and simple men, and Abelard's attempt to *understand* the Trinity as an evil example of intellectual arrogance and an insult to Christian belief. So he can write that 'the mysteries of God are forced open, the deepest things bandied about in discussion without reverence'.[1] It is noticeable that he never asks for Abelard's writings to be examined and judged, only that a stop shall be put to the open discussion they stimulate on sacred subjects.

Abelard sees this as an unjustified personal attack similar to

1. Letter 238 in B. S. James, *The Letters of St Bernard of Clairvaux.*

those he suffered before. He maintains that he is defending Christian faith by making it as intelligible as possible. He always believes that the words of the sacred Scriptures and the testimony of the Fathers must be true, but we must examine the evidence we have (often in the form of corrupt texts and unreliable witnesses) to remove difficulties and contradictions. His famous *Sic et non* (*Yes and No*) had been written with this purpose in mind, though more than anything it had given a false and damaging picture of him as a sceptic. There he had selected and set out 158 problems where there are conflicting authorities; no synthesis is offered nor conclusion drawn – it is a teaching manual, designed for disputation on the question of the manuscripts being faulty or misunderstood, prompted by the belief that by stating propositions and their opposites we can provoke enquiry and arrive at understanding. He says in his preface that his aim is to sharpen the wits of his young readers and incite them to seek for the truth.

It would be equally wrong to suppose Abelard a rationalist in any but the twelfth-century sense of wishing to use his mastery of logic for the better understanding of his faith. He writes sadly in his 'Confession of Faith' (p. 270) that logic has made him hated by the world through misrepresentation, though 'I do not wish to be a philosopher if it means conflicting with Paul, nor to be an Aristotle if it cuts me off from Christ.' And he makes it plain in his philosophical works that he has no use for popular dialecticians who display their expertise on empty topics; properly used, dialectic has a moral basis and examines real problems, and it demands courage and honesty on the part of the user in giving way neither to authority nor to shallow cleverness in argument. But one can see how his scrupulous search for the proper terms in which to discuss theological problems could lay him open to misinterpretation and the charge of tampering with the content of faith.

The earliest reference to contact between Abelard and Bernard is a letter addressed to Bernard by Abelard after Bernard had visited the Paraclete soon after Heloise was installed and before Abelard went to St Gildas.[1] He writes that on a recent visit to the Paraclete Heloise had told him that Bernard had stayed there and had preached to the nuns 'like an angel'. However, she had also informed him privately (*secreto*) that Bernard had taken exception to their use of the Vulgate version of St Matthew, which refers to 'transubstantial' rather than 'daily' bread in the Lord's Prayer. The letter continues politely but firmly to defend Abelard's preference without yielding an inch. We do not know Bernard's reaction. The two men met at the gathering at the abbey of Morigny in 1131 (p. 25). Between 1132 and 1138 Bernard was travelling in France, Italy and Germany, preaching on behalf of Pope Innocent the Second, during the period of papal schism when many of the cardinals and important families in Italy recognized another claimant, Anacletus the Second. It was not until his rival died in 1138 that Innocent was able to live in Rome, and he must have left France deeply grateful for Bernard's campaigns to establish his legitimate claims. During this time Abelard was probably teaching, and certainly writing a great deal. After the burning of his book on the Trinity he started to rewrite and expand it in his *Theologia Christiana* and planned a comprehensive *Theologia* in three parts; both were frequently revised. He also wrote his *Ethica* or *Scito te ipsum* (*Know Yourself*), a Commentary on St Paul's Letter to the Romans, and the unfinished *Dialogue between a Philosopher, a Jew and a Christian*, as well as the hymns, sermons, answers to problems, and the *Hexameron* for the Paraclete.

At some date in 1139 a copy of Abelard's *Theologia* was read by William, the former abbot of St Thierry in the diocese of Rheims, who had resigned to join a remote Cistercian monastery at Signy in the Ardennes. He had known Abelard personally, perhaps when both had been students at Laon, and he was a close friend of Bernard. He was dismayed by what he read and by what he had heard of Abelard's teaching of 'new things' which would endanger the faith; he listed thirteen heretical points which he refuted, and sent the whole

1. P.L. 178, 335–40; Cousin, Vol. I, pp. 618–24.

statement to Bernard and to Bishop Geoffrey of Chartres, the papal legate in France at the time, who had supported Abelard at the Council of Soissons eighteen years previously. We do not know if the bishop replied, but Bernard acted at once.

According to Bernard's biographer, Geoffrey of Auxerre, and other contemporary witnesses, Bernard twice met Abelard and suggested that he should modify his views and restrain his pupils, but to no effect.[1] Bernard then approached first the bishop of Sens, and then the bishop of Paris to obtain permission to preach to the students. Abelard's reply seems to have been to bring out a fourth edition of his *Theologia*, unchanged in all essentials. Bernard then appealed to the Pope, enclosing his treatise against Abelard's heresies, and he also wrote to the cardinals at Rome. He links Abelard's name with the notorious Arnold of Brescia, and his violent abuse and intemperate language are startlingly disagreeable to an unprejudiced reader.[2] Abelard then asked Archbishop Henry of Sens to arrange for a meeting between himself and Bernard on the Sunday after Whitsun (3 June 1140), which should take the form of a public disputation on their disagreements. It was already to be a great occasion: the relics of the cathedral were to be shown to Louis VII and his court in the presence of the bishops and dignitaries of the diocese. Bernard at first

1. *Vita prima Bernardi*, III. 5.14; P.L. 185, 311.

2. See Letters 237–48, B. S. James, op. cit. Arnold was born in 1094 and was a Canon Regular of Brescia in north Italy from 1130. He was a tireless critic of abuses in the Church, and preached in particular that ecclesiastical property was wrongly held and should be transferred to secular authority. His views on Baptism and the Sacrament were held to be heretical, and he was banished from Italy in 1138; he came to France, where he may have been a pupil of Abelard. John of Salisbury (*Historia pontificalis*, M. Chibnall, ed. and trans., pp. 63–4) says that he allied himself against Bernard with Abelard and the Italian Hyacinth Boboni (later Pope Celestine the Third), and that after the Council of Sens he stayed for a while on Mont Ste Geneviève, preaching his anti-authoritarian views to any riff-raff who would listen. He returned to Italy on the death of Innocent the Second, but was arrested and hanged in 1155. Bernard's concern is to present Abelard as an equally dangerous anti-clerical agitator.

refused to attend, on the grounds that he was no match for a skilled dialectician and he disapproved of arguing about matters of faith. His friends persuaded him to change his mind, so he proceeded to lobby the bishops both by letter and by meeting them at Sens on 2 June, to explain what he intended to do and to enlist their support.[1] He also preached publicly to the people assembled in the town.

In a recently published letter[2] addressed to his friends and pupils which Abelard wrote at this time, he made it clear that he looked upon Bernard's attack as yet another instance of misunderstanding and malice, this time from a monk who was greatly his inferior in intellectual capacity and training. He neither shared Bernard's burning conviction that the purity of the faith was jeopardized, nor was he likely to accept that he was 'a man who does not know his own limitations, making void the virtue of the Cross by the cleverness of his words'.[3] He asked his friends to support him at the Council of Sens, and they must have been confident that Bernard would be defeated in the promised disputation.

Instead, there was no disputation, but something much more like a court of inquisition at which Bernard produced a list of Abelard's heresies which he read aloud and called upon Abelard to defend, renounce, or deny that they were his. Abelard refused to make any statement on the grounds that he wished to appeal direct to the Pope, and left the Council. There has been much speculation why he did this. He may have felt that this was going to be another Council of Soissons, and that he could not face it again, or that a large social occasion with people like the king and Count Theobald of Champagne present was no place for subtle theological exposi-

1. Berengar of Poitiers thought that Bernard had rigged the trial, and he was not the only one to think so. In 1148 Gilbert of Poitiers was also brought to trial for heresy by Bernard (at Rheims), but this time the cardinals objected to Bernard's circulating the charges at a meeting before the trial on the grounds that it was an unfair tactic similar to that used on Abelard. See John of Salisbury, *Historia pontificalis*, pp. 19–20.

2. See R. Klibansky, 'Peter Abailard and Bernard of Clairvaux: a Letter by Abailard' in *Mediaeval and Renaissance Studies*, Vol. V, 1961.

3. Bernard, Letter 241, B. S. James, op. cit.

tion and that no one would pay proper attention; this seems likely enough if we believe anything of the highly-coloured satirical account of the Council given by Abelard's pupil, Berengar of Poitiers, who says that the bishops were half asleep and drunk after a heavy meal, mumbling '*namus*' (we swim) instead of '*damnamus*' (we condemn).[1] It has also been suggested that Abelard had long suffered from a progressive disease, named as Hodgkin's Disease, that he had felt exhausted and ill at Sens but had remission afterwards at Cluny.

The Council condemned nineteen points in Bernard's statement as heretical, and Bernard sent off a letter describing the proceedings to the Pope. The archbishops of Sens and Rheims also wrote and Bernard wrote again to the cardinals.[2] Six weeks later, on 16 July, the Pope sent his rescript to the archbishops and to Bernard condemning Abelard as a heretic, excommunicating his followers, ordering his books to be burned, and himself to be confined in a monastery in perpetual silence.[3] The news reached Abelard at Cluny, where he had stopped on the long journey to Rome and stayed on at the invitation of Peter the Venerable. Immediately after the Council of Sens (or possibly just before it) he had written his 'Confession of Faith', addressed to Heloise, a document of great dignity and restraint, which was probably the last personal message she had from him (p. 270). If we accept an earlier dating, Peter the Venerable had already written to the Pope (p. 275) to report that he and the Abbot of Citeaux had mediated between Abelard and Bernard, that the two men had met and were reconciled, and his letter asking permission for Abelard to remain as a monk of Cluny must have crossed the Pope's rescript; the sentence was afterwards lifted.

Abelard died some eighteen months later, in April 1142; Peter the Venerable's letter to Heloise (p. 277) describing his

1. The text is in P.L. 178, 1854–70 and Cousin, Vol. II, pp. 771–86. For Berengar of Poitiers see D. E. Luscombe, *The School of Peter Abelard*, pp. 29 ff.

2. Letter 337 (Benedictine edition). The fact that the bishops' letter contains several of Bernard's abusive phrases and is included in his letter-collection suggests that he may have drafted it.

3. Benedictine edition, 194, P.L. 79, 515–17.

death in a daughter house of Cluny at St Marcel, near Chalon-sur-Saône, pays tribute to the simplicity and piety of his life and to his devotion to his studies, as far as his health permitted, right up to the end. It is uncertain if he actually wrote anything at Cluny and St Marcel. The long, rather platitudinous letter in verse giving advice to his son Astralabe is now generally dated to about 1135 rather than to this period, for the complete text[1] refers to 'the frequent complaint of our Heloise' (*nostrae Eloysae crebra querela*) that she can have no hope of salvation if she cannot repent of what she once did with Abelard, an echo of her second letter (p. 132). Abelard is not likely to have brought this up again some six years later. The *Dialogue between a Philosopher, a Jew and a Christian* and the *Hexameron*, which used to be considered late works, are now also ascribed to the mid thirties.[2] The short general *Confessio fidei universis* (not the one preserved by Berengar of Poitiers) which was Abelard's personal defence, must have been written soon after the Council of Sens, and an *Apologia* was planned but left unfinished – perhaps broken off when Abelard heard of the Pope's sentence.[3] There is no indication that he felt called upon to modify the theological views which he considered had been attacked in envy and ignorance, nor evidence that he put into writing the piety and humility to which Peter the Venerable testifies. He may well have been physically incapable of sustained creative effort.

Peter the Venerable is credited with a somewhat pedestrian verse epitaph which describes Abelard as 'The Socrates of the Gauls, Plato of the West, our Aristotle, prince of scholars . . ., the keen thinker and dialectician who won his greatest victory when he renounced all for the true philosophy of Christ.' One wonders what he had in mind in referring to Socrates – another opponent of self-deception and loose thinking who had been misrepresented as a corrupting influence on the

1. This is in J.-B. Hauréau, *Le Poème addressé par Abélard à son fils Astralabe*, Paris, 1895; see note, p. 287.

2. See D. E. Luscombe, *Peter Abelard's 'Ethics'*, pp. xxvii ff.

3. P.L. 178, 106–7; Cousin, Vol. II, pp. 772 and 719–23. For a different view, Giles Constable, *The Letters of Peter the Venerable*, Vol. II, p. 178.

minds of the young. Five anonymous epitaphs are also preserved, all of which emphasize Abelard's fame as a philosopher and scholar without reference to his chequered career as a teacher of theology.[1]

There remains an exchange of letters between Heloise and Peter the Venerable written sometime in 1144 (pp. 277 ff.), in which Heloise thanks Peter for visiting the Paraclete and bringing with him Abelard's body to rest in the care of the community he had founded. She asks him for a written absolution for Abelard to be hung over the tomb, and for help in getting her son Astralabe a benefice in one of the cathedrals. Peter sends the absolution along with a ratification of his verbal promise that Cluny will say thirty masses for Heloise after her death, and promises to do his best for Astralabe. This is the only time Heloise mentions him, and nothing definite is known about the young man who had played so small a part in his parents' lives.

Peter the Venerable died in 1156 or 7, but Heloise outlived Abelard by some twenty-one years; she is recorded in the necrology of the Paraclete as dying on 16 May in 1163 or 4. The romantics have liked to think that she died, like Abelard, at the age of sixty-three. In her competent hands the Paraclete grew to be one of the most distinguished religious houses in France. Six daughter houses were founded during her lifetime to receive the increasing numbers of postulants, and the Cartulary of the Paraclete in the Bibliothèque de Troyes (MS. 2284) lists twenty-nine documents which refer to the Paraclete when in her care, confirming privileges and registering deeds of gift. Eleven papal charters are among them; the one of Pope Eugenius of 1147 included arable land, meadows, woods, fish ponds, vineyards, farms, mills, tithes and money.[2] It is clear from Peter the Venerable's letter (p. 277)

1. P.L. 178, 103–4; Cousin, Vol. I, pp. 717–18. Peter the Venerable's epitaph is also quoted in full and translated in E. Hamilton, *Héloïse*, pp. 130–31.

2. Details in McLeod, op. cit., pp. 216–19; text in Cousin, Vol. I, pp. 719–26.

that Heloise was one of the Church's great abbesses, revered for her sanctity as well as for her learning.

It is impossible not to speculate about her inner thoughts and to wonder if she found her vocation, but of course there can be no answer. Human love such as hers does not end with separation or the death of the beloved, but it changes in quality as the physical pangs of severance are blunted; at least it seems unlikely that a woman of her character and common sense allowed herself the indulgence of brooding over the irrecoverable past. At a higher level one hopes that reconciliation with Abelard through their exchange of letters made it possible for her to love him on a different plane, as his 'sister in Christ'; at a lower level that her fine intelligence and administrative ability found full scope in what we should now call a rewarding career, and that with passage of time she achieved 'calm of mind, all passion spent'.

Heloise is recorded in the Paraclete's burial record as having been buried alongside Abelard in the abbey church, which was later known as the chapel of St Denis or the Petit Moustier ('Little Monastery'). This was the small oratory built by Abelard's students many years before, to replace the simple reed and thatch structure he had first set up. There is no record of her body having been put into Abelard's tomb. In 1497 the abbess of the time had the bodies moved from what was described as a damp and watery position and placed on either side of the high altar in the new oratory which had been built further away from the Ardusson. They were moved again in 1621 to a crypt below an altar on which stood a stone representing the Three Persons of the Trinity, which was believed to have been carved under Abelard's direction. In 1701 this stone was moved to a better position in the choir, and in 1780 the bodies moved again to a new position, still in the crypt. When the convent was sold at the time of the Revolution and the buildings demolished, apart from the residence of the abbess (the present Château, dating from 1685), the bones were taken to the church of St Laurent in Nogent-sur-Seine, and in 1800 to Paris, to Alexandre Lenoir's Musée des Monuments Français. They were later moved to the cemetery of Mont Louis, now Père Lachaise. There they are still, in a sarcophagus brought from St Marcel which Lenoir believed to have been Abelard's original tomb, beneath a Gothic-style structure and surrounded by modern iron railings, through which flowers are still sometimes placed beside their effigies by tourists who know something of their history, and by Parisians on All Souls' Day.

Text and Translation

There are relatively few tributes to Abelard after his death, either as theologian or philosopher. People would remember or hear of the events at Sens who knew little or nothing of Abelard's last months at Cluny, and Bernard's influence was strong enough for Abelard's name to be virtually erased even if his theological teaching continued in the Cathedral schools where Bernard's traditionalism was not acceptable. The analytical and critical methods of the *Sic et Non* influenced such famous theological manuals as Peter the Lombard's *Books of the Sentences*, and Abelard stands as one of the creators of open-minded thinking which led to the birth of the medieval universities, but as a logician he suffered from the discovery of Aristotle's scientific works within a decade of his death. Once Aristotle's solution to the nature of Universals was known, Abelard's formulation of Conceptualism, which was remarkably Aristotelean, was no longer read.

There are, however, manuscripts of his logical works and his *Apologia* which date back to the late twelfth and early thirteenth century, as well as references to his teaching.[1] The case of the letters is very different. The occasional references

1. 'The names of some twenty-one disciples and sometime pupils under Abelard are known. In addition some fourteen anonymous writers composed works of theology or of logic under Abelard's inspiration.' (Luscombe, *The School of Peter Abelard*, p. 14). There were doubtless more who are unknown, but his logical writings were not copied after the thirteenth century, and eighty manuscripts are known, as compared with some 1,500 of Bernard's. As a largely free-lance teacher Abelard left no school associated with his name, and what he wrote for the Paraclete was unlikely to be widely distributed.

we have to the lovers in the twelfth-century chroniclers are short and factual. William Godel, a monk of St Martin of Limoges, writing in 1173, says that Heloise or Helvisa was 'formerly Abelard's wife and truly his friend' and a religious and learned woman well versed in both Latin and Hebrew. The English ecclesiastic Walter Map (*c.* 1140–1209), author of that weird hotchpotch *Courtiers' Trifles* (*De nugis curialium*), is generally credited with a touching quatrain on the young bride's dismay when her husband leaves her for the monastery:

> The bride asks where is her Philosopher
> Whose every word by God was blessed.
> Why does he leave her like a stranger
> Though she had clasped and held him to her breast?[1]

One thirteenth-century manuscript of the Great Chronicle of Tours, attributed to a Canon of St Martin, in the entry for 1140 describes briefly (as the other MSS. do) how Abelard had built the Paraclete and installed the nuns there with his former wife Heloise as abbess, how she 'who was truly his lover' had his body brought there for burial and prayed constantly for him after his death, and then adds: 'It is said that when she was lying in her last illness she gave instructions that when she was dead she should be laid in the tomb of her husband. And when her dead body was carried to the opened tomb, her husband, who had died long before her, raised his arms to receive her, and so clasped her closely in his embrace.'[2] The legend disregards the fact that she was not buried in Abelard's tomb, and it was still told long after historians ceased to believe in the miraculous. But none of the nine known manuscripts of the letters can be dated before the late thirteenth century at the earliest, 150 years after the letters were written.[3] There is no trace of an independent manuscript of the *Historia calamitatum*, a copy of which Heloise

1. Text quoted in Hamilton, op. cit., p. 50 and Muckle, *Mediaeval Studies*, Vol. XV, p. 49.
2. Text in McLeod, op. cit., note 224, p. 290.
3. For a full account of the MSS see Muckle, *Mediaeval Studies*, Vol. XII, pp. 163 ff., and Monfrin's introduction to his critical edition of the *Historia*.

herself (Letter 1, p. 109) says came into her hands. Jean de Meun must have had a manuscript when he translated the *Historia* and introduced the story of Abelard and Heloise into sixty-four lines of his satirical continuation of the allegorical *Roman de la Rose* about 1280, but he quotes the story not in its own right but to prove a point.

It seems highly probable, as both J. Monfrin and R. W. Southern have suggested,[1] that the personal letters were kept by Heloise at the Paraclete along with the 'Letters of Direction' and the later Rules for the nuns, and that more than a century after her death they were brought to Paris and copied. It would be unlikely that anyone would know of her self-revelations during her lifetime. Peter the Venerable would hardly have thought so highly of her holiness and sense of vocation had he read of her sensual longings and self-reproach for hypocrisy. There seems no reason to suppose that Heloise 'edited' the personal letters in any way, even if we accept that Abelard may have put words into her mouth in the *Historia calamitatum*.[2] My own feeling is that once she had accepted that her relationship with Abelard must be re-established on a different basis and that henceforth she could look to him only for guidance as the founder of the institution of which she was a respected abbess, she would be unwilling to reread those painful outpourings of her heart. From the first paragraph of Letter 5 the correspondence takes on a different tone from which Heloise never wavers.

What became of Abelard's copies of the letters no one can know. It was current practice for medieval writers to keep copies of their own letters and even to revise them for later circulation as a letter-collection. This would be of general interest as showing the learning and expertise in the art of letter-writing of a single individual – such as St Bernard, Peter the Venerable or John of Salisbury – and its importance would be literary rather than historical, with the younger Pliny or Sidonius Apollinaris as models for variety of content

1. R. W. Southern, 'The Letters of Heloise and Abelard' in *Medieval Humanism and Other Studies*, p. 103.

2. See note 42, p. 73.

and elegance of style.[1] It was unusual for answers to be included: they could disturb the literary unity of the collection. Here is a further indication that the letters were not issued either in Heloise's lifetime or later as a literary letter-collection, but for their intrinsic personal interest when they came to light in the late thirteenth century.[2]

Even after Jean de Meun, references remain scanty. Abelard and Heloise are not among the incontinent lovers in the Second Circle of Dante's *Inferno* (Canto 5), though their story has something in common with that of Paolo and Francesca da Rimini. Chaucer does no more than mention 'Helowys That was abbesse nat fer fro Parys' in the Wife of Bath's Prologue (lines 677–8), where she is one of an oddly assorted company in a satire on matrimony. He probably knew of her through the *Roman de la Rose*. The first genuine interest in the lovers was shown by Petrarch. One of the nine good manuscripts,[3] dating from the early fourteenth century, belonged to him, and the marginal Latin notes to the *Historia calamitatum* and the personal letters are believed to be in his hand. It is certainly understandable that the author of the

1. See Giles Constable on 'Medieval Letter Collections': introduction to Vol. II of *The Letters of Peter the Venerable*.

2. The authenticity of the whole correspondence has been questioned by Charrier and others, but so far only to create further problems. The most recent theory supposes that the later Rule preserved at the Paraclete represents a stricter discipline which was observed until the late thirteenth century, when a forger (A) compiled Letter 7 in order to introduce male dominance in the convent and a laxer Rule which would permit the eating of meat. A commissioned a second forger (B), perhaps a member of the university of Paris, to add documents which would authenticate his own work. B forged the *Historia* and the personal letters, drawing on a twelfth-century work of fiction based on Abelard's life and written as a literary exercise by another unknown (C), who in his turn incorporated passages from Abelard's works known to us and from others unknown. A may also have had help from a more literary D. The same theory also conjectures that Abelard never broke with the monks of St Denis, that he founded the Paraclete on the lines of Fontevrault before 1121, and that archaeological exploration south of the existing buildings on the site is likely to reveal the monks' chapel and quarters (John F. Benton in a paper read at a conference at Cluny in 1972).

3. Paris, Bib. Nat., MS. lat. 2923. See Muckle, op. cit., pp. 164–5.

Secretum and of his own intensely personal letters should have read the manuscript closely. About a century later, *c.* 1461, François Villon included these lines in his *Ballade des Dames du Temps Jadis*, his theme being that death is inevitable for all mankind:

> Où est la très sage Hellois
> Pour qui fut chastré, puis moine
> Pierre Esbaillart à Saint-Denis?
> Pour son amour eut cette essoyne...
>   Mais où sont les neiges d'antan?[1]

But this amounts to so little, especially at a time when romances like that of Tristan and Iseult or Aucassin and Nicolette were highly popular, that it seems likely that Abelard and Heloise could not be fitted into the current ideal of courtly love, with its emphasis on the lover's devotion to the chaste and unattainable lady. Abelard and Heloise speak a different language of sensuous frankness, of pagan realism in love and classical Stoic fortitude in adversity. Their relationship found physical expression, and Heloise is neither cold nor remote but loving and generous, eager to give service and not to demand it. By contrast with the cruel reality of their tragedy, courtly love as depicted in the romances of chivalry appears mannered and artificial.

The Latin text of the letters and of Abelard's major works was published for the first time in Paris in 1616 in two practically identical editions, one of François d'Amboise, the other of André Duchesne. Why there were two editions has never been explained. The introductory material in the two differs, but the text is the same, and the notes on the *Historia calamitatum* by Duchesne appear in both. This text remained standard for over two centuries.

In 1718 Richard Rawlinson brought out in London a new edition of the letters which adds nothing to the edition of 1616, and in 1841 John Caspar Orelli of Zurich published the

1. 'Where is that learned lady Heloise, for whose sake Pierre Abelard was first castrated, then became a monk at Saint-Denis? It was through love that he suffered such misfortune... But where are last year's snows?'

Historia and the four personal letters. This was followed in 1849 by Victor Cousin's *Petri Abaelardi opera* (Cousin), in two volumes, published in Paris, which became the standard edition. It includes Duchesne's notes, and the text is based on d'Amboise, plus Cousin's reading of four MSS. It is generally considered a better text than that of J. P. Migne in Volume 178 of his Patrologia Latina (P.L.), though this too is mainly d'Amboise's text with Duchesne's notes.

A new critical edition by J. T. Muckle C.S.B. of the text of the *Historia calamitatum* was brought out in 1950 in Volume XII (pp. 163–213) of *Mediaeval Studies*, issued from the Pontifical Institute of Mediaeval Studies of Toronto, Canada; this was followed by Letters 1–4 in Volume XV (pp. 47–94) in 1953, and by Letters 5 and 6 in Volume XVII (pp. 240–81) in 1955, also with a critical commentary by J. T. Muckle, and finally by Letter 7 in Volume XVIII (pp. 241–92) in 1956, edited by T. P. McLaughlin C.S.B. The *Historia calamitatum* alone, with Letters 1 and 3 by Heloise in an appendix, was edited with a critical introduction by J. Monfrin (Paris, 2nd edition 1962).

The d'Amboise-Duchesne text and the English edition by Rawlinson gave rise to an extraordinary number of translations and romantic paraphrases of the letters.[1] The best translations were the English one by the Reverend Joseph Berington (London, 1787) and the French version by Dom Gervaise (Paris, 1723), but these were less influential than some of the wilder flights of fancy. In 1687 Roger de Rabutin, Comte de Bussy, sent Mme de Sévigné his own version of Heloise's two love-letters and Abelard's reply to the first, in which he had inserted fictitious incidents and reduced the whole story to a contemporary flirtatious intrigue. This continued to be reprinted until the mid-nineteenth century. Another version paraphrased by various hands and printed in Amsterdam in 1695 introduces the name 'Philinthe' for the unknown recipient of the *Historia*, and a re-hash of this

1. A full list is given by C. Charrier in *Héloïse dans l'histoire et dans la legende*, pp. 613–16, and a complete list of the French and English versions in McLeod, op. cit., pp. 301–305.

by F. N. Du Bois of the same year ran into many editions. It was Du Bois's paraphrase which made the romance generally known in England and inspired the version by John Hughes, first published in London in 1714, and entitled *Letters of Abelard and Heloise, to which is prefixed a particular account of their lives, Amours and Misfortunes, extracted chiefly from Monsieur Bayle, translated from the French.* (The later editions of Du Bois also claim to have used Bayle's *Dictionnaire* which had appeared in 1697.)

The fourth edition of this (1722) was reprinted in 1901 by J. M. Dent in the Temple Classics series as *The Love Letters of Abelard and Heloise*, and ran successfully through ten editions until it went out of print in 1945. It is edited by Miss H. Morten, who tells us in her short preface that 'It is rather a paraphrase than a translation, but by its swiftness and sympathy best gives the spirit of the original.' The *Historia calamitatum*, headed 'Abelard to Philintus', opens thus:

> The last time we were together, Philintus, you gave me a melancholy account of your misfortunes; I was sensibly touched with the relation, and like a true friend bore a share in your griefs. What did I not say to stop your tears? I laid before you all the reasons philosophy could furnish, which I thought might anyways soften the strokes of fortune. But all these endeavours have proved useless; grief, I perceive, has wholly seized your spirits, and your prudence, far from assisting, seems to have forsaken you. But my skilful friendship has found out an expedient to relieve you. Attend to me a moment, hear but the story of my misfortunes, and yours, Philintus, will be nothing as compared with those of the loving and unhappy Abelard. Observe, I beseech you, at what expense I endeavour to serve you; and think this no small mark of my affection; for I am going to present you with the relation of such particulars as it is impossible for me to recollect without piercing my heart with the most sensible affliction.[1]

And so it goes on. Heloise is given a maidservant, Agaton; 'She was brown, well-shaped, and a person superior to her rank; her features were regular and her eyes sparkling, fit to raise love in any man whose heart was not prepossessed by

1. Compare p. 57.

another passion.' She also has a singing-master who 'was excellently qualified for conveying a *billet* with the greatest dexterity and secrecy', and Abelard's sister Lucilla is persuaded to support her arguments against marriage. Typical of what flows from Heloise's pen is the following passage from Letter 1:

> Though I have lost my lover I still preserve my love. O vows! O convent! I have not lost my humanity under your inexorable discipline! You have not turned me to marble by changing my habit; my heart is not hardened by my imprisonment; I am still sensible to what has touched me, though, alas! I ought not to be! Without offending your commands permit a lover to exhort me to live in obedience to your rigorous rules.[1]

Hughes's travesty of the letters was apparently accepted as genuine even after Berington's translation of 1787. Its main interest now is that it is generally considered to be the source of Pope's *Eloisa to Abelard* which appeared among his works in 1717 (Rawlinson's Latin text did not appear until the following year). Pope's poem was immediately popular and frequently reprinted; it was also translated into French, German and Italian.[2] There were many other poetic versions of the lovers' story inspired by it, though none which showed the same imaginative intensity:

> The darksome pines that o'er yon rocks reclin'd
> Wave high, and murmur to the hollow wind,
> The wand'ring streams that shine between the hills,
> The grots that echo to the tinkling rills,
> The dying gales that pant among the trees,
> The lakes that quiver to the curling breeze;
> No more these scenes my meditation aid,
> Or lull to rest the visionary maid.
> But o'er the twilight groves and dusky caves,
> Long-sounding aisles, and intermingled graves,
> Black Melancholy sits, and round her throws
> A death-like silence, and a dead repose:

1. The passage comes near the end of the letter but there is nothing in the text for comparison.
2. See Charrier, op. cit., pp. 470–71.

Her gloomy presence saddens all the scene,
Shades ev'ry flow'r, and darkens ev'ry green,
Deepens the murmur of the falling floods,
And breathes a browner horror on the woods.

But this is hardly the atmosphere of the gently undulating fields and farmlands of Champagne, with the Ardusson quietly flowing through the rushes by the Paraclete. Pope conjures up something more like the crags and caverns and rushing torrents of Clisson, already romantically associated with Heloise, and said to have inspired some of Poussin's landscapes. It was there too that Lamartine is said to have written his lines in memory of Heloise. Nor does Pope's Eloisa recall the historic Heloise, but is rather the neo-classical heroine painted by Angelica Kauffman and her contemporaries, languishing over Abelard's tomb or on her own deathbed.[1]

In 1875 Octave Gréard translated Cousin's text into readable and accurate French, and his translation of the *Historia calamitatum* and the personal letters was reprinted by Marcel Jouhandeau in the Bibliothèque de Cluny series in 1959, along with the so-called 'Letters of a Portuguese Nun' of 1669. Heloise and Maria Alcoforada had been published together at that time, and the eighteenth century had often linked their names. But the five letters addressed to the Comte de Chantilly by his abandoned mistress are of doubtful authenticity.

In 1925 *The Letters of Abelard and Heloise* translated by C. K. Scott Moncrieff (the translator of Proust) from Migne's text was published by the Cambridge University Press in an edition limited to 750 copies and now out of print. Scott Moncrieff quotes from Hughes's translation but evidently knows nothing of Berington's, as he claims to be the first to translate from Latin and not to adapt a debased French version. There are no explanatory notes, and as an introduction only a curious and rather facetious exchange of letters with George Moore querying the authenticity of the Letters. Moore's novel *Heloise and Abelard* had appeared in 1921.

1. Illustrated in Charrier, *passim*.

The style of the translation is idiosyncratic to the point of being sometimes barely intelligible; it wavers uneasily between the cadences of the Authorized Version, a literal transcription of the original Latin sentence-structure, and the underpunctuated sentences of Moore himself. Here is a passage from Heloise's first letter:

> There were two things, I confess, in thee especially, wherewith thou couldst at once captivate the heart of any woman; namely the arts of making songs and of singing them. Which we know that other philosophers have seldom followed. Wherewith as with a game, refreshing the labour of philosophic exercise, thou has left many songs composed in amatory measure or rhythm, which for the suavity both of words and of tune being oft repeated, have kept thy name without ceasing on the lips of all; since even illiterates the sweetness of thy melodies did not allow to forget thee. It was on this account chiefly that women sighed for love of thee. And as the greater part of thy songs descanted of our love, they spread my fame in a short time through many lands, and inflamed the jealousy of many women against me.[1]

No other English translation has appeared in the last thirty-five years,[2] though there is no lack of interest in the human tragedy of the lovers and a growing one in Abelard as a logician. George Moore's novel was followed by Helen Waddell's popular *Peter Abelard*, and later by M. Worthington's *The Immortal Lovers*; and in 1970 by Ronald Millar's play which ran successfully in the West End. There have been serious studies of Abelard by Sikes, Gilson and Grane, and of Heloise by Charrier, McLeod, Hamilton and Pernoud.[3]

We now have a good, critical (if not very accessible) text in four volumes of the Toronto *Mediaeval Studies*, though the Latin is not very easy reading. Abelard and Heloise do not write in the unsophisticated Latin of the previous century, and they have not the easy grace of an accomplished letter-

1. Compare p. 115.
2. J. T. Muckle translated the *Historia calamitatum* alone in 1962.
3. See Bibliography, p. 296; a fuller one in McLeod, op. cit., pp. 305 ff, and an exhaustive one on Heloise up to 1933 in Charrier, op. cit. pp. 597–645.

writer such as Peter the Venerable. The composition and style of their letters follows the rules for correct letter-writing of the twelfth century, the *dictamen* (or *ars dictandi*) and *cursus*.[1] The elegance this sought in formal address, proper choice of words and arrangement of material seems to us excessive, and Scott Moncrieff has shown that the frequent use of connecting relative pronouns and elaborate antithesis of clauses have to be eschewed in translation. Abelard's *Historia calamitatum*, being largely narrative, is less rhetorical, and Heloise can write directly in her personal letters. But it was the convention of their day to overload a reasoned argument with strings of stock quotations from the Vulgate and the Christian Fathers, or to introduce a homily on an appropriate topic which reads like a set piece. Heloise, for example, has said something in Letter 5 about the evil of incontinence and the effect of strong drink (pp. 166 ff) which Abelard elaborates on in Letter 7, repeating the same quotations (p. 231 ff.). In addition, their intensive classical education leaves its mark both in quotation and choice of words. In this sense they are both learned clerks and write in 'a mood of literary showmanship'.[2] But they are also individuals who would be exceptional in any age, whose letters move through the widest range of emotions – devotion, disappointment, grief and indignation, self-confidence, ambition, impatience, self-reproach and resignation – all under the discipline of a keen critical intelligence which is as marked in Heloise as in Abelard. They deserve to be heard, even if imperfectly and at second-hand through a translation, in the words they wrote.

1. See Giles Constable, op. cit., on 'Style', pp. 29 ff.
2. Southern, 'The Letters of Heloise and Abelard' in *Medieval Humanism and Other Studies*, p. 102.

Historia calamitatum:

Abelard to a Friend: The Story of His Misfortunes

There are times when example is better than precept for stirring or soothing human passions; and so I propose to follow up the words of consolation I gave you in person with the history of my own misfortunes, hoping thereby to give you comfort in absence. In comparison with my trials you will see that your own are nothing, or only slight, and will find them easier to bear.[1]

I was born on the borders of Brittany, about eight miles I think to the east of Nantes, in a town called Le Pallet.[2] I owe my volatile temperament to my native soil and ancestry and also my natural ability for learning. My father had acquired some knowledge of letters before he was a soldier, and later on his passion for learning was such that he intended all his sons to have instruction in letters before they were trained to arms. His purpose was fulfilled. I was his first-born,[3] and being specially dear to him had the greatest care taken over

1. The traditional title of *Historia calamitatum* and the third-person chapter-headings (omitted in this translation) were well known by Petrarch's time, though the best of the early manuscripts read *Abaelardi ad amicum suum consolatoria* ⟨*epistula*⟩ ('Abelard's letter of consolation to his friend'). This version of the title and the opening paragraph indicate that however personal in content, this letter falls into one of the categories recognized by the art of rhetoric. The 'friend' who reappears as a fellow-monk in the closing paragraphs may be wholly imaginary, as part of the convention.

2. In fact Le Pallet is about twelve miles east and a little south of Nantes, on the way to Poitiers. The ruins to be seen on a hill behind the church are said to be the walls of the castle belonging to Abelard's father Berengar (Berengarius), a member of the minor Breton nobility. Abelard was born in 1079; his mother was Lucie (Lucia).

3. A sister, Denise (Dionisia), appears in the necrology of the Paraclete, and there is documentary evidence of three possible brothers, Dagobert, Porcarius and Radulphus. See Muckle, *Mediaeval Studies*, Vol. XII, note 16, p. 175. Abelard mentions visiting a brother in Nantes on p. 103.

my education. For my part, the more rapid and easy my progress in my studies, the more eagerly I applied myself, until I was so carried away by my love of learning that I renounced the glory of a soldier's life, made over my inheritance and rights of the eldest son to my brothers, and withdrew from the court of Mars in order to kneel at the feet of Minerva. I preferred the weapons of dialectic to all the other teachings of philosophy, and armed with these I chose the conflicts of disputation instead of the trophies of war. I began to travel about in several provinces disputing, like a true peripatetic philosopher, wherever I had heard there was keen interest in the art of dialectic.[1]

At last I came to Paris, where dialectic had long been particularly flourishing, and joined William of Champeaux[2] who at the time was the supreme master of the subject, both in reputation and in fact. I stayed in his school for a time, but though he welcomed me at first he soon took a violent dislike to me because I set out to refute some of his arguments and frequently reasoned against him. On several occasions I proved myself his superior in debate. Those who were considered the leaders among my fellow students were also annoyed, and the more so as they looked on me as the youngest and most recent pupil. This was the beginning of

1. There were schools for grammar and rhetoric available at Nantes, Vannes, Redon, Angers and Chartres, and at Loches Abelard must have been taught logic by the famous Nominalist dialectician Jean Roscelin, who is not named here because of his condemnation in 1093 for denying the unity of the Trinity. He was exiled in England, but later allowed to resume teaching at Loches. Abelard afterwards disassociated himself from Roscelin's teaching, and wrote at some unknown date to the bishop of Meaux demanding a confrontation with Roscelin who had attacked him (P.L. 178, 355 ff.; Cousin, Vol. II, pp. 150–51). An abusive letter by Roscelin to Abelard in which there are distasteful taunts about his mutilation is also extant (P.L. 178, 358 ff; Cousin, Vol. II, p. 792 ff.).

The Peripatetic philosophers were the followers of Aristotle, so named because of the arcade (*peripatos*) for 'walking about' in which he taught in Athens.

2. William of Champeaux (*c.* 1070–*c.*1120), Realist philosopher, archdeacon of Paris, head of the Cloister School of Notre Dame, and then at the Abbey of St Victor; in 1112 or 1113 bishop of Châlons-sur-Marne. He installed Bernard as abbot of Clairvaux and became a close friend.

the misfortunes which have dogged me to this day, and as my reputation grew, so other men's jealousy was aroused.

It ended by my setting my heart on founding a school of my own, young as I was and estimating my capacities too highly for my years; and I had my eye on a site suited to my purpose – Melun, an important town at that time and a royal residence.[1] My master suspected my intentions, and in an attempt to remove my school as far as possible from his own, before I could leave him he secretly used every means he could to thwart my plans and keep me from the place I had chosen. But among the powers in the land he had several enemies, and these men helped me to obtain my desire. I also won considerable support simply through his unconcealed jealousy. Thus my school had its start and my reputation for dialectic began to spread, with the result that the fame of my old fellow-students and even that of the master himself gradually declined and came to an end. Consequently my self-confidence rose still higher, and I made haste to transfer my school to Corbeil, a town nearer Paris, where I could embarrass him through more frequent encounters in disputation.

However, I was not there long before I fell ill through overwork and was obliged to return home. For some time I remained absent from France,[2] sorely missed by those eager for instruction in dialectic. A few years later, when I had long since recovered my health, my teacher William, archdeacon of Paris, changed his former status and joined the order of the Canons Regular,[3] with the intention, it was said, of gaining promotion to a higher prelacy through a reputation for increased piety. He was soon successful when he was made

1. Melun, one of the residences of Philip I. None of Abelard's dates is precise; his school may have been set up in 1102. Corbeil was also a royal fief.

2. About six years. Brittany was an independent duchy, not part of France until the late fifteenth century.

3. The Rule of the Canons Regular was based on that drawn up by St Augustine for secular clergy. It was intended to reform the cathedral clergy and to bridge the growing gap between scholars and monks. The Abbey of St Victor became famous under Hugh of St Victor, who taught there from 1125 to 1141.

bishop of Châlons. But this change in his way of life did not oblige him either to leave Paris or to give up his study of philosophy, and he soon resumed his public teaching in his usual manner in the very monastery to which he had retired to follow the religious life. I returned to him to hear his lectures on rhetoric, and in the course of our philosophic disputes I produced a sequence of clear logical arguments to make him amend, or rather abandon, his previous attitude to universals. He had maintained that in the common existence of universals, the whole species was essentially the same in each of its individuals, and among these there was no essential difference, but only variety due to multiplicity of accidents. Now he modified his view in order to say that it was the same not in essence but through non-difference.[1] This has always been the dialectician's chief problem concerning universals, so much so that even Porphyry did not venture to settle it when he deals with universals in his *Isagoge*,[2] but only mentioned it as a 'very serious difficulty'. Consequently, when William had modified or rather been forced to give up his original position, his lectures fell into such contempt that he was scarcely accepted on any other points of dialectic, as if the whole subject rested solely on the question of universals.

My own teaching gained so much prestige and authority from this that the strongest supporters of my master who had hitherto been the most violent among my attackers now flocked to join my school. Even William's successor[3] as head of the Paris school offered me his chair so that he could join the others as my pupil, in the place where his master and mine had won fame. Within a few days of my taking over the teaching of dialectic, William was eaten up with jealousy and consumed with anger to an extent it is difficult to convey, and being unable to control the violence of his resentment for long, he made another artful attempt to banish me. I had done

1. See Introduction, p. 12.

2. Porphyry, a Greek Neoplatonist of the third century A.D. and pupil of Plotinus, had written an Introduction (*Isagoge*) to the *Categories* of Aristotle which was known at this time through a translation by Boethius.

3. Not identified.

nothing to justify his acting openly against me, so he launched an infamous attack on the man who had put me in his chair, in order to remove the school from him and put it in the hands of one of my rivals. I then returned to Melun and set up my school there as before; and the more his jealousy pursued me, the more widely my reputation spread, for, as the poet says:

> Envy seeks the heights, the winds sweep the summits.[1]

But not long after when he heard that there was considerable doubt about his piety amongst the majority of thoughtful men, and a good deal of gossip about his conversion, as it had not led to his departure from Paris, he removed himself and his little community, along with his school, to a village some distance from the city. I promptly returned to Paris from Melun, hoping for peace henceforth from him, but since he had filled my place there, as I said, by one of my rivals, I took my school outside the city to Mont Ste Geneviève,[2] and set up camp there in order to lay siege to my usurper. The news brought William back to Paris in unseemly haste to restore such scholars as remained to him and his community to their former monastery, apparently to deliver from my siege the soldier whom he had abandoned. But his good intentions did the man very serious harm. He had previously had a few pupils of a sort, largely because of his lectures on Priscian,[3] for which he had some reputation, but as soon as his master arrived he lost them all and had to retire from keeping a school. Soon afterwards he appeared to lose hope of future worldly fame, and he too was converted to the monastic life. The bouts of argument which followed William's return to the city between my pupils and him and his followers, and the successes in these encounters which fortune gave my people (myself among them) are facts which you

1. Ovid, *De remedio amoris*, I. 369.

2. The site of the present University of Paris. It was outside the bounds of the city of Paris until the beginning of the next century.

3. The famous Latin grammarian of the early sixth century A.D., teaching at Constantinople, whose eighteen-book treatise on grammar (*Institutiones grammaticae*) was widely used in the Middle Ages.

have long known. And I shall not go too far if I boldly say with Ajax that

> If you demand the issue of this fight,
> I was not vanquished by my enemy.[1]

Should I keep silence, the facts cry out and tell the outcome.

Meanwhile my dearest mother Lucie begged me to return to Brittany, for after my father Berengar's entry into monastic life she was preparing to do the same. When she had done so I returned to France, with the special purpose of studying theology, to find my master William (whom I have often mentioned) already installed as bishop of Châlons. However, in this field his own master, Anselm of Laon,[2] was then the greatest authority because of his great age.

I therefore approached this old man, who owed his reputation more to long practice than to intelligence or memory. Anyone who knocked at his door to seek an answer to some question went away more uncertain than he came. Anselm could win the admiration of an audience, but he was useless when put to the question. He had a remarkable command of words but their meaning was worthless and devoid of all sense. The fire he kindled filled his house with smoke but did not light it up; he was a tree in full leaf which could be seen from afar, but on closer and more careful inspection proved to be barren. I had come to this tree to gather fruit, but I found it was the fig tree which the Lord cursed, or the ancient oak to which Lucan compares Pompey:

> There stands the shadow of a noble name,
> Like a tall oak in a field of corn.[3]

1. Ovid, *Metamorphoses*, 13. 89–90.

2. Anselm of Laon (died *c.*1117) probably studied under St Anselm at Bec, and taught theology at Laon for many years with far greater distinction than Abelard is willing to allow. He and his brother Ralph conducted the school there and made it famous for theology; but his teaching was based on accepted authorities, while Abelard believed that dialectic offered the proper equipment for arriving at a better understanding of theological problems. Anselm's school produced the standard *Ordinary Gloss* on the Bible; see Introduction, p. 13.

3. Cf. Matthew xxi, 18 ff. (the barren fig tree); Lucan, *Pharsalia*, 1. 135–6.

Once I discovered this I did not lie idle in his shade for long. My attendance at his lectures gradually became more and more irregular, to the annoyance of some of his leading pupils, who took it as a sign of contempt for so great a master. They began secretly to turn him against me, until their base insinuations succeeded in rousing his jealousy. One day it happened that after a session of *Sentences*[1] we students were joking amongst ourselves, when someone rounded on me and asked what I thought of the reading of the Holy Scriptures, when I had hitherto studied only philosophy. I replied that concentration on such reading was most beneficial for the salvation of the soul, but that I found it most surprising that for educated men the writings or glosses of the Fathers themselves were not sufficient for interpreting their commentaries without further instruction. There was general laughter, and I was asked by many of those present if I could or would venture to tackle this myself. I said I was ready to try if they wished. Still laughing, they shouted 'Right, that's settled! Take some commentary on a little-known text and we'll test what you say.' Then they all agreed on an extremely obscure prophecy of Ezekiel. I took the commentary and promptly invited them all to hear my interpretation the very next day. They then pressed unwanted advice on me, telling me not to hurry over something so important but to remember my inexperience and give longer thought to working out and confirming my exposition. I replied indignantly that it was not my custom to benefit by practice, but I relied on my own intelligence, and either they must come to my lecture at the time of my choosing or I should abandon it altogether.

1. Anselm's teaching followed the traditional lines of study of the Scriptures (*lectio divina*), as prescribed by St Benedict in *Regula* 48, with an exposition verse by verse from the teachings of the Fathers of the Church (*glossae*). Sentences (*sententiae*) were the deeper truths of Revelation to be arrived at after a study of the letter and sense of the text; these were stated by the teacher and then expounded and proved through citation from the Bible and the Fathers. Abelard's view was that an educated man should be able to study the Scriptures alone with the aid of a commentary. (He was of course a mature student of thirty-four amongst much younger men.)

At my first lecture there were certainly not many people present, for everyone thought it absurd that I could attempt this so soon, when up to now I had made no study at all of the Scriptures. But all those who came approved, so that they commended the lecture warmly, and urged me to comment on the text on the same lines as my lecture. The news brought people who had missed my first lecture flocking to the second and third ones, all alike most eager to make copies of the glosses which I had begun with on the first day.

Anselm was now wildly jealous, and being already set against me by the suggestions of some of his pupils, as I said before, he began to attack me for lecturing on the Scriptures in the same way as my master William had done previously over philosophy. There were at this time two outstanding students in the old man's school, Alberic of Rheims and Lotulf of Lombardy,[1] whose hostility to me was intensified by the good opinion they had of themselves. It was largely through their insinuations, as was afterwards proved, that Anselm lost his head and curtly forbade me to continue my work of interpretation in the place where he taught,[2] on the pretext that any mistake which I might write down through lack of training in the subject would be attributed to him. When this reached the ears of the students, their indignation knew no bounds – this was an act of sheer spite and calumny, such as had never been directed at anyone before; but the more open it was, the more it brought me renown, and through persecution my fame increased.

A few days after this I returned to Paris, to the school which had long ago been intended for and offered to me,[3] and

1. Very little is known of Lotulf, who came from Novara. Alberic became archdeacon of Rheims in 1113 and ran the school there with Lotulf; in 1137 he was elected archbishop of Bourges. They were two of Abelard's main opponents at the Council of Soissons: see p. 79.

2. Evidently a man could be forbidden to teach by a *magister scholarum*, though at this date it was not yet necessary for him to acquire a licence (*licentia docendi*) to do so from the official responsible for the schools in a diocese or city.

3. As *magister scholarum* at Notre Dame Abelard would be adopted into the Chapter as a canon but this did not mean that he was ordained a priest.

from which I had been expelled at the start. I held my position there in peace for several years, and as soon as I began my course of teaching I set myself to complete the commentaries on Ezekiel which I had started at Laon. These proved so popular with their readers that they judged my reputation to stand as high for my interpretation of the Scriptures as it had previously done for philosophy. The numbers in the school increased enormously as the students gathered there eager for instruction in both subjects, and the wealth and fame this brought me must be well known to you.

But success always puffs up fools with pride, and worldly security weakens the spirit's resolution and easily destroys it through carnal temptations. I began to think myself the only philosopher in the world, with nothing to fear from anyone, and so I yielded to the lusts of the flesh. Hitherto I had been entirely continent, but now the further I advanced in philosophy and theology, the further I fell behind the philosophers and holy Fathers in the impurity of my life. It is well known that the philosophers, and still more the Fathers, by which is meant those who have devoted themselves to the teachings of Holy Scripture, were especially glorified by their chastity. Since therefore I was wholly enslaved to pride and lechery, God's grace provided a remedy for both these evils, though not one of my choosing: first for my lechery by depriving me of those organs with which I practised it, and then for the pride which had grown in me through my learning – for in the words of the Apostle, 'Knowledge breeds conceit'[1] – when I was humiliated by the burning of the book of which I was so proud.[2]

The true story of both these episodes I now want you to

He was already *clericus* – 'clerk' rather than 'cleric' – for at this time *clerici* and *scholares* were synonymous, as the schools were all Church institutions. Masters and students were tonsured and wore clerical habits.

1. 1 Corinthians viii, 1. Abelard and Heloise both quote from the Bible very freely. Their own words have been translated when they are only approximate to the Latin of the Vulgate; otherwise the N.E.B., Knox or Jerusalem Bible has been used.

2. His treatise *On the Unity and Trinity of God*, burnt by order of the Council of Soissons. See p. 83.

know from the facts, in their proper order, instead of from hearsay. I had always held myself aloof from unclean association with prostitutes, and constant application to my studies had prevented me from frequenting the society of gentlewomen: indeed, I knew little of the secular way of life. Perverse Fortune flattered me, as the saying goes, and found an easy way to bring me toppling down from my pedestal, or rather, despite my overbearing pride and heedlessness of the grace granted me, God's compassion claimed me humbled for Himself.

There was in Paris at the time a young girl named Heloise,[1] the niece of Fulbert, one of the canons, and so much loved by him that he had done everything in his power to advance her education in letters. In looks she did not rank lowest, while in the extent of her learning she stood supreme. A gift for letters is so rare in women that it added greatly to her charm and had won her renown throughout the realm. I considered all the usual attractions for a lover and decided she was the one to bring to my bed, confident that I should have an easy success; for at that time I had youth and exceptional good looks as well as my great reputation to recommend me, and feared no rebuff from any woman I might choose to honour with my love. Knowing the girl's knowledge and love of letters I thought she would be all the more ready to consent, and that even when separated we could enjoy each other's presence by exchange of written messages in which we could speak more openly than in person, and so need never lack the pleasures of conversation.

All on fire with desire for this girl I sought an opportunity of getting to know her through private daily meetings and so

1. None of the conjectures about Heloise's birth and parentage can be proved, and as she was a young girl (*adolescentula*), it can only be assumed that she was about seventeen at this time, and born in 1100 or 1101. Her mother's name appears in the necrology of the Paraclete as Hersinde; her father is unknown. It is possible that she was illegitimate, and twice in her letters (p. 129 and p. 130) she implies that her social status was lower than Abelard's. See further McLeod, op. cit., p. 8 ff. and note 219, p. 287 ff. Fulbert presumably lived in the cathedral close, north-east of Notre Dame, traditionally in a house on the Quai aux Fleurs.

more easily winning her over; and with this end in view I came to an arrangement with her uncle, with the help of some of his friends, whereby he should take me into his house, which was very near my school, for whatever sum he liked to ask. As a pretext I said that my household cares were hindering my studies and the expense was more than I could afford. Fulbert dearly loved money, and was moreover always ambitious to further his niece's education in letters, two weaknesses which made it easy for me to gain his consent and obtain my desire: he was all eagerness for my money and confident that his niece would profit from my teaching. This led him to make an urgent request which furthered my love and fell in with my wishes more than I had dared to hope; he gave me complete charge over the girl, so that I could devote all the leisure time left me by my school to teaching her by day and night, and if I found her idle I was to punish her severely. I was amazed by his simplicity – if he had entrusted a tender lamb to a ravening wolf it would not have surprised me more. In handing her over to me to punish as well as to teach, what else was he doing but giving me complete freedom to realize my desires, and providing an opportunity, even if I did not make use of it, for me to bend her to my will by threats and blows if persuasion failed? But there were two special reasons for his freedom from base suspicion: his love for his niece and my previous reputation for continence.

Need I say more? We were united, first under one roof, then in heart; and so with our lessons as a pretext we abandoned ourselves entirely to love. Her studies allowed us to withdraw in private, as love desired, and then with our books open before us, more words of love than of our reading passed between us, and more kissing than teaching. My hands strayed oftener to her bosom than to the pages; love drew our eyes to look on each other more than reading kept them on our texts. To avert suspicion I sometimes struck her, but these blows were prompted by love and tender feeling rather than anger and irritation, and were sweeter than any balm could be. In short, our desires left no stage of love-making untried, and if love could devise something new, we welcomed it. We entered on each joy the more eagerly for our previous inexperience, and were the less easily sated.

Now the more I was taken up with these pleasures, the less time I could give to philosophy and the less attention I paid to my school. It was utterly boring for me to have to go to the school, and equally wearisome to remain there and to spend my days on study when my nights were sleepless with love-making. As my interest and concentration flagged, my lectures lacked all inspiration and were merely repetitive; I could do no more than repeat what had been said long ago, and when inspiration did come to me, it was for writing love-songs, not the secrets of philosophy. A lot of these songs, as you know, are still popular and sung in many places,[1] particularly by those who enjoy the kind of life I led. But the grief and sorrow and laments of my students when they realized my preoccupation, or rather, distraction of mind are hard to realize. Few could have failed to notice something so obvious, in fact no one, I fancy, except the man whose honour was most involved – Heloise's uncle. Several people tried on more than one occasion to draw his attention to it, but he would not believe them; because, as I said, of his boundless love for his niece and my well-known reputation for chastity in my previous life. We do not easily think ill of those whom we love most, and the taint of suspicion cannot exist along with warm affection. Hence the remark of St Jerome in his letter to Sabinian:[2] 'We are always the last to learn of evil in our own home, and the faults of our wife and children may be the talk of the town but do not reach our ears.'

But what is last to be learned is somehow learned eventually, and common knowledge cannot easily be hidden from one individual. Several months passed and then this happened in our case. Imagine the uncle's grief at the discovery, and the lovers' grief too at being separated! How I blushed with shame and contrition for the girl's plight, and what sorrow

1. None of these love-lyrics survives, and there are no love-poems in north France as early as this.

2. *Epistulae* cxlvii, 10. The MSS. read 'to Castrician'.

she suffered at the thought of my disgrace! All our laments were for one another's troubles, and our distress was for each other, not for ourselves. Separation drew our hearts still closer while frustration inflamed our passion even more; then we became more abandoned as we lost all sense of shame and, indeed, shame diminished as we found more opportunities for love-making. And so we were caught in the act as the poet says happened to Mars and Venus.[1] Soon afterwards the girl found that she was pregnant, and immediately wrote me a letter full of rejoicing to ask what I thought she should do. One night then, when her uncle was away from home, I removed her secretly from his house, as we had planned, and sent her straight to my own country. There she stayed with my sister until she gave birth to a boy, whom she called Astralabe.[2]

On his return her uncle went almost out of his mind – one could appreciate only by experience his transports of grief and mortification. What action could he take against me? What traps could he set? He did not know. If he killed me or did me personal injury, there was the danger that his beloved niece might suffer for it in my country. It was useless to try to seize me or confine me anywhere against my will, especially as I was very much on guard against this very thing, knowing that he would not hesitate to assault me if he had the courage or the means.

In the end I took pity on his boundless misery and went to him, accusing myself of the deceit love had made me commit as if it were the basest treachery. I begged his forgiveness and

1. They were found in bed together by Venus' husband, Vulcan. The story we now associate with Homer (*Odyssey*, Book 8) was well known to Abelard through the versions by Ovid in *Ars amatoria*, 2. 561 ff. and *Metamorphoses*, 4. 169 ff.

2. In Letter 4, p. 146, Abelard adds the detail that she was disguised as a nun. The sister was probably the Denise or Dionisia who appears in the necrology of the Paraclete, as does Peter Astralabe or Astrolabe. We can only assume that Heloise stayed at Le Pallet, and there is no historical basis for associating her with the more romantic scenery of Clisson. See Introduction, p. 53. The child's strange name, which Abelard says she chose, remains unexplained.

promised to make any amends he might think fit. I protested that I had done nothing unusual in the eyes of anyone who had known the power of love, and recalled how since the beginning of the human race women had brought the noblest men to ruin. Moreover, to conciliate him further, I offered him satisfaction in a form he could never have hoped for: I would marry the girl I had wronged. All I stipulated was that the marriage should be kept secret so as not to damage my reputation.[1] He agreed, pledged his word and that of his supporters, and sealed the reconciliation I desired with a kiss. But his intention was to make it easier to betray me.

I set off at once for Brittany and brought back my mistress to make her my wife. But she was strongly opposed to the proposal, and argued hotly against it for two reasons: the risk involved and the disgrace to myself. She swore that no satisfaction could ever appease her uncle, as we subsequently found out. What honour could she win, she protested, from a marriage which would dishonour me and humiliate us both? The world would justly exact punishment from her if she removed such a light from its midst. Think of the curses, the loss to the Church and grief of philosophers which would greet such a marriage! Nature had created me for all mankind – it would be a sorry scandal if I should bind myself to a single woman and submit to such base servitude. She absolutely rejected this marriage; it would be nothing but a disgrace and a burden to me. Along with the loss to my reputation she put before me the difficulties of marriage, which the apostle Paul

1. Cf. note 3, p.64. Opinion is divided on whether Abelard was in Orders at this time but, even if he were, the Church was only just beginning to forbid marriage to priests and the higher orders of clergy. It would have been thought unworthy of anyone in Abelard's position not to remain celibate, and would have been a bar to his advancement in the Church, where alone he could find scope for his ambitions. One of Heloise's arguments is that his marriage would mean a loss to the Church, her main one that it would be a betrayal of the philosophic ideal. But obviously a secret marriage would not satisfy Fulbert's demand for public satisfaction for the wrong done to his niece. Abelard's true motive for wanting a marriage is revealed in his second letter, p. 149.

exhorts us to avoid when he says:[1] 'Has your marriage been dissolved? Do not seek a wife. If, however, you do marry, there is nothing wrong in it; and if a virgin marries, she has done no wrong. But those who marry will have pain and grief in this bodily life, and my aim is to spare you.' And again: 'I want you to be free from anxious care.'

But if I would accept neither the advice of the Apostle nor the exhortations of the Fathers on the heavy yoke of marriage, at least, she argued, I could listen to the philosophers, and pay regard to what had been written by them or concerning them on this subject – as for the most part the Fathers too have carefully done when they wish to rebuke us. For example, St Jerome in the first book of his *Against Jovinian*[2] recalls how Theophrastus sets out in considerable detail the unbearable annoyances of marriage and its endless anxieties, in order to prove by the clearest possible arguments that a man should not take a wife; and he brings his reasoning from the exhortations of the philosophers to this conclusion: 'Can any Christian hear Theophrastus argue in this way without a blush?' In the same book Jerome goes on to say that 'After Cicero had divorced Terentia and was asked by Hirtius to marry his sister he firmly refused to do so, on the grounds that he could not devote his attention to a wife and philosophy alike. He does not simply say "devote attention", but adds "alike", not wishing to do anything which would be a rival to his study of philosophy.'

But apart from the hindrances to such philosophic study, consider, she said, the true conditions for a dignified way of life. What harmony can there be between pupils and nursemaids, desks and cradles, books or tablets and distaffs, pen or stylus and spindles? Who can concentrate on thoughts of Scripture or philosophy and be able to endure babies crying, nurses soothing them with lullabies, and all the noisy coming and going of men and women about the house? Will he put up with the constant muddle and squalor which small children bring into the home? The wealthy can do so, you will say, for their mansions and large houses can provide privacy and,

1. 1 Corinthians vii, 27, 28, 32. 2. *Contra Jovinianum*, 47.

being rich, they do not have to count the cost nor be tormented by daily cares. But philosophers lead a very different life from rich men, and those who are concerned with wealth or are involved in mundane matters will not have time for the claims of Scripture or philosophy. Consequently, the great philosophers of the past have despised the world, not renouncing it so much as escaping from it, and have denied themselves every pleasure so as to find peace in the arms of philosophy alone. The greatest of them, Seneca, gives this advice to Lucilius:[1] 'Philosophy is not a subject for idle moments. We must neglect everything else and concentrate on this, for no time is long enough for it. Put it aside for a moment, and you might as well give it up, for once interrupted it will not remain. We must resist all other occupations, not merely dispose of them but reject them.'

This is the practice today through love of God of those among us who truly deserve the name of monks,[2] as it was of distinguished philosophers amongst the pagans in their pursuit of philosophy. For in every people, pagan, Jew or Christian, some men have always stood out for their faith or upright way of life, and have cut themselves off from their fellows because of their singular chastity or austerity. Amongst the Jews in times past there were the Nazirites,[3] who dedicated themselves to the Lord according to the Law, and the sons of the prophets, followers of Elijah or Elisha, whom the Old Testament calls monks, as St Jerome bears witness;[4] and in more recent times the three sects of philosophers described by Josephus in the eighteenth book of his *Antiquities*,[5] the Pharisees, Sadducees and Essenes. Today we have the monks who imitate either the communal life of the apostles or the earlier, solitary life of John. Among the pagans, as I said, are the philosophers: for the name of wisdom or philosophy used to be applied not so much to acquisition of learning as to a religious way of life, as we

1. *Epistulae ad Lucilium*, 72. 3.
2. *Monachus* (monk) originally denotes one who chooses a solitary life.
3. Cf. Numbers vi, 21 and Judges xvi, 17 (Samson).
4. 2 Kings vi, 1; Jerome, *Epistulae* cxxv, 7.
5. *Antiquities*, 18.1.11.

learn from the first use of the word itself and from the testimony of the saints themselves. And so St Augustine, in the eighth book of his *City of God*, distinguishes between types of philosopher:[1]

The Italian school was founded by Pythagoras of Samos, who is said to have been the first to use the term philosophy; before him men were called 'sages' if they seemed outstanding for some praiseworthy manner of life. But when Pythagoras was asked his profession, he replied that he was a philosopher, meaning a devotee or lover of wisdom, for he thought it too presumptuous to call himself a sage.

So the phrase 'if they seemed outstanding for some praiseworthy manner of life' clearly proves that the sages of the pagans, that is, the philosophers, were so called as a tribute to their way of life, not to their learning. There is no need for me to give examples of their chaste and sober lives – I should seem to be teaching Minerva herself. But if pagans and laymen could live in this way, though bound by no profession of faith, is there not a greater obligation on you, as clerk and canon, not to put base pleasures before your sacred duties, and to guard against being sucked down headlong into this Charybdis, there to lose all sense of shame and be plunged forever into a whirlpool of impurity? If you take no thought for the privilege of a clerk, you can at least uphold the dignity of a philosopher, and let a love of propriety curb your shamelessness if the reverence due to God means nothing to you. Remember Socrates' marriage and the sordid episode whereby he did at least remove the slur it cast on philosophy by providing an example to be a warning to his successors. This too was noted by Jerome, when he tells this tale of Socrates in the first book of his *Against Jovinian*:[2] 'One day after he had

1. *De civitate Dei*, 8.2.

2. 1.48. Muckle points out that all these quotations (apart from the one from Seneca) appear in other works by Abelard, and in particular in Book II of his *Theologia Christiana* written ten years previously (*Mediaeval Studies*, Vol. XII, pp. 173–4). This suggests that before circulating the *Historia calamitatum* Abelard had expanded Heloise's arguments and supplied precise quotations.

withstood an endless stream of invective which Xanthippe poured out from a window above his head, he felt himself soaked with dirty water. All he did was to wipe his head and say: "I knew that thunderstorm would lead to rain."'

Heloise then went on to the risks I should run in bringing her back, and argued that the name of mistress instead of wife would be dearer to her and more honourable for me – only love freely given should keep me for her, not the constriction of a marriage tie, and if we had to be parted for a time, we should find the joy of being together all the sweeter the rarer our meetings were. But at last she saw that her attempts to persuade or dissuade me were making no impression on my foolish obstinacy, and she could not bear to offend me; so amidst deep sighs and tears she ended in these words: 'We shall both be destroyed. All that is left us is suffering as great as our love has been.' In this, as the whole world knows, she showed herself a true prophet.

And so when our baby son was born we entrusted him to my sister's care and returned secretly to Paris. A few days later, after a night's private vigil of prayer in a certain church, at dawn we were joined in matrimony in the presence of Fulbert and some of his, and our, friends. Afterwards we parted secretly and went our ways unobserved. Subsequently our meetings were few and furtive, in order to conceal as far as possible what we had done. But Fulbert and his servants, seeking satisfaction for the dishonour done to him, began to spread the news of the marriage and break the promise of secrecy they had given me. Heloise cursed them and swore that there was no truth in this, and in his exasperation Fulbert heaped abuse on her on several occasions. As soon as I discovered this I removed her to a convent of nuns in the town near Paris called Argenteuil, where she had been brought up and educated as a small girl, and I also had made for her a religious habit of the type worn by novices, with the exception of the veil, and made her put it on.[1]

1. Heloise took the veil later when she became a nun, but she could have stayed at the convent without wearing a habit at all. The Convent of Ste Marie of Argenteuil was founded as a monastery in the late seventh

At this news her uncle and his friends and relatives imagined that I had tricked them, and had found an easy way of ridding myself of Heloise by making her a nun. Wild with indignation they plotted against me, and one night as I slept peacefully in an inner room in my lodgings, they bribed one of my servants to admit them and there took cruel vengeance on me of such appalling barbarity as to shock the whole world; they cut off the parts of my body whereby I had committed the wrong of which they complained. Then they fled, but the two who could be caught were blinded and mutilated as I had been, one of them being the servant who had been led by greed while in my service to betray his master.

Next morning the whole city gathered before my house, and the scene of horror and amazement, mingled with lamentations, cries and groans which exasperated and distressed me, is difficult, no, impossible, to describe. In particular, the clerks and, most of all, my pupils tormented me with their unbearable weeping and wailing until I suffered more from their sympathy than from the pain of my wound, and felt the misery of my mutiliation less than my shame and humiliation.[1] All sorts of thoughts filled my mind – how brightly my reputation had shone, and now how easily in an evil moment it had been dimmed or rather completely blotted out; how just a judgement of God had struck me in the parts of the body with which I had sinned, and how just a reprisal had been taken by the very man I had myself betrayed. I thought how my rivals would exult over my fitting punishment, how this bitter blow would bring lasting grief and

---

century by a nobleman Hermenricus and his wife Numma, who presented it to the Abbey of St Denis. In the early ninth century Charlemagne removed it from St Denis and made it independent, with his daughter Theodrada as abbess. She intended it to revert to St Denis at her death, but in the civil wars and the Norman invasions it was destroyed and abandoned for about 150 years. At the end of the tenth century it was restored by Queen Adelaide, wife of Hugh Capet, richly endowed and filled with nuns of the order of St Benedict.

1. A letter of consolation exists, written by Fulk, prior of the Benedictine house of St Eugène at Deuil, near Montmorency. See P.L. 178, 371–2; Cousin, Vol. I, pp. 703–7.

misery to my friends and parents, and how fast the news of this unheard-of disgrace would spread over the whole world. What road could I take now? How could I show my face in public, to be pointed at by every finger, derided by every tongue, a monstrous spectacle to all I met? I was also appalled to remember that according to the cruel letter of the Law, a eunuch is such an abomination to the Lord that men made eunuchs by the amputation or mutilation of their members are forbidden to enter a church as if they were stinking and unclean, and even animals in that state are rejected for sacrifice. 'Ye shall not present to the Lord any animal if its testicles have been bruised or crushed, torn or cut.' 'No man whose testicles have been crushed or whose organ has been severed shall become a member of the assembly of the Lord.'[1]

I admit that it was shame and confusion in my remorse and misery rather than any devout wish for conversion which brought me to seek shelter in a monastery cloister. Heloise had already agreed to take the veil in obedience to my wishes and entered a convent. So we both put on the religious habit, I in the Abbey of St Denis,[2] and she in the Convent of Argenteuil which I spoke of before. There were many people, I remember, who in pity for her youth tried to dissuade her from submitting to the yoke of monastic rule as a penance too hard to bear, but all in vain; she broke out as best she could through her tears and sobs into Cornelia's famous lament:[3]

O noble husband,
Too great for me to wed, was it my fate
To bend that lofty head? What prompted me
To marry you and bring about your fall?
Now claim your due, and see me gladly pay...

1. Leviticus xxii, 24; Deuteronomy xxiii, 1.

2. The Benedictine Abbey of St Denis, built to enshrine the tomb of the first bishop of Paris, had close royal connections (many of the kings of France were crowned and buried there), and at this date (*c.* 1119) was still 'unreformed' and often used as a centre for transacting state business. It was to be splendidly embellished and monastic discipline restored in accordance with St Benedict's Rule by Abbot Suger under the guidance of St Bernard of Clairvaux. See *The Letters of St Bernard*, trans. B. S. James, no. 80.

3. Lucan, *Pharsalia*, 8. 94.

So saying she hurried to the altar, quickly took up the veil blessed by the bishop, and publicly bound herself to the religious life.

I had still scarcely recovered from my wound when the clerks came thronging round to pester the abbot and myself with repeated demands that I should now for love of God continue the studies which hitherto I had pursued only in desire for wealth and fame. They urged me to consider that the talent entrusted to me by God would be required of me with interest; that instead of addressing myself to the rich as before I should devote myself to educating the poor, and recognize that the hand of the Lord had touched me for the express purpose of freeing me from the temptations of the flesh and the distractions of the world so that I could devote myself to learning, and thereby prove myself a true philosopher not of the world but of God.

But the abbey to which I had withdrawn was completely worldly and depraved, with an abbot whose pre-eminent position was matched by his evil living and notorious reputation. On several occasions I spoke out boldly in criticism of their intolerably foul practices, both in private and in public, and made myself such a burden and nuisance to them all that they gladly seized on the daily importunities of my pupils as a pretext for having me removed from their midst. As pressure continued for some time and these demands became insistent, my abbot and the monks intervened, and I retired to a priory[1] where I could devote myself to teaching as before; and there my pupils gathered in crowds until there were too many for the place to hold or the land to support.

I applied myself mainly to study of the Scriptures as being more suitable to my present calling, but I did not wholly abandon the instruction in the profane arts in which I was better practised and which was most expected of me. In fact I used it as a hook, baited with a taste of philosophy, to draw my listeners towards the study of the true philosophy – the practice of the greatest of Christian philosophers, Origen, as

1. At Maisoncelle-en-Brie, near Provins, in the county of Champagne.

recorded by Eusebius in his *History of the Christian Church.*[1] When it became apparent that God had granted me the gift for interpreting the Scriptures as well as secular literature, the numbers in my school began to increase for both subjects, while elsewhere they diminished rapidly. This roused the envy and hatred of the other heads of schools against me; they set out to disparage me in whatever way they could, and two of them[2] especially were always attacking me behind my back for occupying myself with secular literature in a manner totally unsuitable to my monastic calling,[3] and for presuming to set up as a teacher of sacred learning when I had had no teacher myself. Their aim was for every form of teaching in a school to be forbidden me, and for this end they were always trying to win over bishops, archbishops, abbots, in fact anyone of account in the Church whom they could approach.

Now it happened that I first applied myself to lecturing on the basis of our faith by analogy with human reason, and composed a theological treatise *On the Unity and Trinity of God* for the use of my students who were asking for human and logical reasons on this subject, and demanded something intelligible rather than mere words. In fact they said that words were useless if the intelligence could not follow them, that nothing could be believed unless it was first understood, and that it was absurd for anyone to preach to others what neither he nor those he taught could grasp with the understanding: the Lord himself had criticized such 'blind guides of blind men'.[4] After the treatise had been seen and read by many people it began to please everyone, as it seemed to answer all questions alike on this subject. It was generally agreed that the questions were peculiarly difficult and the importance of the problem was matched by the subtlety of my solution.

1. *Historia Ecclesiae*, 6. 8 ff.
2. Presumably Alberic and Lotulf.
3. St Benedict says nothing in the Rule about whether secular literature should be studied or not, and we do not know how general the practice had become.
4. Matthew xv, 14.

My rivals were therefore much annoyed and convened a Council against me, prompted by my two old opponents, Alberic and Lotulf who, now that our former masters, William and Anselm, were dead, were trying to reign alone in their place and succeed them as their heirs. Both of them were heads of the school in Rheims, and there, by repeated insinuations, they were able to influence their archbishop, Ralph, to take action against me and, along with Conon, bishop of Palestrina,[1] who held the office of papal legate in France at the time, to convene an assembly, which they called a Council, in the city of Soissons, where I was to be invited to come bringing my treatise on the Trinity. This was done, but before I could make my appearance, my two rivals spread such evil rumours about me amongst the clerks and people that I and the few pupils who had accompanied me narrowly escaped being stoned by the people on the first day we arrived, for having preached and written (so they had been told) that there were three Gods.

I called on the legate as soon as I entered the town, handed him a copy of the treatise for him to read and form an opinion, and declared myself ready to receive correction and make amends if I had written anything contrary to the Catholic faith. But he told me at once to take the book to the archbishop and my opponents, so that my accusers could judge me themselves and the words 'Our enemies are judges'[2] be fulfilled in me. However, though they read and reread the book again and again they could find nothing they dared charge me with at an open hearing, so they adjourned the condemnation they were panting for until the final meeting of the Council. For my part, every day before the Council sat I spoke in public on the Catholic faith in accordance with what I had written, and all who heard me were full of praise both for my exposition and for my interpretation. When the people and clerks saw this they began to say '"Here he is, speaking openly,"[3] and no one utters a word against him. The Council which we were told was expressly convened

1. Praeneste in central Italy.
2. Deuteronomy xxxii, 31.
3. John vii, 26.

against him is quickly coming to an end. Can the judges have found that the error is theirs, not his?' This went on every day and added fuel to my enemies' fury.

And so one day Alberic sought me out with some of his followers, intent on attacking me. After a few polite words he remarked that something he had noticed in the book had puzzled him very much; namely, that although God begat God, and there is only one God, I denied that God had begotten Himself. I said at once that if they wished I would offer an explanation on this point. 'We take no account of rational explanation, he answered, 'nor of your interpretation in such matters; we recognize only the words of authority.' 'Turn the page,' I said, 'and you will find the authority.' There was a copy of the book at hand, which he had brought with him, so I looked up the passage which I knew but which he had failed to see – or else he looked only for what would damage me. By God's will I found what I wanted at once: a sentence headed 'Augustine, *On the Trinity*, Book One'.[1] 'Whoever supposes that God has the power to beget Himself is in error, and the more so because it is not only God who lacks this power, but also any spiritual or corporeal creature. There is nothing whatsoever which can beget itself.'

When his followers standing by heard this they blushed in embarrassment, but he tried to cover up his mistake as best he could by saying that this should be understood in the right way. To that I replied that it was nothing new, but was irrelevant at the moment as he was looking only for words, not interpretation. But if he was willing to hear an interpretation and a reasoned argument I was ready to prove to him that by his own words he had fallen into the heresy of supposing the Father to be His own Son. On hearing this he lost his temper and turned to threats, crying that neither my explanations nor my authorities would help me in this case. He then went off.

On the last day of the Council, before the session was resumed, the legate and the archbishop began to discuss at length with my opponents and other persons what decision

1. *De Trinitate*, I. I.

to take about me and my book, as this was the chief reason for their being convened. They could find nothing to bring against me either in my words or in the treatise which was before them, and everyone stood silent for a while or began to retract his accusation, until Geoffrey, bishop of Chartres,[1] who was outstanding among the other bishops for his reputation for holiness and the importance of his see, spoke as follows: 'All of you, Sirs, who are here today know that this man's teaching, whatever it is, and his intellectual ability have won him many followers and supporters wherever he has studied. He has greatly lessened the reputation both of his own teachers and of ours, and his vine has spread its branches from sea to sea.[2] If you injure him through prejudice, though I do not think you will, you must know that even if your judgement is deserved you will offend many people, and large numbers will rally to his defence; especially as in this treatise before us we can see nothing which deserves any public condemnation. Jerome has said that "Courage which is unconcealed always attracts envy, and lightning strikes the mountain-peaks."[3] Beware lest violent action on your part brings him even more renown, and we are more damaged ourselves for our envy than he is through the justice of the charge. Jerome also reminds us that "A false rumour is soon stifled, and a man's later life passes judgement on his past."[4] But if you are determined to act canonically against him, let his teaching or his writing be put before us, let him be questioned and allowed to give free reply, so that if he is convicted or confesses his error he can be totally silenced. This will at least be in accordance with the words of holy Nicodemus, when he wished to set free the Lord himself: "Does our law permit us to pass judgement on a man unless we have first given him a hearing and learned the facts?" '[5]

At once my rivals broke in with an outcry: 'Fine advice

1. Geoffrey of Lèves, Bishop of Chartres, 1115–1149.

2. Cf. Psalm lxxx, 8–12. The same phrase is applied to Abelard in the letter sent to Innocent the Second by the Council of Sens in 1141.

3. Cf. Horace, *Odes*, II. 10. 11.

4. *Epistulae* liv, 13.

5. John vii, 51.

that is, to bid us compete with the ready tongue of a man whose arguments and sophistries could triumph over the whole world!' (But it was surely far harder to compete with Christ, and yet Nicodemus asked for him to be given a hearing, as sanctioned by the law.) However, when the bishop could not persuade them to agree to his proposal, he tried to curb their hostility by other means, saying that the few people present were insufficient for discussing a matter of such importance, and this case needed longer consideration. His further advice was that my abbot, who was present, should take me back to my monastery, the Abbey of St Denis, and there a larger number of more learned men should be assembled to go into the case thoroughly and decide what was to be done. The legate agreed with this last suggestion, and so did everyone else. Soon after, the legate rose to celebrate Mass before he opened the Council. Through Bishop Geoffrey he sent me the permission agreed on: I was to return to my monastery and await a decision.

Then my rivals, thinking that they had achieved nothing if this matter were taken outside their diocese, where they would have no power to use force – it was plain that they had little confidence in the justice of their cause – convinced the archbishop that it would be an insult to his dignity if the case were transferred and heard elsewhere, and a serious danger if I were allowed to escape as a result. They hurried to the legate, made him reverse his decision, and persuaded him against his better judgement to condemn the book without any inquiry, burn it immediately in the sight of all, and condemn me to perpetual confinement in a different monastery. They said that the fact that I had dared to read the treatise in public and must have allowed many people to make copies without its being approved by the authority of the Pope or the Church should be quite enough to condemn it, and that the Christian faith would greatly benefit if an example were made of me and similar presumption in many others were forestalled. As the legate was less of a scholar than he should have been, he relied largely on the advice of the archbishop, who in turn relied on theirs. When the bishop of Chartres saw what would happen he told me at once about their intrigues and strongly urged me not to take it too hard, as by now it was apparent to all that they were acting too harshly. He said I could be confident that such violence so clearly prompted by jealousy would discredit them and benefit me, and told me not to worry about being confined in a monastery as he knew that the papal legate was only acting under pressure, and would set me quite free within a few days of his leaving Soissons. So he gave me what comfort he could, both of us shedding tears.

I was then summoned and came at once before the Council. Without any questioning or discussion they compelled me to throw my book into the fire with my own hands, and so it was burnt. But so that they could appear to have something to say, one of my enemies muttered that he understood it was written in the book that only God the Father was Almighty. Overhearing this, the legate replied in great surprise that one would scarcely believe a small child could make such a mistake, seeing that it is a professed tenet of our common faith that there are three Almighties. Thereupon the head of a school, Thierry by name,[1] laughed and quoted the words of Athanasius: 'And yet there are not three Almighties, but one Almighty.'[2] His bishop spoke sharply to him and rebuked him for contempt of court, but he boldly stood his ground and, in the words of Daniel:[3] '"Are you such fools, you Israelites, thus to condemn a woman of Israel, without making careful inquiry and finding out the truth? Re-open the trial,"' he said, 'and judge the judge himself, you who set up such a judge for the establishment of the Faith and the correction of error; instead of passing judgement he has condemned himself out of his own mouth. Today God in his mercy clearly acquits this innocent man as he delivered Susanna of old from the hands of her false accusers!'

1. This has generally been taken to be the Thierry who was chancellor of Chartres from 1141, but there is no real evidence that he was head of the school at Chartres at this time. See R. W. Southern, 'Humanism and the School of Chartres' in *Medieval Humanism and other Studies* (1970), p. 68 ff.

2. In the Athanasian Creed.

3. Susanna 48–9 (Apocrypha).

Then the archbishop rose to his feet and confirmed the opinion of the legate, changing only the wording, as was needed. 'Truly, my lord,' he said, 'the Father is Almighty, the Son is Almighty and the Holy Spirit is Almighty, and whoever does not share this belief is clearly in error and should not be heard. And now, with your permission, it would be proper for our brother to profess his faith before us all, so that it may be duly approved or disapproved and corrected.' I then stood up to make a full profession of my faith and explain it in my own words, but my enemies declared that it was only necessary for me to recite the Athanasian Creed – as any boy could do. They even had the text put before me to read in case I should plead ignorance, as though I were not familiar with the words. I read it as best I could for my tears, choked with sobs. Then I was handed over as if guilty and condemned to the abbot of St Médard,[1] who was present, and taken off to his cloister as if to prison. The Council then immediately dispersed.

The abbot and monks of St Médard welcomed me most warmly and treated me with every consideration, thinking that I should remain with them in future. They tried hard to comfort me, but in vain. God who judges equity, with what bitterness of spirit and anguish of mind did I reproach you in my madness and accuse you in my fury, constantly repeating the lament of St Antony – 'Good Jesus, where were you?' All the grief and indignation, the blushes for shame, the agony of despair I suffered then I cannot put into words. I compared my present plight with my physical suffering in the past, and judged myself the unhappiest of men. My former betrayal seemed small in comparison with the wrongs I now had to endure, and I wept much more for the injury done to my reputation than for the damage to my body, for that I had brought upon myself through my own fault, but this open violence had come upon me only because of the

1. Abbot Geoffrey of St Médard, a Cluniac foundation in Soissons, who was later bishop of Châlons-sur-Marne. The judgement passed on Abelard at the Council of Soissons was contrary to ecclesiastical law and also unjust, as he was given no chance to defend himself.

purity of my intentions and love of our Faith which had compelled me to write.

But as the news spread and everyone who heard it began to condemn outright this wanton act of cruelty, the persons who had been present tried to shift the blame on to others; so much so that even my rivals denied it had been done on their advice, and the legate publicly denounced the jealousy of the French in this affair. He soon regretted his conduct and, some days later, feeling that he had satisfied their jealousy at a time when under constraint, he had me brought out of St Médard and sent back to my own monastery, where, as I said above, nearly all the monks who were there before were now my enemies; for their disgraceful way of life and scandalous practices made them deeply suspicious of a man whose criticisms they could ill endure.

A few months later chance gave them the opportunity to work for my downfall. It happened that one day in my reading I came across a statement of Bede, in his *Commentary on the Acts of the Apostles*,[1] which asserted that Dionysius the Areopagite was bishop of Corinth, not of Athens. This seemed in direct contradiction to their claim that their patron Denis is to be identified with the famous Areopagite whose history shows him to have been bishop of Athens. I showed my discovery, by way of a joke, to some of the brothers who were standing by, as evidence from Bede which was against us. They were very much annoyed and said that Bede was a complete liar and they had a more truthful witness in their own abbot Hilduin,[2] who had spent a long time travelling in

1. Chapter 17. Both Bede and the monks of St Denis were wrong. Dionysius the Areopagite converted by St Paul (Acts xvii, 34) was thought to be bishop of Athens, and there was also a Dionysius bishop of Corinth, but the martyr who was patron saint of France and of the abbey belongs to the third century, and there is no indication that he came from Greece. A fourth Dionysius, now known as Pseudo-Dionysius, was a Syrian of *c.* 500 who left important metaphysical writings.

2. Hilduin was abbot of St Denis from 814 to 840 and chaplain to Louis the Pious, who commissioned him to write a Life of St Denis. He was the first to say categorically that the Areopagite and St Denis of Paris were the same person.

Greece to investigate the matter; he had found out the truth and removed all shadow of doubt in the history of the saint which he had compiled himself. Then one of them abruptly demanded my opinion on the discrepancy between Bede and Hilduin. I replied that the authority of Bede, whose writings are accepted by the entire Latin Church, carried more weight with me.

In their fury at this answer they began to cry that now I had openly revealed myself as the enemy of the monastery, and was moreover a traitor to the whole country in seeking to destroy the glory that was its special pride by denying that their patron was the Areopagite. I said that I had not denied it, nor did it much matter whether he was the Areopagite or came from somewhere else, seeing that he had won so bright a crown in the eyes of God. However, they hurried straight to the abbot[1] and told him what they accused me of. He was only too ready to listen and delighted to seize the opportunity to destroy me, for he had the greater reason to fear me as his own life was even more scandalous than that of the rest. He summoned his council, and the chapter of the brethren, and denounced me severely, saying that he would send me straightaway to the king for punishment on the charge of having designs on the royal dignity and crown. Meanwhile he put me under close surveillance until I could be handed over to the king. I offered to submit myself to the discipline of the Rule if I had done wrong, but in vain.

I was so horrified by their wickedness and in such deep despair after having borne the blows of fortune so long, feeling that the whole world had conspired against me, that with the help of a few brothers who took pity on me and the support of some of my pupils I fled secretly in the night, and took refuge in the neighbouring territory of Count Theobald,[2] where once before I had stayed in a priory. I was slightly

1. Adam, who was succeeded by Suger in 1122. Abelard subsequently wrote him a conciliatory letter (Cousin, Vol. I, pp. 682–6; P.L. 178, 341–4), perhaps to gain his support to his proposal to live as a monk in a place of his choice.

2. Theobald (Thibaud) II, Count of Troyes and Champagne, and also of Blois and Chartres by inheritance from his mother, Adela, daughter

acquainted with the Count personally, and he had heard of my afflictions and took pity on me. There I began to live in the town of Provins, in a community of monks from Troyes[1] whose prior had long been my close friend and loved me dearly. He was overjoyed by my arrival and made every provision for me.

But one day it happened that the abbot of St Denis came to the town to see Count Theobald on some personal business; on hearing this, I approached the count, along with the prior, and begged him to intercede for me with the abbot and obtain his pardon and permission to live a monastic life wherever a suitable place could be found. The abbot and those with him took counsel together on the matter, so as to give the count their answer the same day, before they left. On deliberation they formed the opinion that my intention was to be transferred to another abbey and that this would be a great reproach to them, for they considered that I had brought them great glory when I entered the religious life by coming to them in preference to all other abbeys, and now it would be a serious disgrace if I cast them off and went elsewhere. Consequently they would not hear a word on the subject either from the count or from me. Moreover they threatened me with excommunication if I did not return quickly, and absolutely forbade the prior with whom I had taken refuge to keep me any longer, under penalty of sharing my excommunication.

Both the prior and I were very much alarmed at this. The abbot departed, still in the same mind, and a few days later he died. When his successor was appointed,[2] I met him with the bishop of Meaux, hoping that he would grant what I had

---

of William the Conqueror. He was the nephew of Henry I of England. He administered his vast territories for thirty years as a ruler independent from the king of France, on the whole with piety and justice. St Bernard writes to him affectionately in Letters 39–46 and 341 (B. S. James's translation).

1. The Priory of St Ayoul in the lower town of Provins; the church is still there.

2. Abbot Suger was appointed in March 1122. The bishop of Meaux was Burchard.

sought from his predecessor. He too was unwilling to do so at first; but through the intervention of some of my friends I appealed to the king and his council, and so got what I wanted. A certain Stephen,[1] the king's seneschal at the time, summoned the abbot and his supporters and asked why they wished to hold me against my will when this could easily involve them in scandal and do no good, as my life and theirs could never possibly agree. I knew that the opinion of the king's council was that the more irregular an abbey was, the more reason why it should be subject to the king and bring him profit, at least as regards its worldly goods, and this made me think that I should easily win the consent of the king and his council – which I did. But so that the monastery should not lose the reputation gained from having me as a member, I was given permission to withdraw to any retreat I liked, provided that I did not come under the authority of any abbey. This was agreed and confirmed on both sides in the presence of the king and his council.

And so I took myself off to a lonely spot I had known before in the territory of Troyes, and there, on a piece of land given me, by leave of the local bishop, I built a sort of oratory of reeds and thatch and dedicated it in the name of the Holy Trinity.[2] Here I could stay hidden alone but for one of my clerks, and truly cry out to the Lord 'Lo, I escaped far away and found a refuge in the wilderness.'[3]

No sooner was this known than the students began to gather there from all parts, hurrying from cities and towns to inhabit the wilderness, leaving large mansions to build themselves little huts, eating wild herbs and coarse bread instead of delicate food, spreading reeds and straw in place

1. Stephen de Garlande, a deacon and also archdeacon of Notre Dame and dean of Orleans, who was seneschal of the royal household. St Bernard (Letter 80) protests to Suger about his 'serving God as deacon and Mammon as a minister of state'. The king at this time was Louis VI.

2. This was on the bank of the river Ardusson, four miles south-east of Nogent-sur-Seine, in the parish of Quincey. The bishop was Hato of Troyes, friend and correspondent of both St Bernard and Peter the Venerable.

3. Psalm lv, 7.

of soft beds and using banks of turf for tables. They could rightly be thought of as imitating the early philosophers, of whom Jerome in the second book of his *Against Jovinian* says:[1]

The senses are like windows through which the vices gain entry into the soul. The capital and citadel of the spirit cannot be taken except by a hostile army entering through the gates. If anyone takes pleasure in the circus and athletic contests, an actor's pantomime or a woman's beauty, the splendour of jewels and garments or anything of that sort, the liberty of his soul is captured through the window of the eye, and the word of the prophet is fulfilled: 'Death has climbed in through our windows.'[2] So when the marshalled forces of distraction have marched through these gates into the citadel of the soul, where will its liberty be and its fortitude? Where will be its thoughts of God? Especially when sensibility pictures for itself pleasures of the past and by recalling its vices compels the soul to take part in them and, as it were, to practise what it does not actually do. These are the considerations which have led many philosophers to leave crowded cities and the gardens outside them, where they find that water meadows and leafy trees, twittering of birds, reflections in spring waters and murmuring brooks are so many snares for eye and ear; they fear that amidst all this abundance of riches the strength of the soul will weaken and its purity be soiled. No good comes from looking often on what may one day seduce you, and in exposing yourself to the temptation of what you find it difficult to do without. Indeed, the Pythagoreans used to shun this kind of contact and lived in solitude in the desert. Plato himself was a wealthy man (and his couch was trampled on by Diogenes with muddy feet),[3] yet in order to give all his time to philosophy he chose to set up his Academy some way from the city on a site which was unhealthy as well as deserted, so that the perpetual preoccupation of sickness would break the assaults of lust, and his pupils would know no pleasures but what they had from their studies.

Such too was the life that the sons of the prophets, the followers of Elisha, are said to have led,[4] of whom (amongst

1. Chapter 8 ff. 2. Jeremiah ix, 21.

3. Diogenes Laertius, *Vitae philosophorum*, 6. 26. Diogenes the Cynic said that in doing so he trampled on Plato's pride, and Plato retorted that he showed pride of a different sort.

4. 2 Kings vi, 1; Jerome, *Epistulae* cxxv, 7.

other things) Jerome writes to the monk Rusticus, as if they were the monks of their time, that 'The sons of the prophets, who are called monks in the Old Testament, built themselves huts by the river Jordan, and abandoned city crowds to live on barley meal and wild herbs.' My pupils built themselves similar huts on the banks of the Ardusson, and looked like hermits rather than scholars.

But the greater the crowds of students who gathered there and the harder the life they led under my teaching, the more my rivals thought this brought honour to me and shame upon themselves. They had done all they could to harm me, and now they could not bear to see things turning out for my advantage; and so, in the words of Jerome: 'Remote as I was from cities, public affairs, law-courts and crowds, envy (as Quintilian says)[1] sought me out in my retreat.' They brooded silently over their wrongs, and then began to complain '"Why, all the world has gone after him"[2] – we have gained nothing by persecuting him, only increased his fame. We meant to extinguish the light of his name but all we have done is make it shine still brighter. See how the students have everything they need at hand in the cities, but they scorn the comforts of civilization, flock to the barren wilderness, and choose this wretched life of their own accord.'

Now it was sheer pressure of poverty at the time which determined me to open a school, since I was 'not strong enough to dig and too proud to beg';[3] so I returned to the skill which I knew, and made use of my tongue instead of working with my hands. For their part, my pupils provided all I needed unasked, food, clothing, work on the land as well as building expenses, so that I should not be kept from my studies by domestic cares of any kind. As my oratory could not hold even a modest proportion of their numbers, they were obliged to enlarge it, and improved it by building in wood and stone. It had been founded and dedicated in the name of the Holy Trinity, but because I had come there as a fugitive and in the depths of my despair had been granted

1. *Declamationes*, 13. 2. 2. John xii, 19.
3. Luke xvi, 3.

some comfort by the grace of God, I named it the Paraclete, in memory of this gift. Many who heard the name were astonished, and several people violently attacked me, on the grounds that it was not permissible for my church to be assigned specifically to the Holy Spirit any more than to God the Father, but that it must be dedicated according to ancient custom either to the Son alone or to the whole Trinity.

This false charge doubtless arose from their mistaken belief that there was no distinction between the Paraclete and the Holy Spirit as Paraclete. In fact, the whole Trinity or any member of the Trinity may be addressed as God and Protector and equally properly be addressed as Paraclete, that is, Comforter, according to the words of the Apostle:[1] 'Praise be to the God and Father of our Lord Jesus Christ, the all-merciful Father and the God whose consolation never fails us. He comforts us in all our troubles; and as the Truth says, "And he shall give you another to be your Comforter."' When the whole Church is consecrated in the name of the Father and of the Son and of the Holy Spirit, and is in their possession indivisibly, what is to prevent the house of the Lord from being ascribed to the Father or to the Holy Spirit just as much as to the Son? Who would presume to erase the owner's name from above his door? Or again, when the Son has offered himself as a sacrifice to the Father, and consequently, in celebrations of the Mass it is the Father to whom prayers are specially directed and the Host is offered, why should the altar not properly be particularly his to whom prayer and sacrifice are specially offered? Is it any better to say that the altar belongs to him who is sacrificed than to him to whom sacrifice is made? Would anyone claim that an altar is better named after the Lord's Cross, or the Sepulchre, St Michael, St John or St Peter, or any other saint who is neither sacrificed there nor receives sacrifice, nor has prayers addressed to him? Surely even amongst the idolators, altars and temples were said to belong only to those who received sacrifice and homage. Perhaps someone may say that neither

1. 2 Corinthians i, 3–4; John xiv, 16.

churches nor altars should be dedicated to the Father because no deed of his exists which calls for a special feast in his honour. But this argument detracts from the entire Trinity, not from the Holy Spirit, since the Holy Spirit by its coming has its own feast of Pentecost,[1] just as the Son, by his, has the feast of the Nativity; for the Holy Spirit claims its own feast by coming among the disciples just as the Son came into the world.

In fact it seems more fitting that a temple should be ascribed to the Holy Spirit than to any other member of the Trinity, if we pay careful attention to apostolic authority and the workings of the Holy Spirit itself. To none of the three does the Apostle assign a special shrine except to the Holy Spirit, for he speaks neither of a shrine of the Father nor of the Son as he does of the Holy Spirit when he writes in the First Letter to the Corinthians:[2] 'But he who links himself with Christ is one with him, spiritually,' and again, 'Do you not know that your body is a shrine of the indwelling Holy Spirit, and the spirit is God's gift to you? You do not belong to yourselves.' Everyone knows too that the divine benefits of the sacraments administered in the Church are ascribed particularly to the effective power of divine Grace, by which is meant the Holy Spirit. For by water and the Holy Spirit we are reborn in baptism, after which we first become a special temple for God; and in the sacrament of confirmation the sevenfold grace of the Holy Spirit is conferred on us whereby the temple of God is adorned and dedicated. Is it then surprising that we dedicate a material temple to the one to whom the Apostle has specially ascribed a spiritual one? To whom can a church be more fittingly consecrated than to the one to whose effective power all the benefits of the Church sacraments are particularly ascribed? However, in first giving my oratory the name of Paraclete I had no thought of declaring its dedication to a single person; my reason was simply what I said above – it was in memory of the comfort I had found there. But even if I had done so with the intention

1. Acts ii, 1 ff. 2. 1 Corinthians vi, 17, 19.

which was generally believed, it would not have been unreasonable, though unknown to general custom.

Meanwhile, though my person lay hidden in this place, my fame travelled all over the world, resounding everywhere like that poetic creation Echo, so called because she has so large a voice but no substance.[1] My former rivals could do nothing by themselves, and therefore stirred up against me some new apostles[2] in whom the world had great faith. One of these boasted that he had reformed the life of the Canons Regular, the other the life of the monks. They went up and down the country, slandering me shamelessly in their preaching as much as they could, and for a while brought me into considerable disrepute in the eyes of the ecclesiastical as well as of the secular authorities; and they spread such evil reports of my faith and of my way of life that they also turned some of my chief friends against me, while any who up till now had retained some of their old affection for me took fright and tried to conceal this as best they could. God is my witness that I never heard that an assembly of ecclesiastics had met without thinking this was convened to condemn me. I waited like one in terror of being struck by lightning to be brought before a council or synod and charged with heresy or profanity, and, if I may compare the flea with the lion, the ant with the elephant, my rivals persecuted me with the same cruelty as the heretics in the past did St Athanasius. Often, God knows,

1. Ovid, *Metamorphoses*, 2. 359.

2. The 'former rivals' are probably Alberic and Lotulf, but it is difficult to accept the traditional view that the 'new apostles' are St Norbert of Xanten (*c.*1080–*c.*1134), founder of the Order of Premonstratensian (White) Canons and friend of St Bernard, and Bernard himself. There are no extant texts of Norbert attacking Abelard, and in 1126 he was elected archbishop of Magdeburg and was not in France. Bernard does not appear to have been hostile to Abelard until he received William of St Thierry's letter about 1139 which led to the convening of the Council of Sens, unless an early date (*c.* 1125) is accepted for Bernard's *De baptismo* which criticizes the teaching of Abelard or one of his pupils. See Bernard's Letter 236 (James's translation). Abelard is still at the Paraclete at this time, i.e. before 1128 when we know that the nuns from Argenteuil came there. For a full discussion see Muckle, *Mediaeval Studies*, Vol. XII, Appendix pp. 212–13.

I fell into such a state of despair that I thought of quitting the realm of Christendom and going over to the heathen,[1] there to live a quiet Christian life amongst the enemies of Christ at the cost of what tribute was asked. I told myself they would receive me more kindly for having no suspicion that I was a Christian on account of the charges against me, and they would therefore believe I could more easily be won over to their pagan beliefs.

While I was continuously harrassed by these anxieties and as a last resort had thought of taking refuge with Christ among Christ's enemies, an opportunity was offered me which I believed would bring me some respite from the plots against me; but in taking it I fell among Christians and monks who were far more savage and wicked than the heathen. There was in Brittany, in the diocese of Vannes, the Abbey of St Gildas de Rhuys, which the death of its abbot had left without a superior. I was invited there by the unanimous choice of the monks, with the approval of the lord of the district,[2] and permission from the abbot and brothers of my monastery was easily obtained. Thus the jealousy of the French drove me West as that of the Romans once drove St Jerome East.[3] God knows, I should never have accepted this offer had I not hoped to find some escape from the attacks which, as I said, I had perpetually to endure. The country was

1. i.e. the Saracens. Abelard implies that prejudice and persecution on the part of the ecclesiastical authorities made it impossible for him to carry on with his teaching, but the Lament of his pupil Hilary written when Abelard left the Paraclete suggests that the school was closed because of the disorderly behaviour of the large numbers of undisciplined students assembled there. For Hilary see Luscombe, *The School of Peter Abelard*, p. 52 ff.; the Lament is in P.L. 178, 1855–6; Cousin, Vol. I, p. 708, and *The Oxford Book of Medieval Latin Verse*, pp. 243–5.

2. Either Conon IV, Duke of Brittany, or some local feudal lord. The Romanesque abbey-church and some monastic buildings still stand at St Gildas on the bay of Quiberon.

3. St Jerome was secretary for a time to Pope Damasus the First who encouraged his revision of the Latin New Testament, but the hostility of the Romans after the pope's death in 385 made him leave for Bethlehem along with Paula, Eustachium and other Roman ladies who wished to live a studious, simple life under his direction.

wild and the language unknown to me,[1] the natives were brutal and barbarous, the monks were beyond control and led a dissolute life which was well known to all. Like a man who rushes at a precipice in terror at the sword hanging over him, and at the very moment he escapes one death, meets another, I wilfully took myself from one danger to another, and there by the fearful roar of the waves of the Ocean, at the far ends of the earth where I could flee no further, I used to repeat in my prayers the words of the Psalmist:[2] 'From the end of the earth I have called to thee when my heart was in anguish.'

Everyone knows now, I think, of this anguish which my tormented heart suffered night and day at the hands of that undisciplined community I had undertaken to direct, while I thought of the dangers to my soul as well as to my body. I was certain at any rate that if I tried to bring them back to the life of rule for which they had taken their vows it would cost me my own life; yet if I did not do my utmost to achieve this, I should be damned. In addition, the abbey had long been subject to a certain powerful lord in the country who had taken advantage of the disorder in the monastery to appropriate all its adjoining lands for his own use, and was exacting heavier taxes from the monks than he would have done from Jews subject to tribute.[3] The monks beset me with demands for their daily needs, though there was no common allowance for me to distribute, but each one of them provided for himself, his concubine and his sons and daughters from his own purse. They took delight in distressing me over this, and they also stole and carried off what they could, so that when I had reached the end of my resources I should be forced to abandon my attempt at enforcing discipline or leave them altogether. The entire savage population of the area was similarly lawless and out of control; there was no one I could

1. Le Pallet was very near the French border, and Abelard's family may have been French-speaking. There were also several Breton dialects.

2. Psalm lxi, 2.

3. Evidently the reforms of Gregory the Seventh protecting Church property had not touched Brittany at this period. Jews were subject to special imposts locally, but Abelard is probably speaking generally.

turn to for help since I disapproved equally of the morals of them all. Outside the monastery wall that tyrant and his minions never ceased to harry me, inside it the monks were always setting traps for me, until it seemed that the words of the Apostle applied especially to my case:[1] 'Quarrels all round us, forebodings in our heart.'

I used to weep as I thought of the wretched, useless life I led, as profitless to myself as to others; I had once done so much for the clerks, and now that I had abandoned them for the monastery, all I did for them and for the monks was equally fruitless. I had proved ineffective in all my attempts and undertakings, so that now above all men I justly merited the reproach, 'There is the man who started to build and could not finish.'[2] I was in deep despair when I remembered what I had fled from and considered what I had met with now; my former troubles were as nothing in retrospect, and I often used to groan and tell myself that I deserved my present sufferings for deserting the Paraclete, the Comforter, and plunging myself into certain desolation – in my eagerness to escape from threats I had run into actual dangers.

What tormented me most of all was the thought that in abandoning my oratory I had been unable to make proper provision for celebrating the Divine Office, since the place was so poor that it could barely provide for the needs of one man. But then again the true Paraclete himself brought me true comfort in my great distress, and provided for the oratory as was fitting, for it was his own. It happened that my abbot of St Denis by some means took possession of the Abbey of Argenteuil where Heloise – now my sister in Christ rather than my wife – had taken the veil. He claimed that it belonged to his monastery by ancient right,[3] and forcibly expelled the community of nuns, of which she was prioress,

1. 2 Corinthians vii, 5. 2. Luke xiv, 30.

3. See note 18, p. 74. Suger claimed to have seen charters establishing the ownership by the Abbey of St Denis, and he also attacked the morality of the nuns – with what foundation cannot be known. Pope Honorius the Second and King Louis VI agreed to the transfer in 1129. For a full account, see McLeod, op. cit., p. 93 ff.

so that they were now scattered as exiles in various places. I realized that this was an opportunity sent me by the Lord for providing for my oratory, and so I returned and invited her, along with some other nuns from the same convent who would not leave her, to come to the Paraclete; and once they had gathered there, I handed it over to them as a gift,[1] and also everything that went with it. Subsequently, with the approval of the local bishop acting as intermediary, my deed of gift was confirmed by Pope Innocent the Second by charter[2] in perpetuity to them and their successors.

Their life there was full of hardship at first and for a while they suffered the greatest deprivation, but soon God, whom they served devoutly, in his mercy brought them comfort; he showed himself a true Paraclete to them too in making the local people sympathetic and kindly disposed towards them. Indeed, I fancy that their worldly goods were multiplied more in a single year than mine would have been in a hundred, had I remained there, for a woman, being the weaker sex, is the more pitiable in a state of need, easily rousing human sympathy, and her virtue is the more pleasing to God as it is to man. And such favour in the eyes of all did God bestow on that sister of mine who was in charge of the other nuns, that bishops loved her as a daughter, abbots as a sister,[3] the laity as a mother; while all alike admired her piety and wisdom, and her unequalled gentleness and patience in every situation. The more rarely she allowed herself to be seen (so that she could devote herself without distraction to prayer and meditation on holy things in a closed cell) the more eagerly did those outside demand her presence and her spiritual conversation for their guidance.

But then all the people in the neighbourhood began attacking me violently for doing less than I could and should to

1. This was the first meeting of Abelard and Heloise after a separation of ten years.

2. The charter is dated 28 November 1131. The local bishop was Hato of Troyes.

3. Both St Bernard, abbot of Clairvaux, and Peter the Venerable, abbot of Cluny, visited her at a later date.

minister to the needs of the women, as (they said) I was certainly well able to do, if only through my preaching; so I started to visit them more often to see how I could help them. This provoked malicious insinuations, and my detractors, with their usual perverseness, had the effrontery to accuse me of doing what genuine charity prompted because I was still a slave to the pleasures of carnal desire and could rarely or never bear the absence of the woman I had once loved. I often repeated to myself the lament of St Jerome in his letter to Asella about false friends:[1] 'The only fault found in me is my sex, and that only when Paula comes to Jerusalem.' And again: 'Before I knew the house of saintly Paula, my praises were sung throughout the city, and nearly everyone judged me worthy of the highest office of the Church. But I know well that it is through good and evil report that we make our way to the kingdom of heaven.'

When, as I say, I recalled the injustice of such a calumny against so great a man, I took no small comfort from it. 'If my rivals,' said I, 'were to find such strong grounds for suspicion in my case, how I should suffer from their slander! But now that I have been freed from such suspicion by God's mercy, and the power to commit this sin is taken from me, how can the suspicion remain? What is the meaning of this latest monstrous accusation? My present condition removes suspicion of evil-doing so completely from everyone's mind that men who wish to keep close watch on their wives employ eunuchs, as sacred history tell us in the case of Esther and the other concubines of King Ahasuerus.[2] We also read that it was a eunuch of the Ethiopian Queen Candace, a man of authority in charge of all her treasure, whom the apostle Philip was directed by the angel to convert and baptize.[3] Such men have always held positions of responsibility and familiarity in the homes of modest and honourable women simply because they are far removed from suspicions of this kind, and it was to rid himself of it entirely, when planning to include women in

1. *Epistulae* xlv, 2. 2. Cf. Esther ii, 3.

3. Acts viii, 26 ff. More accurately, the N.E.B. translates 'the Kandake, or Queen, of Ethiopia ...' Cf. Letter 4, p. 154–5.

his teaching of sacred learning that the great Christian philosopher Origen laid violent hands on himself, as Book Six of the *History of the Church* relates.'[1] However, I thought that in this God's mercy had been kinder to me than to him, for he is believed to have acted on impulse and been strongly censured as a result, whereas it had happened to me through no fault of mine, but so that I might be set free for a similar work; and with all the less pain for being quick and sudden, for I was asleep when attacked and felt practically nothing.

Yet though perhaps I suffered less physical pain at the time, I am now the more distressed for the calumny I must endure. My agony is less for the mutilation of my body than for the damage to my reputation, for it is written that 'A good name is more to be desired than great riches.'[2] In his sermon *On the Life and Morals of Clerics*[3] St Augustine remarks that 'He who relies on his conscience to the neglect of his reputation is cruel to himself,' and earlier on says: ' "For our aims," as the Apostle says,[4] "are honourable not only in God's sight but also in the eyes of men." For ourselves, our conscience within us is sufficient. For your sake, our reputation should not be sullied but should be powerful amongst you. Conscience and reputation are two different things; conscience concerns yourself, reputation your neighbour.' But what would my enemies in their malice have said to Christ himself and his followers, to the prophets, the apostles, or the other holy Fathers, had they lived in their times, when these men were seen with their manhood intact consorting with women on the friendliest terms? Here also St Augustine in his book *On the Work of Monks* proves that women too were the inseparable companions of our Lord Jesus Christ and the apostles, even to the extent of accompanying them on their preaching:

To this end, faithful women who had worldly goods went with them and made provision for them so that they should lack none of the necessities of this life. If anyone does not believe that it was

1. Eusebius, *Historia Ecclesiae*, 6.8.
2. Proverbs xxii, 1. 3. Sermon 355. 4. 2 Corinthians viii, 21.

the practice of the apostles to take with them women of holy life wherever they preached the Gospel, he has only to hear the Gospel to know that they did this following the example of the Lord himself. For there it is written:[1] 'After this he went journeying from town to town and village to village, proclaiming the good news of God. With him were the Twelve and a number of women who had been set free from evil spirits and infirmities: Mary, known as Mary of Magdala, ... Joanna, the wife of Chuza, Herod's steward, and Susanna, and many others. These women provided for them out of their own resources.'

Leo the Ninth too, in answer to a letter of Parmenian, of the monastery of Studius,[2] says:

We declare absolutely that no bishop, presbyter, deacon or subdeacon may give up the care of his wife in the name of religion, so as not to provide her with food and clothing, though he may not lie with her carnally. This was the practice of the holy apostles, as we read in St Paul:[3] 'Have I no right to take a Christian wife about with me, like the rest of the apostles and the Lord's brothers and Cephas?' Take note, you fool, that he did not say 'Have I no right to embrace a wife' but 'to take about', meaning that they should support their wives on the profit from their preaching, not that they should have further carnal intercourse with them.

Certainly that Pharisee who said to himself of the Lord,[4] 'If this man were a real prophet he would know who this woman is who touches him, and what sort of woman she is, a sinner,' could have supposed far more easily, as far as human judgement goes, that the Lord was guilty of evil-living than my enemies could imagine the same of me; while anyone who saw the Lord's mother entrusted to the care of a young man or the prophets enjoying the hospitality and conversation of widows[5] would entertain far more probable

1. Luke viii, 1–3.

2. This is not in the extant works of Leo the Ninth. The quotation is from an answer of Cardinal Humbertus to a pamphlet written by one Niceta, a monk of the monastery of Studius, in Constantinople. See Muckle, *Mediaeval Studies*, Vol. XII, note 73, pp. 207–8.

3. 1 Corinthians ix, 5.

4. Luke vii, 39.

5. John xix, 27; 2 Kings xvii, 10.

suspicions. And what would my detractors have said if they had seen Malchus, the captive monk of whom St Jerome writes,[1] living in the same home with his wife? In their eyes it would have been a great crime, though the famous doctor had nothing but high praise for what he saw: 'There was an old man named Malchus there . . . a native of the place, and an old woman living in his cottage . . . Both of them were so eager for the faith, for ever wearing down the threshold of the church, that you would have thought them Zacharias and Elizabeth in the Gospel but for the fact that John was not with them.'

Finally, why do they refrain from accusing the holy Fathers themselves, when we have often read or seen how they founded monasteries for women too and ministered to them there, following the example of the seven deacons, who were appointed to wait at table and look after the women?[2] The weaker sex needs the help of the stronger, so much so that the Apostle lays down that the man must always be over the woman, as her head, and as a sign of this he orders her always to have her head covered.[3] And so I am much surprised that the custom should have been long established in convents of putting abbesses in charge of women just as abbots are set over men, and of binding women by profession according to the same rule, for there is so much in the Rule which cannot be carried out by women, whether in authority or subordinate. In several places too, the natural order is overthrown to the extent that we see abbesses and nuns ruling the clergy[4] who have authority over the people, with opportunities of leading them on to evil desires in proportion to their dominance, holding them as they do beneath a heavy yoke. The satirist

1. In his *Vita Malchi* (P.L. 23, 53). Malchus was taken captive by the Saracens and forced to marry a woman who also wished to remain celibate.

2. Acts vi, 2–3.

3. 1 Corinthians xi, 5.

4. Adjacent monasteries of men and women had existed for a long time (in Whitby in the seventh century the abbess St Hilda had ruled over a small community of monks just outside the convent precinct), and Abelard appears to refer to Fontevrault, founded in 1106, where the abbess was the head of her nuns and also of the priests dedicated to their service. See D. Knowles, *From Pachomius to Ignatius*, p. 34.

has this in mind when he says that[1] 'Nothing is more intolerable than a rich woman.'

After much reflection I decided to do all I could to provide for the sisters of the Paraclete, to manage their affairs, to watch over them in person too, so that they would revere me the more, and thus to minister better to their needs. The persecution I was now suffering at the hands of the monks who were my sons was even more persistent and distressing than what I had endured previously from my brothers, so I thought I could turn to the sisters as a haven of peace and safety from the raging storms, find repose there for a while, and at least achieve something amongst them though I had failed with the monks. Indeed, the more they needed me in their weakness, the more it would benefit me.

But now Satan has put so many obstacles in my path that I can find nowhere to rest or even to live; a fugitive and wanderer I carry everywhere the curse of Cain, forever tormented (as I said above) by 'quarrels all round us, forebodings in our heart',[2] or rather, quarrels and forebodings without and within. The hostility of my sons here is far more relentless and dangerous than that of my enemies, for I have them always with me and must be forever on my guard against their treachery. I can see my enemies' violence as a danger to my person if I go outside the cloister; but it is within the cloister that I have to face the incessant assaults – as crafty as they are violent – of my sons, that is, of the monks entrusted to my care, as their abbot and father. How many times have they tried to poison me – as happened to St Benedict![3] The same reason which led him to abandon his depraved sons might well have encouraged me to follow the example of so great a Father of the Church, lest in exposing myself to certain dangers I should be thought a rash tempter

1. Juvenal, *Satires*, 6. 460.

2. Genesis iv, 14; 2 Corinthians vii, 5.

3. The episode is told in the *Dialogues* of Gregory the Great, 2.3. Benedict was asked to leave his solitary life at Subiaco, east of Rome, to be abbot of a small monastery at Vicovaro, where the monks rebelled against his high standards and tried to poison him.

rather than a true lover of God, or even appear to be my own destroyer. And while I guarded as well as I could against their daily assaults by providing my own food and drink, they tried to destroy me during the very act of sacrament by putting poison in the chalice.[1] On another day, when I had gone into Nantes to visit the count who was ill, and was staying there in the home of one of my brothers in the flesh, they tried to poison me by the hand of one of the servants accompanying me, supposing, no doubt, that I should be less on my guard against a plot of that kind. By God's intervention it happened that I did not touch any of the food prepared for me. But one of the monks I had brought from the abbey who knew nothing of their intentions ate it and dropped dead; and the servant who had dared to do this fled in terror, as much through consciousness of his guilt as because of the evidence of his crime.

From then on their villainy was known to all, and I began to make no secret of the fact that I was avoiding their snares as well as I could; I even removed myself from the abbey and lived in small cells with a few companions. But whenever the monks heard that I was travelling anywhere they would bribe robbers and station them on the roads and byways to murder me. I was still struggling against all these perils when one day the hand of the Lord struck me sharply and I fell from my saddle, breaking a bone in my neck.[2] This fracture caused me far greater pain and weakened me more than my previous injury. Sometimes I tried to put a stop to their lawless insubordination by excommunication, and compelled those of them I most feared to promise me either on their honour or on oath taken before the rest that they would leave the abbey altogether and trouble me no more. But then they would openly and shamelessly violate both the word they had given and the oaths they had sworn, until in the end they were forced to renew their oaths on this and many other

1. Abelard must have been an ordained priest at this time, as he was celebrating Mass. Cf. note 3, p. 64.

2. Petrarch added in the margin of his manuscript *et me nocte*. He fell from his horse in February 1345.

things in the presence of the count and the bishops, by authority of the Roman Pope Innocent, through his special legate[1] sent for this purpose.

Even then they would not live in peace. After those mentioned had been expelled I recently came back to the abbey and entrusted myself to the remaining brothers from whom I thought I had less to fear. I found them even worse than the others. They did not deal with poison but with a dagger held to my throat, and it was only under the protection of a certain lord of the land that I managed to escape. I am still in danger, and every day I imagine a sword hanging over my head, so that at meals I dare scarcely breathe: like the man we read about[2] who supposed the power and wealth of the tyrant Dionysius to constitute the supreme happiness until he looked up and saw a sword suspended by a thread over his own head and realised what sort of happiness it is which accompanies earthly power. This is my experience all the time; a poor monk raised to be an abbot, the more wretched as I have become more wealthy, in order that my example may curb the ambition of those who have deliberately chosen a similar course.

Dearly beloved brother in Christ, close friend and long-standing companion, this is the story of my misfortunes which have dogged me almost since I left my cradle; let the fact that I have written it with your own affliction and the injury you have suffered in mind suffice to enable you (as I said at the beginning of this letter) to think of your trouble as little or nothing in comparison with mine, and to bear it with more patience when you can see it in proportion. Take comfort from what the Lord told his followers about the followers of the Devil:[3] 'As they persecuted me they will persecute you. If the world hates you, it hated me first, as you know well. If you belonged to the world, the world would

1. Geoffrey of Lèves, bishop of Chartres, who had spoken on Abelard's behalf at the Council of Soissons. See p. 81.

2. The well-known story of the sword of Damocles; see Cicero, *Tusculanae Disputationes*, v. 20–21. Note the present tense above; Abelard is still at St Gildas.

3. John xv, 20, 18, 19.

love its own.' And the Apostle says:[1] 'Persecution will come to all who want to live a godly life as Christians,' and elsewhere, 'Do you think I am currying favour with men? If I still sought men's favour I should be no servant of Christ.' The psalmist says that 'They are destroyed who seek to please men, since God has rejected them.'[2] It was with this particularly in mind that St Jerome, whose heir I consider myself as regards slanders and false accusations, wrote in his letter to Nepotian:[3] '"If I still sought men's favour" says the Apostle, "I should be no servant of Christ." He has ceased to seek men's favour and is become the servant of Christ.' He also wrote to Asella, concerning false friends,[4] 'Thank God I have deserved the hatred of the world,' and to the monk Heliodorus: 'You are wrong, brother, wrong if you think that the Christian can ever be free of persecution. Our adversary "like a roaring lion, prowls around, seeking someone to devour", and do you think of peace? "He sits in ambush with the rich."'[5]

Let us then take heart from these proofs and examples, and bear our wrongs the more cheerfully the more we know they are undeserved. Let us not doubt that if they add nothing to our merit, at least they contribute to the expiation of our sins. And since everything is managed by divine ordinance, each one of the faithful, when it comes to the test, must take comfort at least from the knowledge that God's supreme goodness allows nothing to be done outside his plan, and whatever is started wrongly, he himself brings it to the best conclusion. Hence in all things it is right to say to him, 'Thy will be done.'[6] Finally, think what consolation comes to those who love God on the authority of the Apostle, who says:[7] 'As we know, all things work together for good for those who love God.' This is what the wisest of mankind had in mind when he said

1. 2 Timothy iii, 12; Galatians i, 10.
2. Perhaps an echo of Psalm lii, but the wording is very inexact.
3. *Epistulae* lii, 13.
4. *Epistulae* xlv, 6; xiv, 4.
5. 1 Peter v, 8. Cf. Psalm x, 8.
6. Matthew vi, 10 (the Lord's Prayer).
7. Romans viii, 28.

in his *Proverbs*:[1] 'Whatever befalls the righteous man it shall not sadden him.' Here he clearly shows that those who are angered by some personal injury, though they well know it has been laid on them by divine dispensation, leave the path of righteousness and follow their own will rather than God's; they rebel in their secret hearts against the meaning of the words 'Thy will be done', and set their own will above the will of God. Farewell.

1. Proverbs xii, 21: Vulgate version, reading *contristabit*. The N.E.B. translates 'No mischief shall befall the righteous.'

The Personal Letters

Letter 1. Heloise to Abelard

To her master, or rather her father, husband, or rather brother; his handmaid, or rather his daughter, wife, or rather sister; to Abelard, Heloise.

Not long ago, my beloved, by chance someone brought me the letter of consolation you had sent to a friend. I saw at once from the superscription that it was yours, and was all the more eager to read it since the writer is so dear to my heart. I hoped for renewal of strength, at least from the writer's words which would picture for me the reality I have lost. But nearly every line of this letter was filled, I remember, with gall and wormwood, as it told the pitiful story of our entry into religion and the cross of unending suffering which you, my only love, continue to bear.

In that letter you did indeed carry out the promise you made your friend at the beginning, that he would think his own troubles insignificant or nothing, in comparison with your own. First you revealed the persecution you suffered from your teachers, then the supreme treachery of the mutilation of your person, and then described the abominable jealousy and violent attacks of your fellow-students, Alberic of Rheims and Lotulf of Lombardy.[1] You did not gloss over what at their instigation was done to your distinguished theological work or what amounted to a prison sentence passed on yourself. Then you went on to the plotting against you by your abbot and false brethren, the serious slanders from those two pseudo-apostles, spread against you by the same rivals, and the scandal stirred up among many people because you had acted contrary to custom in naming your oratory after the Paraclete. You went on to the incessant, intolerable persecutions which you still endure at the hands of that cruel tyrant and the evil monks you call your sons, and so brought your sad story to an end.

1. See *Historia calamitatum*, p. 79.

No one, I think, could read or hear it dry-eyed; my own sorrows are renewed by the detail in which you have told it, and redoubled because you say your perils are still increasing. All of us here are driven to despair of your life, and every day we await in fear and trembling the final word of your death. And so in the name of Christ, who is still giving you some protection for his service, we beseech you to write as often as you think fit to us who are his handmaids and yours, with news of the perils in which you are still storm-tossed. We are all that are left you, so at least you should let us share your sorrow or your joy.

It is always some consolation in sorrow to feel that it is shared, and any burden laid on several is carried more lightly or removed. And if this storm has quietened down for a while, you must be all the more prompt to send us a letter which will be the more gladly received. But whatever you write about will bring us no small relief in the mere proof that you have us in mind. Letters from absent friends are welcome indeed, as Seneca himself shows us by his own example when he writes these words in a passage of a letter to his friend Lucilius:[1]

> Thank you for writing to me often, the one way in which you can make your presence felt, for I never have a letter from you without the immediate feeling that we are together. If pictures of absent friends give us pleasure, renewing our memories and relieving the pain of separation even if they cheat us with empty comfort, how much more welcome is a letter which comes to us in the very handwriting of an absent friend.

Thank God that here at least is a way of restoring your presence to us which no malice can prevent, nor any obstacle hinder; then do not, I beseech you, allow any negligence to hold you back.

You wrote your friend a long letter of consolation, prompted no doubt by his misfortunes, but really telling of your own. The detailed account you gave of these may have been intended for his comfort, but it also greatly increased

1. *Epistulae ad Lucilium*, 40. 1.

our own feeling of desolation; in your desire to heal his wounds you have dealt us fresh wounds of grief as well as re-opening the old. I beg you, then, as you set about tending the wounds which others have dealt, heal the wounds you have yourself inflicted. You have done your duty to a friend and comrade, discharged your debt to friendship and comradeship, but it is a greater debt which binds you in obligation to us who can properly be called not friends so much as dearest friends, not comrades but daughters, or any other conceivable name more tender and holy. How great the debt by which you have bound yourself to us needs neither proof nor witness, were it in any doubt; if the whole world kept silent, the facts themselves would cry out.[1] For you after God are the sole founder of this place, the sole builder of this oratory, the sole creator of this community. You have built nothing here upon another man's foundation.[2] Everything here is your own creation. This was a wilderness open to wild beasts and brigands, a place which had known no home nor habitation of men. In the very lairs of wild beasts and lurking-places of robbers, where the name of God was never heard, you built a sanctuary to God and dedicated a shrine in the name of the Holy Spirit. To build it you drew nothing from the riches of kings and princes, though their wealth was great and could have been yours for the asking: whatever was done, the credit was to be yours alone. Clerks and scholars came flocking here, eager for your teaching, and ministered to all your needs; and even those who had lived on the benefices of the Church and knew only how to receive offerings, not to make them, whose hands were held out to take but not to give, became pressing in their lavish offers of assistance.

And so it is yours, truly your own, this new plantation for God's purpose, but it is sown with plants which are still very tender and need watering if they are to thrive. Through its feminine nature this plantation would be weak and frail even if it were not new; and so it needs a more careful and regular cultivation, according to the words of the Apostle:

1. Cf. Cicero, *In Catalinam*, 1. 8.   2. Cf. Romans xv, 20.

'I planted the seed and Apollos watered it; but God made it grow.'[1] The Apostle through the doctrine that he preached had planted and established in the faith the Corinthians, to whom he was writing. Afterwards the Apostle's own disciple, Apollos, had watered them with his holy exhortations and so God's grace bestowed on them growth in the virtues. You cultivate a vineyard of another's vines which you did not plant yourself and which has now turned to bitterness against you,[2] so that often your advice brings no result and your holy words are uttered in vain. You devote your care to another's vineyard; think what you owe to your own. You teach and admonish rebels to no purpose, and in vain you throw the pearls of your divine eloquence to the pigs.[3] While you spend so much on the stubborn, consider what you owe to the obedient; you are so generous to your enemies but should reflect on how you are indebted to your daughters. Apart from everything else, consider the close tie by which you have bound yourself to me, and repay the debt you owe a whole community of women dedicated to God by discharging it the more dutifully to her who is yours alone.

Your superior wisdom knows better than our humble learning of the many serious treatises which the holy Fathers compiled for the instruction or exhortation or even the consolation of holy women, and of the care with which these were composed. And so in the precarious early days of our conversion long ago I was not a little surprised and troubled by your forgetfulness, when neither reverence for God nor our mutual love nor the example of the holy Fathers made you think of trying to comfort me, wavering and exhausted as I was by prolonged grief, either by word when I was with you or by letter when we had parted.[4] Yet you must know that

1. 1 Corinthians iii, 6.

2. Cf. Jeremiah ii, 21.

3. Matthew vii, 6.

4. This sentence, often mistranslated as if it refers to the present and so suggesting that Abelard has never visited nor written to her at the Paraclete, has been used as evidence that the letters are a forgery because it contradicts what Abelard says in the *Historia calamitatum* (p. 98). But the tense (*movit*) is past, translated here as 'I was troubled,' and Heloise must be referring to his failure to help her by word before they separated and

you are bound to me by an obligation which is all the greater for the further close tie of the marriage sacrament uniting us, and are the deeper in my debt because of the love I have always borne you, as everyone knows, a love which is beyond all bounds.

You know, beloved, as the whole world knows, how much I have lost in you, how at one wretched stroke of fortune that supreme act of flagrant treachery robbed me of my very self in robbing me of you; and how my sorrow for my loss is nothing compared with what I feel for the manner in which I lost you. Surely the greater the cause for grief the greater the need for the help of consolation, and this no one can bring but you; you are the sole cause of my sorrow, and you alone can grant me the grace of consolation. You alone have the power to make me sad, to bring me happiness or comfort; you alone have so great a debt to repay me, particularly now when I have carried out all your orders so implicitly that when I was powerless to oppose you in anything, I found strength at your command to destroy myself. I did more, strange to say – my love rose to such heights of madness that it robbed itself of what it most desired beyond hope of recovery, when immediately at your bidding I changed my clothing along with my mind, in order to prove you the sole possessor of my body and my will alike. God knows I never sought anything in you except yourself; I wanted simply you, nothing of yours. I looked for no marriage-bond, no marriage portion, and it was not my own pleasures and wishes I sought to gratify, as you well know, but yours. The name of wife may seem more sacred or more binding, but sweeter for me will always be the word mistress, or, if you will permit me, that of concubine or whore. I believed that the more I humbled myself on your account, the more gratitude I should win from you, and also the less damage I should do to the brightness of your reputation.

You yourself on your own account did not altogether forget this in the letter of consolation I have spoken of

---

by letter after she had entered the convent. See McLeod, op. cit., pp. 248–50.

which you wrote to a friend;[1] there you thought fit to set out some of the reasons I gave in trying to dissuade you from binding us together in an ill-starred marriage. But you kept silent about most of my arguments for preferring love to wedlock and freedom to chains. God is my witness that if Augustus, Emperor of the whole world, thought fit to honour me with marriage and conferred all the earth on me to possess for ever, it would be dearer and more honourable to me to be called not his Empress but your whore.

For a man's worth does not rest on his wealth or power; these depend on fortune, but worth on his merits. And a woman should realize that if she marries a rich man more readily than a poor one, and desires her husband more for his possessions than for himself, she is offering herself for sale. Certainly any woman who comes to marry through desires of this kind deserves wages, not gratitude, for clearly her mind is on the man's property, not himself, and she would be ready to prostitute herself to a richer man, if she could. This is evident from the argument put forward in the dialogue of Aeschines Socraticus[2] by the learned Aspasia to Xenophon and his wife. When she had expounded it in an effort to bring about a reconciliation between them, she ended with these words: 'Unless you come to believe that there is no better man nor worthier woman on earth you will always still be looking for what you judge the best thing of all – to be the husband of the best of wives and the wife of the best of husbands.'

These are saintly words which are more than philosophic; indeed, they deserve the name of wisdom, not philosophy. It is a holy error and a blessed delusion between man and wife, when perfect love can keep the ties of marriage unbroken not so much through bodily continence as chastity of spirit. But what error permitted other women, plain truth permitted me,

1. This suggests that Heloise believed the *Historia calamitatum* to be a genuine letter to a real person, and not an example of a conventional epistolatory genre, unless she is writing ironically.

2. Aeschines Socraticus, a pupil of Socrates, wrote several dialogues of which fragments survive. This is however no proof that Heloise knew Greek, as the passage was well known in the Middle Ages from Cicero's translation of it in *De inventione*, 1.31.

and what they thought of their husbands, the world in general believed, or rather, knew to be true of yourself; so that my love for you was the more genuine for being further removed from error. What king or philosopher could match your fame? What district, town or village did not long to see you? When you appeared in public, who did not hurry to catch a glimpse of you, or crane his neck and strain his eyes to follow your departure? Every wife, every young girl desired you in absence and was on fire in your presence; queens and great ladies envied me my joys and my bed.

You had besides, I admit, two special gifts whereby to win at once the heart of any woman – your gifts for composing verse and song, in which we know other philosophers have rarely been successful. This was for you no more than a diversion, a recreation from the labours of your philosophic work, but you left many love-songs and verses which won wide popularity for the charm of their words and tunes and kept your name continually on everyone's lips.[1] The beauty of the airs ensured that even the unlettered did not forget you; more than anything this made women sigh for love of you. And as most of these songs told of our love, they soon made me widely known and roused the envy of many women against me. For your manhood was adorned by every grace of mind and body, and among the women who envied me then, could there be one now who does not feel compelled by my misfortune to sympathize with my loss of such joys? Who is there who was once my enemy, whether man or woman, who is not moved now by the compassion which is my due? Wholly guilty though I am, I am also, as you know, wholly innocent. It is not the deed but the intention of the doer which makes the crime, and justice should weigh not what was done but the spirit in which it is done.[2] What my

1. Cf. *Historia calamitatum*, p. 68 and note. None of Abelard's secular verse survives.

2. Cf. Letter 3, p. 132, Letter 5, p. 175, and Introduction, p. 18. This is the 'ethic of pure intention' strongly held by Heloise and Abelard and set out in his *Ethica* or *Scito te ipsum* (*Know yourself*): our actions must be judged good or bad solely through the spirit in which they are performed and not by their effects. The deed itself is neither good nor bad.

intention towards you has always been, you alone who have known it can judge. I submit all to your scrutiny, yield to your testimony in all things.

Tell me one thing, if you can. Why, after our entry into religion, which was your decision alone, have I been so neglected and forgotten by you that I have neither a word from you when you are here to give me strength nor the consolation of a letter in absence?[1] Tell me, I say, if you can – or I will tell you what I think and indeed the world suspects. It was desire, not affection which bound you to me, the flame of lust rather than love. So when the end came to what you desired, any show of feeling you used to make went with it. This is not merely my own opinion, beloved, it is everyone's. There is nothing personal or private about it; it is the general view which is widely held. I only wish that it *were* mine alone, and that the love you professed could find someone to defend it and so comfort me in my grief for a while. I wish I could think of some explanation which would excuse you and somehow cover up the way you hold me cheap.

I beg you then to listen to what I ask – you will see that it is a small favour which you can easily grant. While I am denied your presence, give me at least through your words – of which you have enough and to spare – some sweet semblance of yourself. It is no use my hoping for generosity in deeds if you are grudging in words. Up to now I had thought I deserved much of you, seeing that I carried out everything for your sake and continue up to the present moment in complete obedience to you. It was not any sense of vocation which brought me as a young girl to accept the austerities of the cloister, but your bidding alone, and if I deserve no gratitude from you, you may judge for yourself how my

1. This is not to be taken as contradicting Abelard's statement on p. 98 that he often visited the Paraclete, and had invited Heloise and her nuns to go there (either by letter or interview). Her complaint is that he never writes her a personal letter nor offers her help in her personal problems. In Letter 4, p. 145, he refers to her 'old perpetual complaint' to him, but he evidently will not be drawn into discussion. As Muckle puts it, 'he did not and would not become her individual spiritual director' (*Mediaeval Studies*, Vol. XV, p. 58). Cf. note 4, p. 112.

labours are in vain. I can expect no reward for this from God, for it is certain that I have done nothing as yet for love of him. When you hurried towards God I followed you, indeed, I went first to take the veil – perhaps you were thinking how Lot's wife turned back[1] when you made me put on the religious habit and take my vows before you gave yourself to God. Your lack of trust in me over this one thing, I confess, overwhelmed me with grief and shame. I would have had no hesitation, God knows, in following you or going ahead at your bidding to the flames of Hell.[2] My heart was not in me but with you, and now, even more, if it is not with you it is nowhere; truly, without you it cannot exist. See that it fares well with you, I beg, as it will if it finds you kind, if you give grace in return for grace,[3] small for great, words for deeds. If only your love had less confidence in me, my dear, so that you would be more concerned on my behalf! But as it is, the more I have made you feel secure in me, the more I have to bear with your neglect.

Remember, I implore you, what I have done, and think how much you owe me. While I enjoyed with you the pleasures of the flesh, many were uncertain whether I was prompted by love or lust; but now the end is proof of the beginning. I have finally denied myself every pleasure in obedience to your will, kept nothing for myself except to prove that now, even more, I am yours. Consider then your injustice, if when I deserve more you give me less, or rather, nothing at all, especially when it is a small thing I ask of you and one you could so easily grant. And so, in the name of God to whom you have dedicated yourself, I beg you to restore your presence to me in the way you can – by writing me some word of comfort, so that in this at least I may find increased strength and readiness to serve God. When in the past you sought me out for sinful pleasures your letters came to me thick and fast, and your many songs put your Heloise on everyone's lips, so that every

1. Cf. Genesis xix, 26.

2. The Latin is *Vulcania loca*, Vulcan's regions, or Tartarus, and illustrates how Heloise's natural manner of expressing herself is classical.

3. John i, 16.

street and house echoed with my name. Is it not far better now to summon me to God than it was then to satisfy our lust? I beg you, think what you owe me, give ear to my pleas, and I will finish a long letter with a brief ending: farewell, my only love.

Letter 2. Abelard to Heloise

To Heloise, his dearly beloved sister in Christ, Abelard her brother in Christ.

If since our conversion from the world to God I have not yet written you any word of comfort or advice, it must not be attributed to indifference on my part but to your own good sense, in which I have always had such confidence that I did not think anything was needed; God's grace has bestowed on you all essentials to enable you to instruct the erring, comfort the weak and encourage the fainthearted, both by word and example, as, indeed, you have been doing since you first held the office of prioress under your abbess. So if you still watch over your daughters as carefully as you did previously over your sisters, it is sufficient to make me believe that any teaching or exhortation from me would now be wholly superfluous. If, on the other hand, in your humility you think differently, and you feel that you have need of my instruction and writings in matters pertaining to God, write to me what you want, so that I may answer as God permits me. Meanwhile thanks be to God who has filled all your hearts with anxiety for my desperate, unceasing perils, and made you share in my affliction; may divine mercy protect me through the support of your prayers and quickly crush Satan beneath our feet. To this end in particular, I hasten to send the psalter you earnestly begged from me,[1] my sister once dear in the world and now dearest in Christ, so that you may offer a perpetual sacrifice of

1. *Psalterium.* Heloise's letter does not mention this, but the request could have been made in person at the time when Abelard was still visiting the Paraclete: the tense (*requisisti*) suggests it was not very recent (*requiris* would be more natural for a request just received). Possibly the bearer of the letter was told to ask for it. Muckle (*Mediaeval Studies*, Vol. XV, pp. 58–9) suggests that the word refers not to a psalter, or Book of Psalms, which the convent would surely already have, but to a 'Chant', that is, the arrangement of versicles and responses at the end of this letter which are to be used in the prayers on his behalf.

prayers to the Lord for our many great aberrations, and for the dangers which daily threaten me.

We have indeed many examples as evidence of the high position in the eyes of God and his saints which has been won by the prayers of the faithful, especially those of women on behalf of their dear ones and of wives for their husbands. The Apostle observes this closely when he bids us pray continually.[1] We read that the Lord said to Moses 'Let me alone, to vent my anger upon them,'[2] and to Jeremiah 'Therefore offer no prayer for these people nor stand in my path.'[3] By these words the Lord himself makes it clear that the prayers of the devout set a kind of bridle on his wrath and check it from raging against sinners as fully as they deserve; just as a man who is willingly moved by his sense of justice to take vengeance can be turned aside by the entreaties of his friends and forcibly restrained, as it were, against his will. Thus when the Lord says to one who is praying or about to pray, 'Let me alone and do not stand in my path'[4], he forbids prayers to be offered to him on behalf of the impious; yet the just man prays though the Lord forbids, obtains his requests and alters the sentence of the angry judge. And so the passage about Moses continues: 'And the Lord repented and spared his people the evil with which he had threatened them.'[5] Elsewhere it is written about the universal works of God, 'He spoke, and it was.'[6] But in this passage it is also recorded that he had said the people deserved affliction, but he had been prevented by the power of prayer from carrying out his words.

Consider then the great power of prayer, if we pray as we are bidden, seeing that the prophet won by prayer what he was forbidden to pray for, and turned God aside from his declared intention. And another prophet says to God: 'In thy wrath remember mercy.'[7] The lords of the earth should listen and take note, for they are found obstinate rather than just in the execution of the justice they have decreed and

1. 1 Thessalonians v, 16. 2. Exodus xxxii, 10.
3. Jeremiah vii, 16, loosely quoted. 4. Exodus xxxii, 10.
5. Exodus xxxii, 14. 6. Psalm xxxiii, 9. 7. Habbakuk, iii, 2.

pronounced; they blush to appear lax if they are merciful, and untruthful if they change a pronouncement or do not carry out a decision which lacked foresight, even if they can emend their words by their actions. Such men could properly be compared with Jephtha, who made a foolish vow and in carrying it out even more foolishly, killed his only daughter.[1] But he who desires to be a 'member of his body'[2] says with the Psalmist 'I will sing of mercy and justice unto thee, O Lord.'[3] 'Mercy', it is written, 'exalts judgement,' in accordance with the threat elsewhere in the Scriptures: 'In that judgement there will be no mercy for the man who has shown no mercy.'[4] The Psalmist himself considered this carefully when at the entreaty of the wife of Nabal the Carmelite, as an act of mercy he broke the oath he had justly sworn concerning her husband and the destruction of his house.[5] Thus he set prayer above justice, and the man's wrongdoing was wiped out by the entreaties of his wife.

Here you have an example, sister, and an assurance how much your prayers for me may prevail on God, if this woman's did so much for her husband, seeing that God who is our father loves his children more than David did a suppliant woman. David was indeed considered a pious and merciful man, but God is piety and mercy itself. And the woman whose entreaties David heard then was an ordinary lay person, in no way bound to God by the profession of holy devotion; whereas if you alone are not enough to win an answer to your prayer, the holy convent of widows and virgins which is with you will succeed where you cannot by yourself. For when the Truth says to the disciples, 'When two or three have met together in my name, I am there among them,'[6] and again, 'If two of you agree about any request you have to make, it shall be granted by my Father,'[7] we can all see how the com-

1. Judges xi, 30 ff. Abelard was to write a *Lament* for Jephtha's daughter, one of a set of six Laments (P.L. 178, 1819–20; Cousin, Vol. I, p. 334–9).

2. Cf. Ephesians v, 30. 3. Psalm ci, 1. 4. James ii, 13.

5. 1 Samuel, xxv, 32 ff: the meeting of David and Abigail.

6. Matthew xviii, 20. 7. Matthew xviii, 19.

munal prayer of a holy congregation must prevail upon God. If, as the apostle James says, 'A good man's prayer is powerful and effective,'[1] what should we hope for from the large numbers of a holy congregation? You know, dearest sister, from the thirty-eighth homily of St Gregory how much support the prayers of his fellow brethren quickly brought a brother, although he was unwilling and resisted. The depths of his misery, the fear of peril which tormented his unhappy soul, the utter despair and weariness of life which made him try to call his brethren from their prayers – all the details set out there cannot have escaped your understanding.

May this example give you and your convent of holy sisters greater confidence in prayer, so that I may be preserved alive for you all, through him, from whom, as Paul bears witness, women have even received back their dead raised to life.[2] For if you turn the pages of the Old and New Testaments you will find that the greatest miracles of resurrection were shown only, or mostly, to women, and were performed for them or on them. The Old Testament records two instances of men raised from the dead at the entreaties of their mothers, by Elijah and his disciple Elisha.[3] The Gospel, it is true, has three instances only of the dead being raised by the Lord but, as they were shown to women only, they provide factual confirmation of the Apostle's words I quoted above: 'Women received back their dead raised to life.' It was to a widow at the gate of the city of Nain that the Lord restored her son, moved by compassion for her,[4] and he also raised Lazarus his own friend at the entreaty of his sisters Mary and Martha.[5] And when he granted this same favour to the daughter of the ruler of the synagogue at her father's petition,[6] again 'women received back their dead raised to life', for in being brought back to life she received her own body from death just as those other women received the bodies of their dead.

Now these resurrections were performed with only a few interceding; and so the multiplied prayers of your shared devo-

1. James v, 16. 2. Hebrews xi, 35.
3. 1 Kings xvii, 17 ff.; 2 Kings iv, 32 ff. 4. Luke vii, 15.
5. John xi, 1 ff. 6. Mark v, 22 ff.

tion should easily win the preservation of my own life. The more God is pleased by the abstinence and continence which women have dedicated to him, the more willing he will be to grant their prayers. Moreover, it may well be that the majority of those raised from the dead were not of the faith, for we do not read that the widow mentioned above whose son was raised without her asking was a believer. But in our case we are bound together by the integrity of our faith and united in our profession of the same religious life.

Let me now pass from the holy convent of your community, where so many virgins and widows are dedicated to continual service of the Lord, and come to you alone, you whose sanctity must surely have the greatest influence in the eyes of God, and who are bound to do everything possible on my behalf, especially now when I am in the toils of such adversity. Always remember then in your prayers him who is especially yours; watch and pray the more confidently as you recognize your cause is just, and so more acceptable to him to whom you pray. Listen, I beg you, with the ear of your heart to what you have so often heard with your bodily ear. In the book of Proverbs it is written that 'A capable wife is her husband's crown,'[1] and again, 'Find a wife and you find a good thing; so you will earn the favour of the Lord;'[2] yet again, 'Home and wealth may come down from ancestors; but an intelligent wife is a gift from the Lord.'[3] In Ecclesiasticus too it says that 'A good wife makes a happy husband,' and a little later, 'A good wife means a good life.'[4] And we have it on the Apostle's authority that 'the unbelieving husband now belongs to God through his wife'.[5] A special instance of this was granted by God's grace in our own country of France, when Clovis the king was converted to the Christian faith more by the prayers of his wife than by the preaching of holy men;[6] his entire

1. Proverbs xii, 4. 2. Proverbs xviii, 22. 3. Proverbs xix, 14.
4. xxvi, 1; xxvi, 31. 5. 1. Corinthians vii, 14.
6. Clovis (481–511), founder of the Merovingian House of France, was converted to Christianity after his victory over the Alamanni in 496; his wife Clotild, a princess of Burgundy, was already a Catholic and had long begged him to renounce his pagan ways. The story was well known from Gregory of Tours, *History of the Franks*, II. 29–31.

kingdom was then placed under divine law so that humbler men should be encouraged by the example of their betters to persevere in prayer. Indeed, such perseverance is warmly recommended to us in a parable of the Lord which says: 'If the man perseveres in his knocking, though he will not provide for him out of friendship, the very shamelessness of the request will make him get up and give him all he needs.'[1] It was certainly by what I might call this shamelessness in prayer that Moses (as I said above) softened the harshness of divine justice and changed its sentence.

You know, beloved, the warmth of charity your convent once used to show me in their prayers at the times I could be with you. At the conclusion of each of the Hours every day they would offer this special prayer to the Lord on my behalf; after the proper response and versicle were pronounced and sung they added prayers and a collect, as follows:

RESPONSE: Forsake me not, O Lord: Keep not far from me, my God.[2]

VERSICLE: Make haste, O Lord, to help me.[3]

PRAYER: Save thy servant, O my God, whose hope is in thee; Lord hear my prayer, and let my cry for help reach thee.[4]

(LET US PRAY) O God, who through thy servant hast been pleased to gather together thy handmaidens in thy name, we beseech thee to grant both to him and to us that we persevere in thy will. Through our Lord, etc.

But now that I am not with you, there is all the more need for the support of your prayers, the more I am gripped by fear of greater peril. And so I ask of you in entreaty, and entreat you in asking, particularly now that I am absent from you, to show me how truly your charity extends to the absent by adding this form of special prayer at the conclusion of each hour:

RESPONSE: O Lord, Father and Ruler of my life, do not desert me, lest I fall before my adversaries and my enemy gloats over me.[5]

1. Luke xi, 8.
2. Psalm xxxviii, 21.
3. Psalm lxx, 1.
4. Psalm cii, 1.
5. Cf. Ecclesiasticus xxiii, 3.

VERSICLE: Grasp shield and buckler and rise up to help me, lest my enemy gloats.[1]

PRAYER: Save thy servant, O my God, whose hope is in thee. Send him help, O Lord, from thy holy place, and watch over him from Zion. Be a tower of strength to him, O Lord, in the face of his enemy. Lord hear my prayer, and let my cry for help reach thee.

(LET US PRAY) O God who through thy servant hast been pleased to gather together thy handmaidens in thy name, we beseech thee to protect him in all adversity and restore him in safety to thy handmaidens. Through our Lord, etc.

But if the Lord shall deliver me into the hands of my enemies so that they overcome and kill me, or by whatever chance I enter upon the way of all flesh while absent from you, wherever my body may lie, buried or unburied, I beg you to have it brought to your burial-ground, where our daughters, or rather, our sisters in Christ may see my tomb more often and thereby be encouraged to pour out their prayers more fully to the Lord on my behalf. There is no place, I think, so safe and salutary for a soul grieving for its sins and desolated by its transgressions than that which is specially consecrated to the true Paraclete, the Comforter, and which is particularly designated by his name. Nor do I believe that there is any place more fitting for Christian burial among the faithful than one amongst women dedicated to Christ. Women were concerned for the tomb of our Lord Jesus Christ, they came ahead and followed after, bringing precious ointments,[2] keeping close watch around this tomb, weeping for the death of the Bridegroom, as it is written: 'The women sitting at the tomb wept and lamented for the Lord.'[3] And there they were first reassured about his resurrection by the appearance of an angel and the words he spoke to them; later on they were found worthy both to taste the joy of his resurrection when he twice appeared to them, and also to touch him with their hands.

1. Psalm xxxv, 2.
2. Cf. Mark xvi, 1.
3. Not in the Gospels. It is the antiphon for the Benedictus in the Roman Breviary for Holy Saturday.

Finally, I ask this of you above all else: at present you are over-anxious about the danger to my body, but then your chief concern must be for the salvation of my soul, and you must show the dead man how much you loved the living by the special support of prayers chosen for him.

Live, fare you well, yourself and your sisters with you,
Live, but I pray, in Christ be mindful of me.

Letter 3. Heloise to Abelard

To her only one after Christ, she who is his alone in Christ.

I am surprised, my only love, that contrary to custom in letter-writing and, indeed, to the natural order, you have thought fit to put my name before yours in the greeting which heads your letter, so that we have woman before man, wife before husband, handmaid before master, nun before monk, deaconess[1] before priest and abbess before abbot. Surely the right and proper order is for those who write to their superiors or equals to put their names before their own, but in letters to inferiors, precedence in order of address follows precedence in rank.[2]

We were also greatly surprised when instead of bringing us the healing balm of comfort you increased our desolation and made the tears to flow which you should have dried. For which of us could remain dry-eyed on hearing the words you wrote towards the end of your letter: 'But if the Lord shall deliver me into the hands of my enemies so that they overcome and kill me . . .'? My dearest, how could you think such a thought? How could you give voice to it? Never may God be so forgetful of his humble handmaids as to let them outlive you; never may he grant us a life which would be harder to bear than any form of death. The proper course would be for you to perform our funeral rites, for you to commend our souls to God, and to send ahead of you those whom you

1. It is not clear what Heloise means here by 'deaconess', though subservience is implied from its use in the early Church. In Letter 7 Abelard uses the term for an abbess; see p. 199 and note.

2. Heloise shows her knowledge of the rules for composing formal letters (*Dictamen* or *Ars dictandi*) which are found in several treatises from the eleventh century onwards, notably in that by Alberic (later Cardinal), theologian and monk of Monte Cassino, born in 1008. The rule of precedence is generally observed; it is a tribute to Heloise's status and reputation when Peter the Venerable, abbot of Cluny, in writing to her as abbess of the Paraclete, puts her name before his own.

assembled for God's service – so that you need no longer be troubled by worries for us, and follow after us the more gladly because freed from concern for our salvation. Spare us, I implore you, master, spare us words such as these which can only intensify our existing unhappiness; do not deny us, before death, the one thing by which we live. 'Each day has trouble enough of its own,'[1] and that day, shrouded in bitterness, will bring with it distress enough to all it comes upon. 'Why is it necessary,' says Seneca, 'to summon evil'[2] and to destroy life before death comes?

You ask us, my love, if you chance to die when absent from us, to have your body brought to our burial-ground so that you may reap a fuller harvest from the prayers we shall offer in constant memory of you. But how could you suppose that our memory of you could ever fade? Besides, what time will there be then which will be fitting for prayer, when extreme distress will allow us no peace, when the soul will lose its power of reason and the tongue its use of speech? Or when the frantic mind, far from being resigned, may even (if I may say so) rage against God himself, and provoke him with complaints instead of placating him with prayers? In our misery then we shall have time only for tears and no power to pray; we shall be hurrying to follow, not to bury you, so that we may share your grave instead of laying you in it. If we lose our life in you, we shall not be able to go on living when you leave us. I would not even have us live to see that day, for if the mere mention of your death is death for us, what will the reality be if it finds us still alive? God grant we may never live on to perform this duty, to render you the service which we look for from you alone; in this may we go before, not after you!

And so, I beg you, spare us – spare her at least, who is yours alone, by refraining from words like these. They pierce our hearts with swords of death, so that what comes before is more painful than death itself. A heart which is exhausted with grief cannot find peace, nor can a mind preoccupied with anxieties genuinely devote itself to God. I beseech you

1. Matthew vi, 34. 2. Seneca, *Epistulae ad Lucilium*, 24. 1.

not to hinder God's service to which you specially committed us. Whatever has to come to us bringing with it total grief we must hope will come suddenly, without torturing us far in advance with useless apprehension which no foresight can relieve. This is what the poet has in mind when he prays to God:

> May it be sudden, whatever you plan for us; may man's mind
> Be blind to the future. Let him hope on in his fears.[1]

But if I lose you, what is left for me to hope for? What reason for continuing on life's pilgrimage, for which I have no support but you, and none in you save the knowledge that you are alive, now that I am forbidden all other pleasures in you and denied even the joy of your presence which from time to time could restore me to myself? O God – if I dare say it – cruel to me in everything! O merciless mercy! O Fortune who is only ill-fortune, who has already spent on me so many of the shafts she uses in her battle against mankind that she has none left with which to vent her anger on others. She has emptied a full quiver on me, so that henceforth no one else need fear her onslaughts, and if she still had a single arrow she could find no place in me to take a wound. Her only dread is that through my many wounds death may end my sufferings; and though she does not cease to destroy me, she still fears the destruction which she hurries on.

Of all wretched women I am the most wretched, and amongst the unhappy I am unhappiest. The higher I was exalted when you preferred me to all other women, the greater my suffering over my own fall and yours, when I was flung down; for the higher the ascent, the heavier the fall. Has Fortune ever set any great or noble woman above me or made her my equal, only to be similarly cast down and crushed with grief? What glory she gave me in you, what ruin she brought upon me through you! Violent in either extreme, she showed no moderation in good or evil. To make me the saddest of all women she first made me blessed above all, so that when I thought how much I had lost, my consuming grief would match my crushing loss, and my sorrow for what

1. Lucan, *Pharsalia* 2, 14–15.

was taken from me would be the greater for the fuller joy of possession which had gone before; and so that the happiness of supreme ecstasy would end in the supreme bitterness of sorrow.

Moreover, to add to my indignation at the outrage you suffered, all the laws of equity in our case were reversed. For while we enjoyed the pleasures of an uneasy love and abandoned ourselves to fornication (if I may use an ugly but expressive word) we were spared God's severity. But when we amended our unlawful conduct by what was lawful, and atoned for the shame of fornication by an honourable marriage, then the Lord in his anger laid his hand heavily upon us, and would not permit a chaste union though he had long tolerated one which was unchaste. The punishment you suffered would have been proper vengeance for men caught in open adultery. But what others deserve for adultery came upon you through a marriage which you believed had made amends for all previous wrong doing; what adulterous women have brought upon their lovers, your own wife brought on you. Nor was this at the time when we abandoned ourselves to our former delights, but when we had already parted and were leading chaste lives, you presiding over the school in Paris and I at your command living with the nuns at Argenteuil. Thus we were separated, to give you more time to devote yourself to your pupils, and me more freedom for prayer and meditation on the Scriptures, both of us leading a life which was holy as well as chaste. It was then that you alone paid the penalty in your body for a sin we had both committed. You alone were punished though we were both to blame, and you paid all, though you had deserved less, for you had made more than necessary reparation by humbling yourself on my account and had raised me and all my kind to your own level – so much less then, in the eyes of God and of your betrayers, should you have been thought deserving of such punishment.

What misery for me – born as I was to be the cause of such a crime! Is it the general lot of women to bring total ruin on great men? Hence the warning about women in Proverbs:[1]

1. Proverbs vii, 24–7.

'But now, my son, listen to me, attend to what I say: do not let your heart entice you into her ways, do not stray down her paths; she has wounded and laid low so many, and the strongest have all been her victims. Her house is the way to hell, and leads down to the halls of death.' And in Ecclesiastes:[1] 'I put all to the test . . . I find woman more bitter than death; she is a snare, her heart a net, her arms are chains. He who is pleasing to God eludes her, but the sinner is her captive.'

It was the first woman in the beginning who lured man from Paradise, and she who had been created by the Lord as his helpmate became the instrument of his total downfall. And that mighty man of God, the Nazarite whose conception was announced by an angel,[2] Delilah alone overcame; betrayed to his enemies and robbed of his sight, he was driven by his suffering to destroy himself along with his enemies. Only the woman he had slept with could reduce to folly Solomon, wisest of all men; she drove him to such a pitch of madness that although he was the man whom the Lord had chosen to build the temple in preference to his father David, who was a righteous man, she plunged him into idolatry until the end of his life, so that he abandoned the worship of God which he had preached and taught in word and writing.[3] Job, holiest of men, fought his last and hardest battle against his wife, who urged him to curse God.[4] The cunning arch-tempter well knew from repeated experience that men are most easily brought to ruin through their wives, and so he directed his usual malice against us too, and attacked you by means of marriage when he could not destroy you through fornication. Denied the power to do evil through evil, he effected evil through good.

At least I can thank God for this: the tempter did not prevail on me to do wrong of my own consent, like the women I have mentioned, though in the outcome he made me the instrument of his malice. But even if my conscience is clear through innocence, and no consent of mine makes me guilty of this crime, too many earlier sins were committed

1. Ecclesiastes vii, 26.
2. Samson, in Judges xiii, 3.
3. 1 Kings xi, 1–8.
4. Job ii, 9–10.

to allow me to be wholly free from guilt. I yielded long before to the pleasures of carnal desires, and merited then what I weep for now. The sequel is a fitting punishment for my former sins, and an evil beginning must be expected to come to a bad end. For this offence, above all, may I have strength to do proper penance, so that at least by long contrition I can make some amends for your pain from the wound inflicted on you; and what you suffered in the body for a time, I may suffer, as is right, throughout my life in contrition of mind, and thus make reparation to you at least, if not to God.

For if I truthfully admit to the weakness of my unhappy soul, I can find no penitence whereby to appease God, whom I always accuse of the greatest cruelty in regard to this outrage. By rebelling against his ordinance, I offend him more by my indignation than I placate him by making amends through penitence. How can it be called repentance for sins, however great the mortification of the flesh, if the mind still retains the will to sin and is on fire with its old desires?[1] It is easy enough for anyone to confess his sins, to accuse himself, or even to mortify his body in outward show of penance, but it is very difficult to tear the heart away from hankering after its dearest pleasures. Quite rightly then, when the saintly Job said 'I will speak out against myself,' that is, 'I will loose my tongue and open my mouth in confession to accuse myself of my sins,' he added at once 'I will speak out in bitterness of soul.'[2] St Gregory comments on this: 'There are some who confess their faults aloud but in doing so do not know how to groan over them – they speak cheerfully of what should be lamented. And so whoever hates his faults and confesses them must still confess them in bitterness of spirit, so that this bitterness may punish him for what his tongue, at his mind's bidding, accuses him.'[3] But this bitterness of true repentance is very rare, as St Ambrose observes, when he says: 'I have more easily found men who have preserved

1. Heloise's concern for true repentance is closely linked with her belief in the ethic of intention. See Letter I, note 2, p. 115. Inner contrition for sin is all-important.

2. Cf. Job x, 1. 3. *Moralia*, 9. 43.

their innocence than men who have known repentance.'[1]

In my case, the pleasures of lovers which we shared have been too sweet – they can never displease me, and can scarcely be banished from my thoughts. Wherever I turn they are always there before my eyes, bringing with them awakened longings and fantasies which will not even let me sleep. Even during the celebration of the Mass, when our prayers should be purer, lewd visions of those pleasures take such a hold upon my unhappy soul that my thoughts are on their wantonness instead of on prayers. I should be groaning over the sins I have committed, but I can only sigh for what I have lost. Everything we did and also the times and places are stamped on my heart along with your image, so that I live through it all again with you. Even in sleep I know no respite. Sometimes my thoughts are betrayed in a movement of my body, or they break out in an unguarded word. In my utter wretchedness, that cry from a suffering soul could well be mine: 'Miserable creature that I am, who is there to rescue me out of the body doomed to this death?'[2] Would that in truth I could go on: 'The grace of God through Jesus Christ our Lord.' This grace, my dearest, came upon you unsought – a single wound of the body by freeing you from these torments has healed many wounds in your soul. Where God may seem to you an adversary he has in fact proved himself kind: like an honest doctor who does not shrink from giving pain if it will bring about a cure. But for me, youth and passion and experience of pleasures which were so delightful intensify the torments of the flesh and longings of desire, and the assault is the more overwhelming as the nature they attack is the weaker.

Men call me chaste; they do not know the hypocrite I am. They consider purity of the flesh a virtue, though virtue belongs not to the body but to the soul. I can win praise in the eyes of men but deserve none before God, who searches our hearts and loins[3] and sees in our darkness. I am judged religious at a time when there is little in religion which is not hypocrisy, when whoever does not offend the opinions

1. *De paenitentia*, 2.10.
2. Romans vii, 24. 3. Psalm viii, 10.

of men receives the highest praise. And yet perhaps there is some merit and it is somehow acceptable to God, if a person whatever his intention gives no offence to the Church in his outward behaviour, does not blaspheme the name of the Lord in the hearing of unbelievers nor disgrace the Order of his profession amongst the worldly. And this too is a gift of God's grace and comes through his bounty – not only to do good but to abstain from evil – though the latter is vain if the former does not follow from it, as it is written: 'Turn from evil and do good.'[1] Both are vain if not done for love of God.

At every stage of my life up to now, as God knows, I have feared to offend you rather than God, and tried to please you more than him. It was your command, not love of God which made me take the veil. Look at the unhappy life I lead, pitiable beyond any other, if in this world I must endure so much in vain, with no hope of future reward. For a long time my pretence deceived you, as it did many, so that you mistook hypocrisy for piety; and therefore you commend yourself to my prayers and ask me for what I expect from you. I beg you, do not feel so sure of me that you cease to help me by your own prayers. Do not suppose me healthy and so withdraw the grace of your healing. Do not believe I want for nothing and delay helping me in my hour of need. Do not think me strong, lest I fall before you can sustain me. False praise has harmed many and taken from them the support they needed. The Lord cries out through Isaiah: 'O my people! Those who call you happy lead you astray and confuse the path you should take.'[2] And through Ezekiel he says: 'Woe upon you women who hunt men's lives by sewing magic bands upon the wrists and putting veils over the heads of persons of every age.'[3] On the other hand, through Solomon it is said that

1. Psalm xxxvii, 27. 2. Isaiah iii, 12 (Vulgate version).

3. Ezekiel xiii, 18, a much disputed verse. This is the N.E.B. translation; the Knox translation of the Vulgate says 'stitching an elbow cushion for every comer, making a soft pillow for the heads of young and old' and suggests that these are stuffed with magical herbs. Heloise appears to understand it as an attack on those who raise false hopes by superstitious practices.

'The sayings of the wise are sharp as goads, like nails driven home.'[1] That is to say, nails which cannot touch wounds gently, but only pierce through them.

Cease praising me, I beg you, lest you acquire the base stigma of being a flatterer or the charge of telling lies, or the breath of my vanity blows away any merit you saw in me to praise. No one with medical knowledge diagnoses an internal ailment by examining only outward appearance. What is common to the damned and the elect can win no favour in the eyes of God: of such a kind are the outward actions which are performed more eagerly by hypocrites than by saints. 'The heart of man is deceitful and inscrutable; who can fathom it?'[2] And: 'A road may seem straightforward to a man, yet may end as the way to death.'[3] It is rash for man to pass judgement on what is reserved for God's scrutiny, and so it is also written: 'Do not praise a man in his lifetime.'[4] By this is meant, do not praise a man while in doing so you can make him no longer praiseworthy.

To me your praise is the more dangerous because I welcome it. The more anxious I am to please you in everything, the more I am won over and delighted by it. I beg you, be fearful for me always, instead of feeling confidence in me, so that I may always find help in your solicitude. Now particularly you should fear, now when I no longer have in you an outlet for my incontinence. I do not want you to exhort me to virtue and summon me to the fight, saying 'Power comes to its full strength in weakness'[5] and 'He cannot win a crown unless he has kept the rules.'[6] I do not seek a crown of victory; it is sufficient for me to avoid danger, and this is safer than engaging in war. In whatever corner of heaven God shall place

1. Ecclesiastes xii, 11.

2. Jeremiah xvii, 9.

3. Proverbs xiv, 12; xvi, 25.

4. Ecclesiasticus xi, 28: the Vulgate (verse 30) reads *Ante mortem ne laudes hominem quemquam*, which cannot bear the explanation Heloise gives it. The N.E.B. translates the Hebrew 'Call no man happy before his death'. It continues 'for it is by his end that a man is known for what he is.' The similar classical tag means of course that death is the only guarantee against a reversal of fortune.

5. 2 Corinthians xii, 9.

6. 2 Timothy ii, 5.

me, I shall be satisfied. No one will envy another there, and what each one has will suffice. Let the weight of authority reinforce what I say – let us hear St Jerome: 'I confess my weakness, I do not wish to fight in hope of victory, lest the day comes when I lose the battle. What need is there to forsake what is certain and pursue uncertainty?'[1]

1. *Adversus Vigilantium*, 16.

Letter 4. Abelard to Heloise

To the bride of Christ, Christ's servant.

The whole of your last letter is given up to a recital of your misery over the wrongs you suffer, and these, I note, are on four counts. First you complain that contrary to custom in letter-writing, or indeed against the natural order of the world, my letter to you put your name before mine in its greeting. Secondly, that when I ought to have offered you some remedy for your comfort I actually increased your sense of desolation and made the tears flow which I should have checked. This I did by writing 'But if the Lord shall deliver me into the hands of my enemies, so that they overcome and kill me ...' Thirdly you went on to your old perpetual complaint against God concerning the manner of our entry into religious life and the cruelty of the act of treachery performed on me. Lastly, you set your self-accusations against my praise of you, and implored me with some urgency not to praise you again.

I have decided to answer you on each point in turn, not so much in self-justification as for your own enlightenment and encouragement, so that you will more willingly grant my own requests when you understand that they have a basis of reason, listen to me more attentively on the subject of your own pleas as you find me less to blame in my own, and be less ready to refuse me when you see me less deserving of reproach.

What you call the unnatural order of my greeting, if you consider it carefully, was in accordance with your own view as well as mine. For it is common knowledge, as you yourself have shown, that in writing to superiors one puts their name first, and you must realize that you became my superior from the day when you began to be my lady on becoming the bride of my Lord; witness St Jerome, who writes to Eustochium 'This is my reason for writing "my lady Eustochium". Surely I must address as "my lady" her who is the bride of my Lord.'[1] It was a happy transfer of your married state, for you were previously the wife of a poor mortal and now are raised to the bed of the King of kings. By the privilege of your position you are set not only over your former husband but over every servant of that King. So you should not be surprised if I commend myself in life as in death to the prayers of your community, seeing that in common law it is accepted that wives are better able than their households to intercede with their husbands, being ladies rather than servants. As an illustration of this, the Psalmist says of the queen and bride of the King of kings: 'On your right stands the queen,'[2] as if it were clearly stated that she is nearest to her husband and close to his side, and moves forward with him, while all the rest stand apart or follow behind. The bride in the Canticles, an Ethiopian (such as the one Moses took as a wife)[3] rejoices in the glory of her special position and says: 'I am black but lovely, daughters of Jerusalem; therefore the king has loved me and brought me into his chamber.' And again, 'Take no notice of my darkness, because the sun has discoloured me.'[4] In general it is the contemplative soul which is described in these words and especially called the bride of Christ, but your outer habit indicates that they have particular application to you all. For that outer garb of coarse black clothing, like the mourning worn by good widows who weep for the dead husbands they had loved, shows you to be, in the words of the Apostle, truly widowed and desolate and such as the Church should be charged to support.[5] The Scriptures also record the grief of these widows for their spouse who was slain, in the words: 'The women sitting at the tomb wept and lamented for the Lord.'[6]

The Ethiopian woman is black in the outer part of her flesh and as regards exterior appearance looks less lovely than other women; yet she is not unlike them within, but in several respects she is whiter and lovelier, in her bones, for instance, or her teeth. Indeed, whiteness of teeth is also

1. *Epistulae*, 22. 2. 2. Psalm xlv, 9. 3. Numbers xii, 1.
4. Canticles (Song of Solomon) i, 4–5. 5. 1 Timothy v, 16
6. Not in the Gospels. Cf. Letter 2, note 3, p. 125.

praised in her spouse, in reference to 'his teeth whiter than milk'.[1] And so she is black without but lovely within; for she is blackened outside in the flesh because in this life she suffers bodily affliction through the repeated tribulations of adversity, according to the saying of the Apostle: 'Persecution will come to all who want to live a godly life as Christians.'[2] As prosperity is marked by white, so adversity may properly be indicated by black, and she is white within in her bones because her soul is strong in virtues, as it is written that 'The king's daughter is all glory within.'[3] For the bones within, surrounded by the flesh without, are the strength and support of the very flesh they wear or sustain, and can properly stand for the soul which gives life and sustenance to the flesh itself in which it is, and to which it gives movement and direction and provision for all its well-being. Its whiteness or beauty is the sum of the virtues which adorn it.

She is black too in outward things because while she is still an exile on life's pilgrimage, she keeps herself humble and abject in this life so that she may be exalted in the next, which is hidden with Christ in God, once she has come into her own country. So indeed the true sun changes her colour because the heavenly love of the bridegroom humbles her in this way, or torments her with tribulations lest prosperity lifts her up. He changes her colour, that is, he makes her different from other women who thirst for earthly things and seek worldly glory, so that she may truly become through her humility a lily of the valley, and not a lily of the heights like those foolish virgins who pride themselves on purity of the flesh or an outward show of self denial, and then wither in the fire of temptation. And she rightly told the daughters of Jerusalem, that is, the weaker amongst the faithful who deserve to be called daughters rather than sons, 'Take no notice of my darkness, because the sun has discoloured me.' She might say more openly: 'The fact that I humble myself in this way or bear adversity so bravely is due to no virtue

1. Genesis xlix, 12. 2. 2 Timothy iii, 12.

3. Psalm xlv, 14 (Vulgate xliv, 14, in the Latin *ab intus*). The N.E.B. gives 'as probable reading' 'In the palace honour awaits her.'

of mine but to the grace of him whom I serve.' This is not the way of heretics and hypocrites who (at any rate when others are present) humiliate themselves to excess in hopes of earthly glory, and endure much to no purpose. The sort of abjection or tribulation they put up with is indeed surprising, and they are the most pitiable of men, enjoying the good things neither of this life nor of the life to come. It is with this in mind that the bride says 'Do not wonder that I do so;' but we must wonder at those who vainly burn with desire for worldly praise and deny themselves advantages on earth so that they are as unhappy in their present life as they will be in the next. Such self denial is that of the foolish virgins who found the door shut against them.[1]

And she did well to say that, because she is black, as we said, and lovely, she is chosen and taken into the king's bed-chamber, that is, to that secret place of peace and contemplation, and into the bed, of which she says elsewhere, 'Night after night on my bed I have sought my true love.'[2] Indeed, the disfigurement of her blackness makes her choose what is hidden rather than open, what is secret and not known to all, and any such wife desires private, not public delights with her husband, and would rather be known in bed than seen at table. Moreover it often happens that the flesh of black women is all the softer to touch though it is less attractive to look at, and for this reason the pleasure they give is greater and more suitable for private than for public enjoyment, and their husbands take them into a bedroom to enjoy them rather than parade them before the world. Following this metaphor, when that spiritual bride said 'I am black but lovely,' she rightly added at once 'Therefore the king has loved me and brought me into his chamber.'[3] She relates each point to the other: because she was lovely he loved her, and because she was black he brought her into his chamber. She is lovely, as we said before, with virtues within which the bridegroom

1. Matthew xxv, 1 ff.

2. Canticles iii, 1, but not a very apt quotation, as the context makes it clear that the 'bride' is longing for her lover on her solitary bed.

3. From Canticles i, 4–5.

loves, and black outside from the adversity of bodily tribulation. Such blackness of bodily tribulation easily turns the minds of the faithful away from love of earthly things and attaches them to the desire for eternal life, often leading them from the stormy life of the world to retirement for contemplation. Thus St Jerome writes that our own, that is, the monastic life, took its beginning from Paul.[1]

The humiliation of coarse garments also looks to retirement rather than to public life, and is to be preserved as being most suitable for the life of humility and withdrawal which especially befits our profession. The greatest encouragement to public display is costly clothing, which is sought by none except for empty display and worldly ceremony, as St Gregory clearly shows in saying that 'No one adorns himself in private, only where he can be seen.'[2] As for the chamber of the bride, it is the one to which the bridegroom himself in the Gospel invites anyone who prays, saying 'But when you pray, go into a room by yourself, shut the door and pray to your Father.'[3] He could have added 'not like the hypocrites, at street corners and in public places'. So by a room he means a place that is secluded from the tumult and sight of the world, where prayer can be offered more purely and quietly, such as the seclusion of monastic solitude, a place where we are told to shut the door, that is, to close up every approach, lest something happen to hinder the purity of prayer and what we see distract the unfortunate soul.

Yet there are many wearing our habit who despise this counsel, or rather, this divine precept, and we find them hard to tolerate when they celebrate the divine offices with cloister or choir wide open and conduct themselves shamelessly in full view of both men and women, especially during the Mass when they are decked out in valuable ornaments like those of the worldly men to whom they display them. In their view a fast is best celebrated if it is rich in external ornament and

1. Jerome, *Vita Pauli Primi Eremitae*, 5. (Not, of course, the Apostle, but one of the early Desert Fathers).

2. *Homilia in Lucam*, 40.16. (In his copy Petrarch noted in the margin that Seneca said the same thing.)

3. Matthew vi, 6.

lavish in food and drink. Better to keep silence, as it is shameful to speak of their wretched blindness that is wholly contrary to the religion of Christ which belongs to the poor. At heart they are Jews, following their own custom instead of a rule, making a mockery of God's command in their practices, looking to usage, not duty; although, as St Augustine reminds us,[1] the Lord said 'I am truth'[2] not 'I am custom.' Anyone who cares to may entrust himself to the prayers of these men, which are offered with doors open, but you who have been led by the King of heaven himself into his chamber and rest in his embrace, and with the door always shut are wholly given up to him, are more intimately joined to him, in the Apostle's words, 'But anyone who is joined to the Lord is one spirit with him.'[3] So much the more confidence, then, have I in the purity and effectiveness of your prayers, and the more urgently I demand your help. And I believe these prayers are offered more devoutly on my behalf because we are bound together in such great mutual love.

But if I have distressed you by mentioning the dangers which beset me or the death I fear, it was done in accordance with your own request, or rather, entreaty. For the first letter you wrote me has a passage which says: 'And so in the name of Christ, who is still giving you some protection for his service, we beseech you to write as often as you think fit to us who are his handmaids and yours, with news of the perils in which you are still storm-tossed. We are all that are left you, so at least you should let us share your sorrow or your joy. It is always some consolation in sorrow to feel that it is shared, and any burden laid on several is carried more lightly or removed.'[4] Why then do you accuse me of making you share my anxiety when I was forced to do so at your own behest? When I am suffering in despair of my life, would it be fitting for you to be joyous? Would you want to be partners only in joy, not grief, to join in rejoicing without weeping with those who weep?[5] There is no wider distinction

1. *De baptismo*, 3.6.9. 2. Cf. John xiv, 16.
3. 1 Corinthians vi, 17. 4. Letter 1, p. 110. 5. Cf. Romans xii, 15.

between true friends and false than the fact that the former share adversity, the latter only prosperity.

Say no more, I beg you, and cease from complaints like these which are so far removed from the true depths of love! Yet even if you are still offended by this, I am so critically placed in danger and daily despair of life that it is proper for me to take thought for the welfare of my soul, and to provide for it while I may. Nor will you, if you truly love me, take exception to my forethought. Indeed, had you any hope of divine mercy being shown me, you would be all the more anxious for me to be freed from the troubles of this life as you see them to be intolerable. At least you must know that whoever frees me from life will deliver me from the greatest suffering. What I may afterwards incur is uncertain, but from what I shall be set free is not in question. Every unhappy life is happy in its ending, and those who feel true sympathy and pain for the anxieties of others want to see these ended, even to their own loss, if they really love those they see suffer and think more of their friends' advantage than of their own. So when a son has long been ill a mother wants his illness to end even in death, for she finds it unbearable, and can more easily face bereavement than have him share her misery. And anyone who takes special pleasure in the presence of a friend would rather have him happy in absence than present and unhappy, for he finds suffering intolerable if he cannot relieve it. In your case, you are not even permitted to enjoy my presence, unhappy though it is, and so, when any provision you are able to make for me is to your own advantage, I cannot see why you should prefer me to live on in great misery rather than be happier in death. If you see your advantage in prolonging my miseries, you are proved an enemy, not a friend. But if you hesitate to appear in such a guise, I beg you, as I said before, to cease your complaints.

However, I approve of your rejection of praise, for in this very thing you show yourself more praiseworthy. It is written that 'He who is first in accusing himself is just'[1] and 'Who-

1. Proverbs xviii, 17. The N.E.B. translates the whole verse: 'In a lawsuit the first speaker seems right, until another steps forward and

ever humbles himself will be exalted.'[1] May your written words be reflected in your heart! If they are, yours is true humility and will not vanish with anything I say. But be careful, I beg you, not to seek praise when you appear to shun it, and not to reject with your lips what you desire in your heart. St Jerome writes to the virgin Eustochium on this point, amongst others: 'We are led on by our natural evil. We give willing ear to our flatterers, and though we may answer that we are unworthy and an artful blush suffuses our cheeks, the soul inwardly delights in its own praise.'[2] Such artfulness Virgil describes in wanton Galatea, who sought what she wanted by flight, and by feigning rejection led on her lover more surely towards her:

> She flees to the willows and wishes first to be seen.[3]

Before she hides she wants to be seen fleeing, so that the very flight whereby she appears to reject the youth's company ensures that she obtains it. Similarly, when we seem to shun men's praise we are directing it towards ourselves, and when we pretend that we wish to hide lest anyone discovers what to praise in us, we are leading the unwary[4] on to give us praise because in this way we appear to deserve it. I mention this because it is a common occurrence, not because I suspect such things of you; I have no doubts about your humility. But I want you to refrain from speaking like this, so that you do not appear to those who do not know you so well to be seeking fame by shunning it, as Jerome says. My praise will never make you proud, but will summon you to higher things, and the more eager you are to please me, the more anxious you will be to embrace what I praise. My praise is not a tribute to your piety which is intended to bolster up your pride, and we

---

cross-questions him.' The Knox translation of the Vulgate has a note on the obscurity of the Hebrew, and translates the Latin as 'An innocent man is the first to lay bare the truth.' Neither seems to suit the interpretation given by Abelard.

1. Luke xviii, 14. 2. *Epistulae* xxii, 24. 3. *Eclogues*, 3. 65.
4. Latin *imprudentes*. The alternative reading is *impudentes* (wanton).

ought not in fact to believe in our friends' approval any more than in our enemies' abuse.

I come at last to what I have called your old perpetual complaint, in which you presume to blame God for the manner of our entry into religion instead of wishing to glorify him as you justly should.[1] I had thought that this bitterness of heart at what was so clear an act of divine mercy had long since disappeared. The more dangerous such bitterness is to you in wearing out body and soul alike, the more pitiful it is and distressing to me. If you are anxious to please me in everything, as you claim, and in this at least would end my torment, or even give me the greatest pleasure, you must rid yourself of it. If it persists you can neither please me nor attain bliss with me. Can you bear me to come to this without you – I whom you declare yourself ready to follow to the very fires of hell? Seek piety in this at least, lest you cut yourself off from me who am hastening, you believe, towards God; be the readier to do so because the goal we must come to will be blessed, and our companionship the more welcome for being happier. Remember what you have said, recall what you have written, namely that in the manner of our conversion, when God seems to have been more my adversary, he has clearly shown himself kinder.[2] For this reason at least you must accept his will, that it is most salutary for me, and for you too, if your transports of grief will see reason. You should not grieve because you are the cause of so great a good, for which you must not doubt you were specially created by God. Nor should you weep because I have to bear this, except when our blessings through the martyrs in their sufferings and the Lord's death sadden you. If it had befallen me justly, would you find it easier to bear? Would it distress you less? In fact if it had been so, the result would have been greater disgrace for me and more credit to my enemies, since justice would have won them approval while my guilt would have brought me into contempt. And no one would be stirred by pity for me to condemn what was done.

However, it may relieve the bitterness of your grief if I

1. Cf. Letter 1, note 1, p. 116. 2. Cf. Letter 3, p. 133.

prove that this came upon us justly, as well as to our advantage, and that God's punishment was more properly directed against us when we were married than when we were living in sin. After our marriage, when you were living in the cloister with the nuns at Argenteuil and I came one day to visit you privately, you know what my uncontrollable desire did with you there, actually in a corner of the refectory, since we had nowhere else to go. I repeat, you know how shamelessly we behaved on that occasion in so hallowed a place, dedicated to the most holy Virgin. Even if our other shameful behaviour was ended, this alone would deserve far heavier punishment. Need I recall our previous fornication and the wanton impurities which preceded our marriage, or my supreme act of betrayal, when I deceived your uncle about you so disgracefully, at a time when I was continuously living with him in his own house? Who would not judge me justly betrayed by the man whom I had first shamelessly betrayed? Do you think that the momentary pain of that wound is sufficient punishment for such crimes? Or rather, that so great an advantage was fitting for such great wickedness? What wound do you suppose would satisfy God's justice for the profanation such as I described of a place so sacred to his own Mother? Surely, unless I am much mistaken, not that wound which was wholly beneficial was intended as a punishment for this, but rather the daily unending torment I now endure.

You know too how when you were pregnant and I took you to my own country you disguised yourself in the sacred habit of a nun, a pretence which was an irreverent mockery of the religion you now profess. Consider, then, how fittingly divine justice, or rather, divine grace brought you against your will to the religion which you did not hesitate to mock, so that you should willingly expiate your profanation in the same habit, and the truth of reality should remedy the lie of your pretence and correct your falsity. And if you would allow consideration of our advantage to be an element in divine justice, you would be able to call what God did to us then an act not of justice, but of grace.

See then, my beloved, see how with the dragnets of his

mercy the Lord has fished us up from the depth of this dangerous sea, and from the abyss of what a Charybdis he has saved our shipwrecked selves, although we were unwilling, so that each of us may justly break out in that cry: 'The Lord takes thought for me'.[1] Think and think again of the great perils in which we were and from which the Lord rescued us; tell always with the deepest gratitude how much the Lord has done for our souls. Comfort by our example any unrighteous who despair of God's goodness, so that all may know what may be done for those who ask with prayer, when such benefits are granted sinners even against their will. Consider the magnanimous design of God's mercy for us, the compassion with which the Lord directed his judgement towards our chastisement, the wisdom whereby he made use of evil itself and mercifully set aside our impiety, so that by a wholly justified wound in a single part of my body he might heal two souls. Compare our danger and manner of deliverance, compare the sickness and the medicine. Examine the cause, our deserts, and marvel at the effect, his pity.

You know the depths of shame to which my unbridled lust had consigned our bodies, until no reverence for decency or for God even during the days of Our Lord's Passion, or of the greater sacraments could keep me from wallowing in this mire.[2] Even when you were unwilling, resisted to the utmost of your power and tried to dissuade me, as yours was the weaker nature I often forced you to consent with threats and blows. So intense were the fires of lust which bound me to you that I set those wretched, obscene pleasures, which we blush even to name, above God as above myself; nor would it seem that divine mercy could have taken action except by forbidding me these pleasures altogether, without future hope. And so it was wholly just and merciful, although by means of the supreme treachery of your uncle, for me to be reduced in that part of my body which was the seat of lust and sole reason for those desires, so that I could increase in many ways;

1. Vulgate only, the last verse of Psalm xxxix (xl).

2. Intercourse even between married couples was forbidden by the Church during Lent, the Passion, and on the vigils of the major feasts.

in order that this member should justly be punished for all its wrongdoing in us, expiate in suffering the sins committed for its amusement, and cut me off from the slough of filth in which I had been wholly immersed in mind as in body. Only thus could I become more fit to approach the holy altars, now that no contagion of carnal impurity would ever again call me from them. How mercifully did he want me to suffer so much only in that member, the privation of which would also further the salvation of my soul without defiling my body nor preventing any performance of my duties! Indeed, it would make me readier to perform whatever can be honourably done by setting me wholly free from the heavy yoke of carnal desire.

So when divine grace cleansed rather than deprived me of those vile members which from their practice of utmost indecency are called 'the parts of shame' and have no proper name of their own, what else did it do but remove a foul imperfection in order to preserve perfect purity? Such purity, as we have heard, certain sages have desired so eagerly that they have mutilated themselves, so as to remove entirely the shame of desire. The Apostle too is recorded as having besought the Lord to rid him of this thorn in the flesh, but was not heard.[1] The great Christian philosopher Origen provides an example,[2] for he was not afraid to mutilate himself in order to quench completely this fire within him, as if he understood literally the words that those men were truly blessed who castrated themselves for the Kingdom of Heaven's sake,[3] and believed them to be truthfully carrying out the bidding of the Lord about offending members, that we should cut them off and throw them away;[4] and as if he interpreted as historic fact, not as a hidden symbol, that prophecy of Isaiah in which the Lord prefers eunuchs to the rest of the faithful: 'The eunuchs who keep my sabbaths, and choose to do my will I will give a place in my own house and within my walls and a name better than sons and daughters. I will

1. 2 Corinthians xii, 7–8.
2. Cf. Eusebius, *Historia Ecclesiae*, 6. 8.
3. Matthew xix, 12.
4. Matthew xviii, 8.

give them an everlasting name which shall not perish.'[1] Yet Origen is seriously to be blamed because he sought a remedy for blame in punishment of his body. True, he has zeal for God, but an ill-informed zeal,[2] and the charge of homicide can be proved against him for his self mutilation. Men think he did this either at the suggestion of the devil or in grave error but, in my case, through God's compassion, it was done by another's hand. I do not incur blame, I escape it. I deserve death and gain life. I am called but hold back; I persist in crime and am pardoned against my will. The Apostle prays and is not heard, he persists in prayer and is not answered. Truly the Lord takes thought for me.[3] I will go then and declare how much the Lord has done for my soul.[4]

Come too, my inseparable companion, and join me in thanksgiving, you who were made my partner both in guilt and in grace. For the Lord is not unmindful also of your own salvation, indeed, he has you much in mind, for by a kind of holy presage of his name he marked you out to be especially his when he named you Heloise, after his own name, Elohim. In his mercy, I say, he intended to provide for two people in one, the two whom the devil sought to destroy in one; since a short while before this happening he had bound us together by the indissoluble bond of the marriage sacrament. At the time I desired to keep you whom I loved beyond measure for myself alone, but he was already planning to use this opportunity for our joint conversion to himself. Had you not been previously joined to me in wedlock, you might easily have clung to the world when I withdrew from it, either at the suggestion of your relatives or in enjoyment of carnal delights. See then, how greatly the Lord was concerned for us, as if he were reserving us for some great ends, and was indignant or grieved because our knowledge of letters, the talents which he had entrusted to us, were not being used to glorify his name; or as if he feared for his humble and incontinent

1. Isaiah lvi, 4–5.
2. Cf. Romans x, 2.
3. Psalms xl, 18.
4. Cf. Psalms lxvi, 16.

servant, because it is written 'Women make even the wise forsake their faith.'[1] Indeed, this is proved in the case of the wisest of men, Solomon.[2]

How great an interest the talent of your own wisdom pays daily to the Lord in the many spiritual daughters you have borne for him, while I remain totally barren and labour in vain amongst the sons of perdition! What a hateful loss and grievous misfortune if you had abandoned yourself to the defilement of carnal pleasures only to bear in suffering a few children for the world, when now you are delivered in exultation of numerous progeny for heaven! Nor would you have been more than a woman, whereas now you rise even above men, and have turned the curse of Eve into the blessing of Mary. How unseemly for those holy hands which now turn the pages of sacred books to have to perform degrading services in women's concerns! God himself has thought fit to raise us up from the contamination of this filth and the pleasures of this mire and draw us to him by force – the same force whereby he chose to strike and convert Paul[3] – and by our example perhaps to deter from our audacity others who are also trained in letters.

I beg you then, sister, do not be aggrieved, do not vex the Father who corrects us in fatherly wise; pay heed to what is written: 'Whom the Lord loves he reproves'[4] and 'He lays the rod on every son whom he acknowledges.'[5] And elsewhere: 'A father who spares the rod hates his son.'[6] This punishment is momentary, not eternal, and for our purification, not damnation. Hear the prophet and take heart: 'The Lord will not judge twice on the same issue and no second tribulation shall arise.'[7] Listen too to that supreme and mighty exhortation of the Truth: 'By your endurance you will possess your souls.'[8] Solomon, too: 'Better be slow to anger than be a fighter; and master one's heart rather than storm a city.'[9] Are you not moved to tears or remorse by the only begotten Son

1. Ecclesiasticus xix, 2.
2. 1 Kings xi, 1 ff.
3. Cf. Acts xxvi, 12 ff.
4. Proverbs iii, 12.
5. Hebrews xii, 16.
6. Proverbs xiii, 24.
7. Cf. Nahum i, 9.
8. Luke xxi, 19 (Vulgate).
9. Proverbs xvi, 32.

of God who, for you and for all mankind, in his innocence was seized by the hands of impious men, dragged along and scourged, blindfolded, mocked at, buffeted, spat upon, crowned with thorns, finally hanged between thieves on the Cross, at the time so shameful a gibbet, to die a horrible and accursed form of death? Think of him always, sister, as your true spouse and the spouse of all the Church. Keep him in mind. Look at him going to be crucified for your sake, carrying his own cross. Be one of the crowd, one of the women who wept and lamented over him, as Luke tells: 'A great crowd of people followed, many women among them, who wept and lamented over him.'[1] To these he graciously turned and mercifully foretold the destruction which would come to avenge his death, against which they could provide, if they understood. 'Daughters of Jerusalem,' he said, 'do not weep for me; no, weep for yourselves and your children. For the days are surely coming when they will say, "Happy are the barren, the wombs that never bore a child, the breasts that never fed one." Then they will start saying to the mountains, "Fall on us," and to the hills, "Cover us." For if these things are done when the wood is green, what will happen when it is dry?'[2]

Have compassion on him who suffered willingly for your redemption, and look with remorse on him who was crucified for you. In your mind be always present at his tomb, weep and wail with the faithful women, of whom it is written, as I said, 'The women sitting at the tomb wept and lamented for the Lord.'[3] Prepare with them the perfumes for his burial, but better perfumes, which are of the spirit, not of the body, for this is the fragrance he needs though he rejected the other. Be remorseful over this with all your powers of devotion, for he exhorts the faithful to this remorse and compassion in the words of Jeremiah: 'All you who pass by, look and see if there is any sorrow like my sorrow.'[4] That is, if there is

1. Luke xxiii, 27. Compare this passage with Abelard's hymn translated on p. 295.
2. Luke xxiii, 28–31.
3. Cf. Letter 2, note 3, p. 125.
4. Lamentations i, 12 (Vulgate).

some sufferer for whom you should sorrow in compassion when I alone, for no guilt of mine, atone for the sins of others. He himself is the way whereby the faithful pass from exile to their own country. He too has set up the Cross, from which he summons us, as a ladder for us to use. On this, for you, the only begotten Son of God was killed; he was made an offering because he wished it. Grieve with compassion over him alone and share his sufferings in your grief. Fulfil what was foretold of devout souls through the prophet Zachariah: 'They shall wail for him as over an only child, and shall grieve for him as for the death of a first born son.'[1]

See, sister, what great mourning there is amongst those who love their king over the death of his only and first begotten son. Behold the lamentation and grief with which the whole household and court are consumed; and when you come to the bride of the only son who is dead, you will find her wailing intolerable and more than you can bear. This mourning, sister, should be yours and also the wailing, for you were joined to this bridegroom in blessed matrimony. He bought you not with his wealth, but with himself. He bought and redeemed you with his own blood. See what right he has over you, and know how precious you are. This is the price which the Apostle has in mind when he considers how little he is worth for whom the price was paid, and what return he should make for such a gift: 'God forbid that I should boast of anything but the Cross of our Lord Jesus Christ, through whom the world is crucified to me and I to the world!'[2] You are greater than heaven, greater than the world, for the Creator of the world himself became the price for you. What has he seen in you, I ask you, when he lacks nothing, to make him seek even the agonies of a fearful and inglorious death in order to purchase you? What, I repeat, does he seek in you except yourself? He is the true friend who desires yourself and nothing that is yours, the true friend who said when he was about to die for you: 'There is no greater love than this, that a man should lay down his life for his friends.'[3]

1. Zachariah xii, 10. 2. Galatians vi, 14. 3. John xv, 13.

It was he who truly loved you, not I. My love, which brought us both to sin, should be called lust, not love. I took my fill of my wretched pleasures in you, and this was the sum total of my love. You say I suffered for you, and perhaps that is true, but it was really through you, and even this, unwillingly; not for love of you but under compulsion, and to bring you not salvation but sorrow. But he suffered truly for your salvation, on your behalf of his own free will, and by his suffering he cures all sickness and removes all suffering. To him, I beseech you, not to me, should be directed all your devotion, all your compassion, all your remorse. Weep for the injustice of the great cruelty inflicted on him, not for the just and righteous payment demanded of me, or rather, as I said, the supreme grace granted us both. For you are unrighteous if you do not love righteousness, and most unrighteous if you consciously oppose the will, or more truly, the boundless grace of God. Mourn for your Saviour and Redeemer, not for the seducer who defiled you, for the Master who died for you, not for the servant who lives and, indeed, for the first time is truly freed from death. I beg you, beware lest Pompey's reproach to weeping Cornelia is applied to you, to your shame:

> The battle ended, Pompey the Great
> Lives, but his fortune died. It is this you now mourn
> And loved.[1]

Take this to heart, I pray, and blush for shame, unless you would commend the wanton vileness of our former ways. And so I ask you, sister, to accept patiently what mercifully befell us. This is a father's rod, not a persecutor's sword. The father strikes to correct, and to forestall the enemy who strikes to kill. By a wound he prevents death, he does not deal it; he thrusts in the steel to cut out disease. He wounds the body, and heals the soul; he makes to live what he should have destroyed, cuts out impurity to leave what is pure. He punishes once so that he need not punish forever. One suffers the wound

1. Lucan, *Pharsalia*, 8. 84–5. This is the nearest Abelard comes to a direct rebuke to Heloise for indulging in her memories.

so that two may be spared death; two were guilty, one pays the penalty. That, too, was granted by divine mercy to your weaker nature and, in a way, with justice, for you were naturally weaker in sex and stronger in continence, and so the less deserving of punishment. For this I give thanks to the Lord, who both spared you punishment then and reserved you for a crown to come, and who also by a moment of suffering in my body cooled once and for all the fires of that lust in which I had been wholly absorbed through my excessive incontinence, lest I be consumed. The many greater sufferings of the heart through the continual prompting of the flesh of your own youth he has reserved for a martyr's crown. Though you may weary of hearing this and forbid it to be said, the truth of it is clear. For the one who must always strive there is also a crown; and the athlete cannot win his crown unless he has kept to the rules.[1] But no crown is waiting for me, because no cause for striving remains. The matter for strife is lacking in him from whom the thorn of desire is pulled out.

Yet I think it is something, even though I may receive no crown, if I can escape further punishment, and by the pain of a single momentary punishment may perhaps be let off much that would be eternal. For it is written of the men, or rather, the beasts of this wretched life, 'The beasts have rotted in their dung.'[2] Then too, I complain less that my own merit is diminished when I am confident that yours is increasing; for we are one in Christ, one flesh according to the law of matrimony. Whatever is yours cannot, I think, fail to be mine, and Christ is yours because you have become his bride. Now, as I said before, you have as a servant me whom in the past you recognized as your master, more your own now when bound to you by spiritual love than one subjected by fear. And so I have increasing confidence that you will plead for us both before him and, through your prayer, I may be granted what I cannot obtain through my own; especially now, when the daily pressure of dangers and disturbances threaten my life and give me no time for prayer. Nor can I imitate that blessed eunuch, the high official of Candace,

1. Cf. 2 Timothy ii, 5. 2. Joel i, 17 (Vulgate).

Queen of Ethiopia,[1] who had charge of all her wealth, and had come from so far to worship in Jerusalem. He was on his way home when the apostle Philip was sent by the angel to convert him to the faith, as he had already deserved by his prayers and his assiduous reading of the Scriptures. Because he did not want to take time from this even on his journey, although he was a man of great wealth and a gentile, it came about through the great goodness of Providence that the passage of Scripture was before him which gave the apostle the perfect opportunity for his conversion.

So that nothing may delay my petition nor defer its fulfilment, I hasten to compose and send to you this prayer, which you may offer to the Lord in supplication on our behalf:

God, who at the beginning of human creation, in forming woman from a rib of man didst sanctify the great sacrament of the marriage bond, and who didst glorify marriage with boundless honours either by being born of one given in marriage, or by the first of thy miracles; thou who moreover didst grant this remedy for the incontinence of my frailty, in such manner as pleased thee, despise not the prayers of thy humble handmaid which I pour out as a suppliant in the presence of thy majesty for my own excesses and those of my beloved. Pardon, O most gracious, who art rather graciousness itself, pardon our many great offences, and let the ineffable immensity of thy mercy test the multitude of our faults. Punish the guilty now, I beseech thee, that thou mayst spare them hereafter. Punish now, lest thou punish in eternity. Take to thy servants the rod of correction, not the sword of wrath. Afflict their flesh that thou mayst preserve their souls. Come as a redeemer, not an avenger; gracious rather than just; the merciful Father, not the stern Lord. Prove us, Lord, and test us, in the manner in which the prophet asks for himself,[2] as if he said openly: First consider my strength and measure accordingly the burden of my testing. This is what St Paul promises to the faithful, when he says 'God keeps faith, and he will not allow you to be tested beyond your powers, but when the test comes he will also provide a way out, so that you are able to sustain it.'[3] Thou hast joined us, Lord, and hast parted

1. Acts 8. 26 ff. See *Historia calamitatum*, note 3, p. 98. The passage the eunuch was reading was Isaiah liii, 7–8.

2. Psalm xxvi, 2.

3. 1 Corinthians x, 13.

us, when and in what manner it pleased thee. Now, Lord, what thou hast mercifully begun, most mercifully end, and those whom thou hast parted for a time on earth, unite forever to thyself in heaven: thou who art our hope, our portion, our expectation and our consolation, O Lord, who art blessed world without end. Amen.

Farewell in Christ, bride of Christ; in Christ fare well and live in Christ.

The Letters of Direction

Letter 5. Heloise to Abelard

God's own in species, his own as individual.[1]

I would not want to give you cause for finding me disobedient in anything, so I have set the bridle of your injunction on the words which issue from my unbounded grief; thus in writing at least I may moderate what it is difficult or rather impossible to forestall in speech. For nothing is less under our control than the heart – having no power to command it we are forced to obey. And so when its impulses move us, none of us can stop their sudden promptings from easily breaking out, and even more easily overflowing into words which are the every-ready indications of the heart's emotions:[2] as it is written, 'A man's words are spoken from the overflowing of the heart.'[3] I will therefore hold my hand from writing words which I cannot restrain my tongue from speaking; would that a grieving heart would be as ready to obey as a writer's hand! And yet you have it in your power to remedy my grief, even if you cannot entirely remove it. As one nail drives out another hammered in,[4] a new thought expels an old, when the mind is intent on other things and forced to dismiss or interrupt its recollection of the past. But the more fully any thought occupies the mind and distracts it from other things, the more worthy should be the subject of such a thought and the more important it is where we direct our minds.

And so all we handmaids of Christ, who are your daughters in Christ, come as suppliants to demand of your paternal interest two things which we see to be very necessary for ourselves. One is that you will teach us how the order of nuns began and what authority there is for our profession.

1. i.e. Abelard's own. These cryptic words (*Domino specialiter, sua singulariter*) have also been translated as 'To him who is especially her lord, she who is uniquely his'.

2. An idea taken from Boethius' translation of Aristole's *De interpretatione*, Book I.

3. Matthew xii, 34.

4. Cicero, *Tusculanae disputationes*, IV. 35. 75.

The other, that you will prescribe some Rule for us and write it down, a Rule which shall be suitable for women, and also describe fully the manner and habit of our way of life, which we find was never done by the holy Fathers. Through lack and need of this it is the practice today for men and women alike to be received into monasteries to profess the same Rule, and the same yoke of monastic ordinance is laid on the weaker sex as on the stronger.

At present the one Rule of St Benedict is professed in the Latin Church by women equally with men, although, as it was clearly written for men alone, it can only be fully obeyed by men, whether subordinates or superiors. Leaving aside for the moment the other articles of the Rule: how can women be concerned with what is written there about cowls, drawers or scapulars?[1] Or indeed, with tunics or woollen garments worn next to the skin, when the monthly purging of their superfluous humours must avoid such things? How are they affected by the ruling for the abbot,[2] that he shall read aloud the Gospel himself and afterwards start the hymn? What about the abbot's table, set apart for him with pilgrims and guests? Which is more fitting for our religious life: for an abbess never to offer hospitality to men, or for her to eat with men she has allowed in? It is all too easy for the souls of men and women to be destroyed if they live together in one place, and especially at table, where gluttony and drunkenness are rife, and wine which leads to lechery[3] is drunk with enjoyment. St Jerome warns us of this when he writes to remind a mother and daughter that 'It is difficult to preserve modesty at table.'[4] And the poet himself, that master of sensuality and shame, in his book called *The Art of Love* describes in detail what an opportunity for fornication is provided especially by banquets:[5]

When wine has sprinkled Cupid's thirsty wings
He stays and stands weighed down in his chosen place ...
Then laughter comes, then even the poor find plenty,

1. *Regula*, chapter 55.
2. *Regula*, chapter 11.
3. Ephesians v, 18.
4. *Epistulae* cxvii, 6.
5. Ovid, *Ars amatoria* 1, 233–4, 239–40, 243–4.

Then sorrow and care and wrinkles leave the brow ...
That is the time when girls bewitch men's hearts,
And Venus in the wine adds fire to fire.

And even if they admit to their table only women to whom they have given hospitality, is there no lurking danger there? Surely nothing is so conducive to a woman's seduction as woman's flattery, nor does a woman pass on the foulness of a corrupted mind so readily to any but another woman; which is why St Jerome particularly exhorts women of a sacred calling to avoid contact with women of the world.[1] Finally, if we exclude men from our hospitality and admit women only, it is obvious that we shall offend and annoy the men whose services are needed by a convent of the weaker sex, especially if little or no return seems to be made to those from whom most is received.

But if we cannot observe the tenor of this Rule, I am afraid that the words of the apostle James may be quoted to condemn us also:[2] 'For if a man keeps the whole law but for one single point, he is guilty of breaking all of it.' That is to say, although he carries out much of the law he is held guilty simply because he fails to carry out all of it, and he is turned into a law-breaker by the one thing he did not keep unless he fulfilled all the law's precepts. The apostle is careful to explain this at once by adding:[3] 'For the One who said "Thou shalt not commit adultery" said also "Thou shalt not commit murder." You may not be an adulterer, but if you commit murder you are a law-breaker all the same.' Here he says openly that a man becomes guilty by breaking any one of the law's commandments, for the Lord himself who laid down one also laid down the other, and whatever commandment of the law is violated, it shows disregard of him who laid down the law in all its commandments, not in one alone.

However, to pass over those provisions of the Rule which we are unable to observe in every detail, or cannot observe without danger to ourselves: what about gathering in the harvest – has it ever been the custom for convents of

1. *Epistulae* xxii, 16. 2. James ii, 10. 3. James ii, 11.

nuns to go out to do this, or to tackle the work of the fields? Again, are we to test the constancy of the women we receive during the space of a single year, and instruct them by three readings of the Rule, as it says there?[1] What could be so foolish as to set out on an unknown path, not yet defined, or so presumptuous as to choose and profess a way of life of which you know nothing, or to take a vow you are not capable of keeping? And since discretion is the mother of all the virtues and reason the mediator of all that is good, who will judge anything virtuous or good which is seen to conflict with discretion and reason? For the virtues which exceed all bounds and measure are, as Jerome says,[2] to be counted among vices. It is clearly contrary to reason and discretion if burdens are imposed without previous investigation into the strength of those who are to bear them, to ensure that human industry may depend on natural constitution. No one would lay on an ass a burden suitable for an elephant, or expect the same from children and old people as from men, the same, that is, from the weak as from the strong, from the sick as from the healthy, from women, the weaker sex, as from men, the stronger one. The Pope St Gregory was careful to make this distinction as regards both admonition and precept in the twenty-fourth chapter of his *Pastoral*: 'Therefore men are to be admonished in one way, women in another; for heavy burdens may be laid on men and great matters exercise them, but lighter burdens on women, who should be gently converted by less exacting means.'

Certainly those who laid down rules for monks were not only completely silent about women but also prescribed regulations which they knew to be quite unsuitable for them, and this showed plainly enough that the necks of bullock and heifer should in no sense be brought under the same yoke of a common Rule, since those whom nature created unequal cannot properly be made equal in labour. St Benedict, who is imbued with the spirit of justice in everything, has this discretion in mind when he moderates everything in the Rule according to the quality of men or the times, so that, as he

1. *Regula*, chapter 58. 2. *Epistulae* cxxx, 11.

says himself at one point,[1] all may be done in moderation. And so first of all, starting with the abbot himself, he lays down that he shall preside over his subordinates in such a way that (he says)[2]

> he will accommodate and adapt himself to them all in accordance with the disposition and intelligence of each individual. In this way he will suffer no loss in the flock entrusted to him but will even rejoice to see a good flock increase ... At the same time he must always be conscious of his own frailty and remember that the bruised reed must not be broken ... He must also be prudent and considerate, bearing in mind the good sense of holy Jacob when he said[3] 'If I drive my herds too hard on the road they will all die in a single day.' Acting on this, and on other examples of discretion, the mother of the virtues, he must arrange everything so that there is always what the strong desire and the weak do not shrink from.

Such modification of regulations[4] is the basis of the concessions granted to children, and the old and the weak in general, of the feeding of the lector or weekly server in the kitchen before the rest,[5] and in the monastery itself, the provision of food and drink in quality or quantity adapted to the diversity of the people there. All these matters are precisely set out in the Rule. He also relaxes the set times for fasting according to the season or the amount of work to be done, to meet the needs of natural infirmity. What, I wonder, when he adapts everything to the quality of men and seasons, so that all his regulations can be carried out by everyone without complaint – what provision would he make for women if he laid down a Rule for them like that for men? For if in certain respects he is obliged to modify the strictness of the Rule for the young, the old and weak, according to their natural frailty or infirmity, what would he provide for the weaker sex whose frailty and infirmity is generally known?

Consider then how far removed it is from all reason and good sense if both women and men are bound by profession of a common Rule, and the same burden is laid on the weak as

1. *Regula*, chapter 48.
2. *Regula*, chapters 2 and 64; Isaiah xlii, 3.
3. Genesis xxxiii, 13.
4. *Regula*, chapters 35–41.
5. *Regula*, chapter 36.

on the strong. I think it should be sufficient for our infirmity if the virtue of continence and also of abstinence makes us the equals of the rulers of the Church themselves and of the clergy who are confirmed in holy orders, especially when the Truth says:[1] 'Everyone will be fully trained if he reaches his teacher's level.' It would also be thought a great thing if we could equal religious laymen; for what is judged unimportant in the strong is admired in the weak. In the words of the Apostle:[2] 'Power comes to its full strength in weakness.' But lest we should underestimate the religion of the laity, of men like Abraham, David and Job, although they had wives, Chrysostom reminds us in his seventh sermon on the Letter to the Hebrews:

There are many ways whereby a man may struggle to charm that beast. What are they? Toil, study, vigils. 'But what concern are they of ours, when we are not monks?' Do you ask me that? Rather, ask Paul, when he says[3] 'Be watchful in all tribulation and persevere in prayer' and 'Give no more thought to satisfying the bodily appetites.' For he wrote these things not only for monks but for all who were in the cities, and the layman should not have greater freedom than the monk, apart from sleeping with his wife. He has permission for this, but not for other things; and in everything he must conduct himself like a monk. The Beatitudes too, which are the actual words of Christ, were not addressed to monks alone, otherwise the whole world must perish ... and he would have confined the things which belong to virtue within narrow limits. And how can marriage be honourable[4] when it weighs so heavily on us?

From these words it can easily be inferred that anyone who adds the virtue of continence to the precepts of the Gospel will achieve monastic perfection. Would that our religion could rise to this height – to carry out the Gospel, not to go beyond it, lest we attempt to be more than Christians! Surely this is the reason (if I am not mistaken) why the holy Fathers decided not to lay down a general Rule for us as for men, like a new law, nor to burden our weakness with a great

1. Luke vi, 40. 2. 2 Corinthians xii, 9.
3. Cf. Ephesians vi, 18; Romans xiii, 14. 4. Cf. Hebrews xiii, 4.

number of vows; they looked to the words of the Apostle:[1] 'Because law can bring only retribution; but where there is no law there can be no breach of law.' And again, 'Law intruded to multiply law-breaking.' The same great preacher of continence also shows great consideration for our weakness and appears to urge the younger widows to a second marriage, when he says[2] 'It is my wish, therefore, that young widows shall marry again, have children and preside over a home. Then they will give no opponent occasion for slander.' St Jerome also believes this to be salutary advice, and tells Eustochium of the rash vows taken by women, in these words:[3] 'But if those who are virgins are still not saved, because of other faults, what will become of those who have prostituted the members of Christ and turned the temple of the Holy Spirit into a brothel? It were better for a man to have entered matrimony and walked on the level than to strain after the heights and fall into the depths of hell.' St Augustine too has women's rashness in taking vows in mind when he writes to Julian in his book *On the Continence of Widows*:[4] 'Let her who has not begun, think it over, and her who has made a start, continue. No opportunity must be given to the enemy, no offering taken from Christ.'

Consequently, canon law has taken our weakness into account, and laid down that deaconesses must not be ordained before the age of forty,[5] and only then after thorough probation, while deacons may be promoted from the age of twenty. And in the monasteries there are those called the Canons Regular of St Augustine who claim to profess a certain rule and think themselves in no way inferior to monks although we see them eating meat and wearing linen. If our weakness can match their virtue, it should be considered no small thing. And Nature herself has made provision for our being safely granted a mild indulgence in any kind of food, for our sex is protected by greater sobriety. It is well

1. Romans iv, 15; v, 20. 2. 1 Timothy v, 14.
3. *Epistulae* xxii. 4. *De bono viduitatis*, 9.12.
5. The Council of Chalcedon in 451 lowered the age from sixty to forty (Muckle).

known that women can be sustained on less nourishment and at less cost than men, and medicine teaches that they are not so easily intoxicated. And so Macrobius Theodosius in the seventh book of his *Saturnalia*[1] notes that:

> Aristotle says that women are rarely intoxicated, but old men often. Woman has an extremely humid body, as can be known from her smooth and glossy skin, and especially from her regular purgations which rid the body of superfluous moisture. So when wine is drunk and merged with so general a humidity, it loses its power and does not easily strike the seat of the brain when its strength is extinguished.

Again:

> A woman's body which is destined for frequent purgations is pierced with several holes, so that it opens into channels and provides outlets for the moisture draining away to be dispersed. Through these holes the fumes of wine are quickly released. By contrast, in old men the body is dry, as is shown by their rough and wrinkled skin.

From this it can be inferred how much more safely and properly our nature and weakness can be allowed any sort of food and drink; in fact we cannot easily fall victims to gluttony and drunkenness, seeing that our moderation in food protects us from the one and the nature of the female body as described from the other. It should be sufficient for our infirmity, and indeed, a high tribute to it, if we live continently and without possessions, wholly occupied by service of God, and in doing so equal the leaders of the Church themselves in our way of life or religious laymen or even those who are called Canons Regular and profess especially to follow the apostolic life.

Finally, it is a great sign of forethought in those who bind themselves by vow to God if they perform more than they vow, so that they add something by grace to what they owe. For the Truth says in his own words:[2] 'When you have carried out all your orders, say "We are useless servants and have only done our duty." ' Or, in plain words, 'We are useless

1. *Saturnalia*, VII, 6. 16–17; 18. 2. Luke xvii, 10.

and good for nothing, and deserve no credit, just because we were content only to pay what we owed and added nothing extra as a gift.' The Lord himself, speaking in a parable, says of what should be freely added:[1] 'But if you give more in addition, I will repay you on my return.'

If indeed many of those who rashly profess monastic observance today would pay more careful attention to this, would consider beforehand what it is that they profess in their vows, and study closely the actual tenor of the Rule, they would offend less through ignorance, and sin less through negligence. As things are, they all hurry almost equally indiscriminately to enter monastic life: they are received without proper discipline and live with even less, they profess a Rule they do not know and are equally ready to despise it and set up as law the customs they prefer. We must therefore be careful not to impose on a woman a burden under which we see nearly all men stagger and even fall. We see that the world has now grown old, and that with all other living creatures men too have lost their former natural vigour: and, in the words of the Truth, amongst many or indeed almost all men love itself has grown cold.[2] And so it would seem necessary today to change or to modify those Rules which were written for men in accordance with men's present nature.

St Benedict himself was also well aware of this need to discriminate, and admits that he has so tempered the rigour of monastic strictness that he regards the Rule he has set out, in comparison with earlier institutes, as no more than a basis for virtuous living and the beginning of a monastic life. He says that[3] 'We have written down this Rule in order that by practising it we may show that we have attained some degree of virtue and the rudiments of monastic observance. But for anyone who would hasten towards perfection of the monastic life, there are the teachings of the holy Fathers, observance of which may lead a man to the summit of perfec-

1. Luke x, 35.

2. Matthew xxiv, 12. This pagan commonplace, a nostalgia for a Golden Age, would be known to Heloise through her classical reading, but it is equally common in the Middle Ages.

3. *Regula*, chapter 73.

tion.' And again, 'Whoever you are, then, who hasten to the heavenly kingdom, observe, with Christ's help, this minimum Rule as a beginning, and then you will come finally to the higher peaks of doctrine and virtue, under the protection of God.' He also says specifically[1] that whereas we read that the holy Fathers of old used to complete the psalter in a single day, he has modified psalmody for the lukewarm so as to spread the psalms over a week; the monks may then be content with a smaller number of them, as the clergy are.

Moreover, what is so contrary to the religious life and peace of the monastery as the thing which most encourages sensuality and starts up disturbances, which destroys our reason, the very image of God in us, whereby we are raised above the rest of creation? That thing is wine, which the Scriptures declare to be the most harmful of any form of nourishment, warning us to beware of it. The wisest of wise men refers to it in Proverbs in these words:[2]

> Wine is reckless and strong drink quarrelsome; no one who delights in it grows wise . . . Who will know woe, as his father will, and quarrels, brawls, bruises without cause and bloodshot eyes? Those who linger late over their wine, and look for ready-mixed wine. Do not look at the wine when it glows and sparkles in the glass. It goes down smoothly, but in the end it will bite like a snake and spread venom like a serpent. Then your eyes will see strange sights, and your mind utter distorted words; you will be like a man sleeping in mid-ocean, like a drowsy helmsman who has lost his rudder, and you will say: 'They struck me and it did not hurt, dragged me off and I felt nothing. When I wake up I shall turn to wine again . . .'

And again:[3]

> Do not give wine to kings, O Lemuel, never to kings, for there is no privy council where drinking prevails. If they drink they may forget what they have decreed and neglect the pleas of the poor for their sons.

In Ecclesiasticus too it is written:[4] 'Wine and women rob the wise of their wits and are a hard test for good sense.'

1. *Regula*, chapter 18.
2. Proverbs xx, 1; xxiii, 29 ff.
3. Proverbs xxxi, 4.
4. Ecclesiasticus xix, 2.

Jerome himself also, when writing to Nepotian about the life of the clergy, and apparently highly indignant because the priests of the Law abstain from anything which could intoxicate them and surpass our own priests in such abstinence, says:[1]

Never smell of wine, lest you hear said of you those words of the philosopher:[2] 'This is not offering a kiss but proffering a cup.' The Apostle equally condemns priests who are given to drink, and the Old Law forbids it:[3] 'Those who serve the altar shall not drink wine nor strong drink.' By 'strong drink' in Hebrew is understood any drink which can intoxicate, whether produced by fermentation, or from apple juice, or from honey-comb which has been distilled into a sweet, rough drink, or when the fruit of the date palm is pressed into liquid, or water is enriched with boiled grain. Whatever intoxicates and upsets the balance of the mind, shun it like wine.

See how what is forbidden kings to enjoy is wholly denied to priests, and is known to be more dangerous than any food. And yet so spiritual a man as St Benedict himself is compelled to allow it to monks as a sort of concession to the times in which he lived.[4] 'Although,' he says, 'we read that wine is no drink for monks, yet because nowadays monks cannot be persuaded of this etc.' He had read, if I am not mistaken, these passages in the *Lives of the Fathers*:[5]

Certain people told abba Pastor that a particular monk drank no wine, to which he replied that wine was not for monks.

And further on:

There was once a celebration of the Mass on the Mount of abba Antony, and a jar of wine was found there. One of the elders took a small vessel, carried a cupful to abba Sisoi and gave it to him. He drank once, and a second time he took it and drank, but when it was offered a third time he refused, saying 'Peace, brother, do you not know it is Satan?'

1. *Epistulae* lii.
2. Not identifiable.
3. Cf. 1 Timothy iii, 3: Leviticus x, 9.
4. *Regula*, chapter 40.
5. *Vitae patrum*, V, 4. 31.

It is also said of abba Sisoi:

> His disciple Abraham then asked, 'If this happens on the Sabbath and the Lord's Day in church, and he drinks three cups, is that too much?' 'If it were not Satan,' the old man replied, 'it would not be much.'

On the question of meat: where, I ask you, has this ever been condemned by God or forbidden to monks? Look, pray, and mark how of necessity St Benedict modifies the Rule on this point too (though it is more dangerous for monks and he knew it was not for them), because in his day it was impossible to persuade monks to abstain from meat. I would like to see the same dispensation granted in our own times, with a similar modification regarding matters which fall between good and evil and are called indifferent, so that vows would not compel what cannot now be gained by persuasion. If concession were made without scandal on neutral points, it would be enough to forbid only what is sinful. Thus the same dispensations could be made for food as for clothing, so that provision could be made of what can be purchased more cheaply, and, in everything, necessity not superfluity could be our consideration. For things which do not prepare us for the Kingdom of God or commend us least to God call for no special attention. These are all outward works which are common to the damned and elect alike, as much to hypocrites as to the religious.[1] For nothing so divides Jew from Christian as the distinction between outward and inner works, especially since between the children of God and those of the devil love alone distinguishes: what the Apostle calls the sum of the law and the object of what is commanded.[2] And so he also disparages pride in works in order to set above it the righteousness of faith, and thus addresses Jewry:[3]

> What room then is left for human pride? It is excluded. And on what principle? Of works? No, but through the principle of faith. For our argument is that a man is justified by faith without observances of the law.

1. Cf. Letter 3, p. 135.
2. Cf. Romans xiii, 10; 1 Timothy i, 5.
3. Romans iii, 27–8.

And again:[1]

For if Abraham was justified by works, then he has a ground for pride, but not before God: for what does Scripture say? 'Abraham put his faith in the Lord and that faith was counted to him as righteousness.'

Once more:[2]

But if without any work he simply puts his faith in him who makes a just man of the sinner, then his faith is indeed 'counted as righteousness' according to God's gracious plan.

The Apostle also allows Christians to eat all kinds of food and distinguishes from it those things which count as righteous. 'The Kingdom of God,' he says,[3] 'is not eating and drinking, but justice, peace, and joy in the Holy Spirit . . . Everything is pure in itself, but anything is bad for the man who gives offence by his eating. It is a good thing not to eat meat and not to drink wine, nor to do anything which may offend or scandalize or weaken your brother.' In this passage there is no eating of food forbidden, only the giving of offence by eating, because certain converted Jews were scandalized when they saw things being eaten which the Law had forbidden. The apostle Peter was also trying to avoid giving such offence when he was seriously rebuked and wholesomely corrected, as Paul himself recounts in his letter to the Galatians.[4] Paul also writes to the Corinthians:[5] 'Certainly food does not commend us to God,' and again: 'You may eat anything sold in the meat market . . . The earth is the Lord's and all that is in it.' To the Colossians he says:[6] 'Allow no one therefore to take you to task about what you eat or drink,' and later on, 'If you died with Christ and passed beyond the elements of this world, why do you behave as though still living the life of the world? "Do not touch this, do not taste that, do not handle the other" – these are all things which perish as we use them, all based on the injunctions and

1. Romans iv, 2–3. 2. Romans iv, 5.
3. Romans xiv, 12, 20–21. 4. Galatians ii, 11 ff.
5. 1 Corinthians viii, 8; x, 25–6. 6. Colossians ii, 16; xx, 22.

teaching of men.' The elements of the world are what he calls the first rudiments of the law dealing with carnal observances, in the practice of which, as in learning the rudiments of letters, the world, that is, a people still carnal, was engaged. But those who are Christ's own are dead as regards these rudiments or carnal observances, for they owe them nothing, as they no longer live in this world among carnal people who pay heed to forms and distinguish or discriminate between certain foods and similar things, and so say 'Do not touch this or that.' For such things when touched or tasted or handled, says the Apostle, are destructive to the soul in the act of using them for some purpose only in accordance with the precepts and teaching of men, that is, of carnal beings who interpret the law in a worldly sense and not in the way of Christ or of his own.

When Christ sent his apostles out to preach, at a time when it was even more necessary to avoid any scandal, he allowed them to eat any kind of food, so that wherever they might be shown hospitality they could live like their hosts, eating and drinking what was in the house.[1] Paul certainly foresaw through the Holy Spirit that they would fall away from this, the Lord's teaching and his own, and wrote on the subject to Timothy:[2]

> The Spirit says expressly that in after-times some will desert from the faith and give their minds to subversive doctrines inspired by devils who speak lies in hypocrisy ... They forbid marriage and demand abstinence from certain foods, though God created them to be enjoyed with thanksgiving by believers who have inward knowledge of the truth. For everything that God created is good, and nothing is to be rejected when it is taken with thanksgiving, since it is hallowed by God's own word and by prayer. By offering such advice as this to the brotherhood you will prove a good servant of Jesus Christ, bred in the precepts of our faith and of the sound instruction which you have followed.

But if anyone turns his bodily eye to the display of outward abstinence, he would then prefer John and John's disciples wasting away through excessive fasting, to Christ and his

1. Luke x, 7. 2. 1 Timothy iv, 1–6.

disciples: and indeed, John's disciples who were apparently still following Jewish custom in outward matters grumbled against Christ and his disciples, and even questioned the Lord himself:[1] 'Why is it that John's disciples and the disciples of the Pharisees are fasting but yours are not?' In examining this passage and determining the difference between virtue and exhibition of virtue, St Augustine concludes that as regards outward matters, works add nothing to merit. In his book *On the Good of Marriage* he says that:

> Continence is a virtue not of the body but of the soul. But the virtues of the spirit are displayed sometimes in works, sometimes in natural habit, as when the virtue of martyrs has been seen in their endurance of suffering. Also, patience was already in Job; the Lord knew this and gave proof of knowing it, but he made it known to men through the ordeal of Job's testing.[2]

And again:

> So that it may truly be better understood how virtue may be in natural habit though not in works, I will quote an example of which no Catholic is in doubt. That the Lord Jesus, in the truth of the flesh, was hungry and thirsty and ate and drank, no one can fail to know who is faithful to his Gospel. Yet surely the virtue of continence was as great in him as in John the Baptist? 'For John came neither eating nor drinking and men said he was possessed. The Son of man came eating and drinking and they said, "Look at him, a glutton and a drinker, a friend of taxgatherers and sinners!"'[3] After which he added, 'And yet God's wisdom is proved right by its own children,' for they see that the virtue of continence ought always to exist in natural habit but is shown in practice only in appropriate times and seasons, as was the virtue of endurance in the holy martyrs ... And so just as the merit of endurance is not greater in the case of Peter who suffered martyrdom than in John who did not, so John who never married wins no greater merit for continence than Abraham who fathered children, for the celibacy of the one and the marriage of the other both fought for Christ in accordance with the difference of their times. Yet John was continent in practice as well, Abraham only as a habit. At the time after the days of the Patriarchs, when the Law declared a man

1. Mark ii, 18, referring to John the Baptist.
2. Job i, 8.
3. Matthew xi, 18–19.

to be accursed if he did not perpetuate his race in Israel, a man who could have continence did not reveal himself, but even so, he had it.[1] Afterwards 'the term was completed'[2] when it could be said, 'Let the man accept it who can;'[3] and if he can, put it into practice, but if he does not wish to do so, he must not claim it untruthfully.

From these words it is clear that virtues alone win merit in the eyes of God, and that those who are equal in virtue, however different in works, deserve equally of him.

Consequently, those who are true Christians are wholly occupied with the inner man, so that they may adorn him with virtues and purify him of vices, but they have little or no concern for the outer man. We read[4] that the apostles themselves were so simple and almost rough in their manner even when in the company of the Lord, that they were apparently forgetful of respect and propriety, and when walking through the cornfields were not ashamed to pick the ears of corn and strip and eat them like children. Nor were they careful about washing their hands before taking food; but when they were rebuked by some for what was thought an unclean habit, the Lord made excuses for them, saying that 'To eat without first washing his hands does not defile a man.'[5] He then added the general ruling that the soul is not defiled by any outward thing but only by what proceeds from the heart, 'wicked thoughts, adultery, murder' and so on. For unless the spirit be first corrupted by evil intention, whatever is done outwardly in the body cannot be a sin. He also rightly says that even adultery or murder proceed from the heart and can be perpetrated without bodily contact, as in the words:[6] 'If a man looks upon a woman with a lustful eye he has already committed adultery with her in his heart,' and 'Everyone who hates his brother is a murderer.' Such

1. Deuteronomy xxv, 5–10: St Augustine means that a man could have the habit of continence though the Law forbade him to show it in practice. But the text quoted refers only to the brother-in-law of a widow.

2. Galatians iv, 4.

3. Matthew xix, 12, during a discussion of celibacy.

4. Matthew xii, 1 ff.

5. Matthew xv, 19–20.

6. Matthew v, 28; 1 John iii, 15.

acts are not necessarily committed by contact with or injury to the body, as when, for instance, a woman is violently assaulted or a judge compelled in justice to kill a man. 'No murderer', it is written,[1] 'has a place in the Kingdom of Christ and of God.'

And so it is not so much what things are done as the spirit in which they are done that we must consider, if we wish to please him who tests the heart and the loins and sees in hidden places, 'who will judge the secrets of men', says Paul, 'in accordance with my gospel',[2] that is, according to the doctrine of his preaching. Consequently, the modest offering of the widow, which was two tiny coins worth a farthing,[3] was preferred to the lavish offerings of all the rich by him of whom it is said that he has no need of any possessions, and who takes pleasure in the offering because of the giver, rather than in the giver because of his offering: as it is written 'The Lord received Abel and his gift with favour,'[4] that is, he looked first at the devotion of the giver and was pleased with the gift offered because of him. Such devotion of the heart is valued the more highly by God the less it is concerned with outward things, and we serve him with greater humility and think more of our duty to him the less we put our trust in outward things. The Apostle too, after writing to Timothy on the subject of a general indulgence about food, as I said above, went on to speak of training the body:[5] 'Keep yourself in training for the practice of religion. The training of the body brings limited benefit, but the benefits of religion are without limit, since it holds promise not only for this life but for the life to come.' For the pious devotion of the mind to God wins from him both what is necessary in this life and things eternal in the life to come. By these examples are we not surely taught to think as Christians, and like Jacob to provide for our Father a meal from domestic animals and not go after wild game with Esau,[6] and act the Jew in outward things? Hence the verse of the Psalmist:[7] 'I have bound

1. Cf. 1 John iii, 15.
2. Romans ii, 16.
3. Cf. Mark xii, 42–4.
4. Genesis iv, 4.
5. 1 Timothy iv, 7–8.
6. Genesis xxvii, 6 ff.
7. Psalm lvi, 12.

myself with vows to thee, O God, and will redeem them with due thank-offerings.' To this add the words of the poet:[1] 'Do not look outside yourself.'

There are many, indeed innumerable testimonies from the learned, both secular and ecclesiastic, to teach us that we should care little for what is performed outwardly and called indifferent, otherwise the works of the Law and the insupportable yoke of its bondage, as Peter calls it,[2] would be preferable to the freedom of the Gospel and the easy yoke and light burden of Christ. Christ himself invites us to this easy yoke and light burden in the words:[3] 'Come to me, all you whose work is hard, whose load is heavy . . .' The apostle Peter also sharply rebuked certain people who were already converted to Christ but believed they should still keep to the works of the Law, as it is recorded in the Acts of the Apostles:[4] 'My brothers . . . why do you provoke God by laying on the shoulders of these converts a yoke which neither we nor our fathers were able to bear? No, we believe that it is by the grace of the Lord Jesus that we are saved, and so are they.'

Do you then also, I beg you, who seek to imitate not only Christ but also this apostle, in discrimination as in name, modify your instructions for works to suit our weak nature, so that we can be free to devote ourselves to the offices of praising God. This is the offering which the Lord commends, rejecting all outward sacrifices, when he says:[5] 'If I am hungry I will not tell you, for the world and all that is in it are mine. Shall I eat the flesh of your bulls or drink the blood of he-goats? Offer to God the sacrifice of thanksgiving and pay your vows to the Most High. Call upon me in time of trouble and I will come to your rescue, and you shall honour me.'

We do not speak like this with the intention of rejecting physical labour when necessity demands it, but so as not to attach importance to things which serve bodily needs and obstruct the celebration of the divine office, particularly when on apostolic authority the special concession was granted to

1. Persius, *Satires*, 1.7.
2. Cf. Acts xv, 10.
3. Matthew xi, 28–30.
4. Acts xv, 10–11.
5. Psalm l, 12–15.

devout women of being supported by services provided by others rather than on the result of their own labour. Thus Paul writes to Timothy:[1] 'If any among the faithful has widows in the family, he must support them himself: the Church must be relieved of the burden, so that it may be free to support those who are widows in the full sense.' By widows in the full sense he means all women devoted to Christ, for whom not only are their husbands dead but the world is crucified and they too to the world. It is right and proper that they should be supported from the funds of the Church as if from the personal resources of their husbands. Hence the Lord provided his mother with an apostle to care for her instead of her own husband,[2] and the apostles appointed seven deacons, or ministers of the Church, to minister to devout women.[3]

We know of course that when writing to the Thessalonians the Apostle sharply rebuked certain idle busybodies by saying that[4] 'A man who will not work shall not eat', and that St Benedict instituted manual labour for the express purpose of preventing idleness.[5] But was not Mary sitting idle in order to listen to the words of Christ, while Martha was working for her as much as for the Lord and grumbling rather enviously about her sister's repose, as if she had to bear the burden and heat of the day alone?[6] Similarly today we see those who work on external things often complaining as they serve the earthly needs of those who are occupied with divine offices. Indeed, people often protest less about what tyrants seize from them than about what they are compelled to pay to those whom they call lazy and idle, although they observe them not only listening to Christ's words but also busily occupied in reading and chanting them. They do not see that it is no great matter, as the Apostle says,[7] if they have to make material provision for those to whom they look for things of the spirit, nor is it unbecoming for men occupied with earthly matters to serve those who are devoted to the

1. 1 Timothy v, 16. 2. John xix, 26. 3. Acts vi, 5.
4. 2 Thessalonians iii, 10. 5. *Regula*, chapter 48.
6. Cf. Luke x, 39 ff. 7. Cf. 1 Corinthians ix, 11.

spiritual. That is why the ministers of the Church were also granted by the sanction of the Law this salutary concession of freedom through leisure, whereby the tribe of Levi should have no patrimony in the land, the better to serve the Lord, but should receive tithes and offerings from the labour of others.[1]

As regards fasts, which Christians hold to be abstinence from vices rather than from food, you must consider whether anything should be added to what the Church has instituted, and order what is suitable for us.

But it is chiefly in connection with the offices of the Church and ordering of the psalms that provision is needed, so that here at least, if you think fit, you may allow some concession to our weakness, and when we recite the psalter in full within a week it shall not be necessary to repeat the same psalms. When St Benedict divided up the week according to his view, he left instructions[2] that others could order the psalms differently, if it seemed better to do so, for he expected that with passage of time the ceremonies of the Church would become more elaborate, and from a rough foundation would arise a splendid edifice.

Above all, we want you to decide what we ought to do about reading the Gospel in the Night Office.[3] It seems to us hazardous if priests and deacons, who should perform the reading, are allowed among us at such hours, when we should be especially segregated from the approach and sight of men in order to devote ourselves more sincerely to God and to be safer from temptation.

It is for you then, master, while you live, to lay down for us what Rule we are to follow for all time, for after God you are the founder of this place, through God you are the creator of our community,[4] with God you should be the director of our religious life. After you we may perhaps have another to guide us, one who will build something upon another's

1. Cf. Numbers xviii, 21.

2. *Regula*, chapter 18.

3. Cf. *Regula*, chapter 11.

4. Cf. Heloise's first letter (p. 111) where the sentence appears in much the same form.

foundation, and so, we fear, he may be less likely to feel concern for us, or be less readily heard by us; or indeed, he may be no less willing, but less able. Speak to us then, and we shall hear. Farewell.

Letter 6. Abelard to Heloise

This long letter is Abelard's answer to Heloise's first question about the origin of nuns. To us it seems prolix and not very logical in the arrangement of the many examples it gives of the specially favoured position of women amongst the followers of Christ and in the early Church. It also draws comparisons between Christian women and the heroines of the Old Testament and classical antiquity. The following is a summary of its main points. (Ed.)

Nuns can be said to have their origin in the special attention Christ paid to women, for example, Mary the sister of Martha and Lazarus, Mary Magdalene, the woman who poured ointment on Christ's head (with a long digression on the importance of anointing as a sacrament), the women who remained at the Cross after the disciples had fled, and who saw the angel at the tomb at the Resurrection. In the Acts the mother of Jesus and other women form part of the devout group of followers after the Ascension, and special provision was made for widows of the faithful through the appointment of deacons (Acts vi, I ff.).

St Augustine in his *On the Work of Monks* is certain that women accompanied the disciples to administer to their needs, and Philo of Alexandria is quoted by Eusebius in his *History of the Church* (ii, 17) as praising the early Church of Alexandria in which women took part in chanting and hymn singing. (Such women are compared with women from the Old Testament, Miriam, sister of Aaron, who led the women in song and dance in praise of God [Exodus xv, 20], Deborah, Hannah mother of Samuel, Judith, and Anna of the Temple of Jerusalem who recognized the divinity of the infant Jesus [Luke ii, 36].)

St Paul accepts older women as deaconesses, advises Timothy on caring for widows (1 Timothy v, 3ff.) and commends Phoebe, a deaconess, to the Church in Rome (Romans xvi, 1). Jerome addresses Eustochium as 'my lady' (cf. Letter

4, p. 137) and writes to her at length about virginity. God takes special pleasure in the virtues of women which they achieve in spite of being the weaker sex. St Ambrose in his *De paradisis* notes that woman was created inside Paradise, and God restored woman in Mary before man in Christ. No deeds performed by men have been greater than those of Deborah, Judith, Esther, the daughter of Jephtha who died to save her father from perjury (Judges xi, 30), and the mother of seven sons who watched them tortured and killed by King Antiochus rather than eat food forbidden to Jews (Maccabees vii).

The highest honour has been paid to woman in the person of Mary, the mother of God, and in Elizabeth the mother of John the Baptist, who prophesied the divinity of Christ (Luke i, 42). Prophecy was also granted to women of pagan antiquity, the Sibyls: St Augustine in *The City of God* (Book 18, 23 ff.) and Lactantius both quote the Erechthean Sibyl as prophesying the birth of Christ, and the Cumaean Sibyl in Virgil's *Fourth Eclogue* tells of a miraculous birth which will take away the sins of the world.

Christ extended his concern to Gentile women in the episode of accepting a drink of water from the Samaritan woman (John iv, 8 ff.), and in his raising of the dead he answers the prayers especially of women, as did Elijah and Elisha (1 Samuel xvii, 22; 2 Kings iv, 22). Women were also among the early martyrs: for example, St Agnes, and St Agatha who saved the heathen from the fires of Etna by means of her veil, a miracle which no monk's cowl has ever achieved.

The Church in its orders and sacraments has taken much both from the Jews and from the pagans: bishops and archbishops have replaced *flamines* and *archiflamines*, and temples erected to demons have been consecrated and dedicated to saints. There were communities of dedicated virgins in antiquity, such as the Vestal Virgins and the priestesses of Juno, and the Ten Sibyls listed by Varro. A Vestal named Claudia was able to draw along a boat by her girdle or her hair (an episode on which are quoted verses by Sidonius Apollinaris) and another, as St Augustine, quoting Varro, relates (*City of God*, 22.11), proved her innocence when accused of unchasitity by carrying water in a sieve. Thus God has conceded miraculous powers to unbelievers in virtue of their continence and disregarded the error of their unbelief. (Similarly, the Emperor Vespasian was said by Suetonius [*Life*, ch. 7] to have the power of healing, and St Gregory prayed for the soul of Trajan to enter heaven. Horace [*Epistles* I, 16, 52] is quoted as saying that 'through love of virtue the good hate to sin'.) But God also punishes those who violate their vows, just as the Vestal Virgins were burned alive if they were unchaste: Juvenal (*Satires* 4, 8–9) and St Augustine (*City of God*, 3.5) are quoted in proof of this. The Fathers of the Church hold that an adulteress against Christ is far more guilty than one against her husband.

The great Doctors of the Church, Origen, Ambrose and Jerome, all showed special concern for women. Origen's self-mutilation was inflicted to end false suspicion putting a stop to his instruction of women. Many of Jerome's books were written at the request of Paula and Eustochium, and none of his *Lives* of holy Fathers is written as warmly as his *Life* of Paula. Ambrose wrote to the sisters of the Emperor Valentinian after his death, promising them he would gain salvation as he died a catechumen; in this Ambrose went further than the Catholic faith and the gospels concede. Women have even been granted special treatment when they have shown special zeal for chastity: for example, St Eugenia was encouraged by her bishop, St Helenus, to put on male attire so that she could be admitted into a monastery of monks.

'Dearest sister in Christ, I think I have written enough in answer to the first of your latest requests, concerning the authority for your order, and also in recommendation of its special position, so that you may more warmly embrace the calling of your profession through better understanding of its excellence. Now let me have the support of your merits and your prayers so that, God willing, I may also carry out the second. Farewell.'

Letter 7. Abelard to Heloise

Some part of your request has already been answered, as far as I was able, and it remains, God willing, for me to turn my attention to the rest of it by fulfilling the wishes of your spiritual daughters and yourself. For I still have to meet the second part of your demand by writing out some regulations to be a kind of Rule for your calling and to deliver this to you, so that the written word may give you more certainty than custom about what you should follow. Relying, therefore, partly on good practices and partly on the testimony of the Scriptures with the support of reason, I have decided to put all these together, in order to adorn the spiritual temple of God which you are[1] by embellishing it with certain choice pictures, and from several imperfect elements to create as far as I can a single, complete work. In this I intend to imitate the painter Zeuxis, and work on the spiritual temple as he planned his achievement on a material one. For, as Tully records in his *Rhetoric*,[2] the people of Crotona appointed him to decorate with the best possible pictures a certain temple for which they had the highest veneration. So that he might do so more surely he chose from the people the five most beautiful maidens and looked at them as they sat by him while he worked, so that he could copy their beauty in his painting. This was probably done for two reasons: first, as the philosopher I quoted above remarks, Zeuxis had developed his greatest skill in portraying women, secondly because maidenly beauty is naturally considered more refined and delicate than the male figure. Moreover, Tully says that he chose several girls because he did not believe he could find all the members of a single one equally lovely, since so much grace and beauty had never been conferred by nature on any one so as to give her equal beauty in every feature; for nature in creating bodies

1. Cf. 2 Corinthians vi, 16.
2. Cicero, *De inventione rhetorica*, II. I.

produces nothing which is perfect in every detail, as though she would have nothing left to bestow on the rest if she conferred all her advantages on one.

I too, then, in wishing to depict the beauty of the soul and describe the perfection of the bride of Christ, in which you may discover your own beauty or blemish as in the mirror of one spiritual virgin always held before your eyes, propose to instruct your way of life through the many documents of the holy Fathers and the best customs of monasteries, gathering each blossom as it comes to mind and collecting in a single bunch what I shall see will accord with the sanctity of your calling; and choosing what was instituted not only for nuns but also for monks. For as in name and profession of continence you are one with us, so nearly all our institutions are suitable for you. Gathering from these then, as I said, many things as if they were flowers with which to adorn the lilies of your chastity, I must describe the virgin of Christ with far greater care than that which Zeuxis applied to painting the likeness of an idol. Indeed, he believed that five maidens were sufficient for him to copy their beauty; but I have abundant riches in the records of the Fathers and, trusting in God's aid, do not despair of leaving you a more finished work, whereby you may be able to attain to the lot or description of those five wise virgins whom the Lord sets before us in the Gospel[1] in depicting the virgin of Christ. May I be granted the power to achieve this through your prayers. Greetings[2] to you in Christ, Brides of Christ.

I have decided that in describing and fortifying your religion and arranging the celebration of divine service, the treatise for your instruction shall be divided into three parts, in which I believe the sum of monastic faith to rest: that is, a life of continence and one without personal possessions and, above all, the observance of silence. This is, in accordance with the Lord's teaching in the commandments of the

1. Matthew xxv, 1 ff.

2. *Valete.* The valediction is suprising here, and has suggested to some that it marks the end of a separate short letter; but it may be intended to round off the formal introductory passage.

Gospel, to be ready with belts fastened, to forsake everything and to avoid idle talk.[1]

Continence is indeed the practice of chastity which the Apostle enjoins when he says:[2] 'The unmarried woman cares for the Lord's business and her aim is to be dedicated to him in body as in spirit.' In body, he says, as a whole, and not in one member, so that none of her members may fall into lasciviousness in deed or word. She is dedicated in spirit when her mind is neither defiled by compliance nor puffed up with pride, like the minds of those five foolish virgins who ran back to the oil-sellers and then were left outside the door. They beat vainly upon the door which was already shut and cried 'Lord, Lord, open to us,' but the bridegroom himself gave a terrible reply: 'Truly I know you not.'

Then too, in forsaking everything we follow naked a naked Christ, as the holy apostles did, when for his sake we put behind us not only our earthly possessions and affection for our kindred in the flesh, but also our own wishes, so that we may not live by our own will but be ruled by the command of our superior, and may wholly submit ourselves for Christ to him who presides over us in the place of Christ, as if to Christ. For Christ himself says that[3] 'Whoever listens to you, listens to me; whoever rejects you, rejects me'. Even if he lives an evil life (which God forbid), so long as his precepts are good, God's utterance must not be rejected because of the vice of the man. God himself enjoins this, saying:[4] 'What they tell you, observe and do; but do not follow their practices.' This spiritual conversion from the world to God he also describes accurately himself, saying that[5] 'Unless a man part with all his possessions he cannot be a disciple of mine'; and again, 'If anyone comes to me and does not hate his father and mother, wife and children, brothers and sisters, even his own life, he cannot be a disciple of mine.' Now, to hate father or mother etc. is to refuse to yield to affection for kindred in the flesh, just as to hate one's own life is to re-

1. Luke xii, 35; xiv, 33; Matthew xii, 36.
2. 1 Corinthians vii, 34.
3. Luke x, 16.
4. Matthew xxiii, 3.
5. Luke xiv, 33; xiv, 26.

nounce one's own will. This too he enjoins elsewhere, saying:[1] 'If anyone wishes to be a follower of mine, he must leave self behind, take up his cross and come with me.' For in thus drawing near to him we are his followers, that is, by closely imitating him we follow him, who says[2] 'I have come not to do my own will but the will of him who sent me.' It is as if he said, let everything be done under obedience.

For what is 'renouncing self' if not for a man to put behind him carnal affections and his own will and commit himself to being ruled by another's judgement and not his own? And so he does not receive his cross from another but takes it up himself, so that through it the world may be crucified to him and he to the world,[3] when by the voluntary offering of his own profession he denies himself worldly and earthly desires: which is a renunciation of his own will. For what else do the carnal seek, except to carry out their will, and what is earthly pleasure if not the fulfilment of our will, even when we attain our desires only with the greatest risk or effort? What is bearing a cross, that is, enduring some form of suffering, if not doing something against our will, however easy or profitable it seems to us? The other Jesus, who was by far the lesser, warns us of this in Ecclesiasticus when he says:[4] 'Do not let your passions be your guide, but restrain your desires. If you indulge yourself with all that passion fancies, it will make you the butt of your enemies.'

It is only when we wholly renounce both our possessions and ourselves that all that we own is cast away and we truly enter into the apostolic life which reduces everything to a common store; as it is written,[5] 'The whole body of believers was united in heart and soul. Not a man of them claimed any of his possessions as his own, but everything was held in common . . . It was distributed to each according to his need.' For they were not equally in want, and so it was not distributed in equal shares to all, but in accordance with each man's need. They were united in heart through faith, because

1. Luke ix, 23. 2. John vi, 38. 3. Cf. Galatians vi, 14.
4. Ecclesiasticus xviii, 30–31. The lesser Jesus is Jesus son of Sirach, the author of Ecclesiasticus named in its preface. 5. Acts iv, 32, 35.

it is through the heart that we believe; and united in soul because there was one mutual will through love, since each man wished the same for his neighbour as for himself and did not seek his own advantage rather than another's, or because everything was brought together by all for the common good, and no one sought or pursued what was his but what was of Jesus Christ. Otherwise they could never have lived without property, which consists in ambition rather than possession.

An idle or superfluous word and too much talk are the same thing. Hence St Augustine says in the first book of his *Retractions*:[1] 'Far be it from me to hold that there is too much talk when necessary words are spoken, however long-winded and prolix they may be.' And in the person of Solomon it is also said that[2] 'Where men talk too much sin is not far away; the man who holds his tongue is wise.' We must therefore guard against what is sinful and take all the greater precautions against this evil, the more dangerous and difficult it is to avoid. St Benedict provides for this when he says that[3] 'At all times monks ought to practise silence.' Evidently to practise or study silence means more than to keep silence, for study is the intense concentration of the mind on doing something. We do many things carelessly or unwillingly, but nothing studiously unless we are willing and apply ourselves.

Just how difficult it is to bridle the tongue, but how beneficial, the apostle James carefully considers when he says that[4] 'All of us often go wrong: the man who never says a wrong thing is perfect.' Again, he says: 'Beasts and birds of every kind, creatures that crawl on the ground and all others are tamed and have been tamed by mankind.' Between these two statements, when he considers how much matter for evil there is in the tongue and destruction of all that is good, he says: 'The tongue is a small member of the body, but how great a fire! How vast a forest it can set alight! . . . It is a world of wickedness, an intractable evil, charged with deadly venom.' What is more dangerous than venom or more to be

1. *Retractiones*, 1, preface.
2. Proverbs x, 19 (Vulgate).
3. *Regula*, chapter 42.
4. James iii, 2; 7–8; 5.

shunned? As venom destroys life, so idle talk means the complete destruction of religion. And so James says earlier on:[1] 'A man may think he is religious, but if he has no control over his tongue he is deceiving himself, and his religion is futile.' Hence it is said in Proverbs:[2] 'Like a city that is breached and left unwalled is a man who cannot control his temper in speech.' This is what the old man had in mind when he made the following reply to Antony who had asked about the talkative brethren accompanying him on his way:[3] 'Have you found good brethren to be with you, Father?' 'No doubt they are good but their dwelling has no door. Anyone who likes can go into the stable and untie the ass.' It is as though our soul were tethered to the manger of the Lord, refreshing itself there by ruminating on sacred thoughts, but once untied from the manger it runs here and there all over the world in its thought, unless the bar of silence keeps it in. Words do indeed impart understanding to the soul, so that it may direct itself towards what it understands and adhere to this by thinking; and by thinking we speak to God as we do in words to men. While we tend towards the words of men it is necessary for us to be led from there, for we cannot tend towards God and man at the same time.

Not only idle words but also those which seem to have some purpose should be avoided, because it is easy to pass from the necessary to the idle, and from the idle to the harmful. The tongue, as James says, is an intractable evil, and being smaller and more sensitive than all the other parts of the body it is the more mobile, so that whereas the others are wearied by movement, it does not tire when moving and finds inactivity a burden. The more sensitive it is in you, and the more flexible from your softness of body, the more mobile and given to words it is, and can be seen to be the seedbed of all evil. The Apostle marks this vice especially in you when he absolutely forbids women to speak in church, and even on matters which concern God he permits them only to question their husbands at home. In learning such things, or

1. James i, 26. 2. Proverbs xxv, 28. 3. *Vitae patrum*, V, 4. 1.

whatever things are to be done, he particularly subjects them to silence, writing thus to Timothy on the point:[1] 'A woman must be a learner, listening quietly and with due submission. I do not permit a woman to be a teacher, nor must woman domineer over man; she should be quiet.'

If he has made these provisions for silence in the case of lay and married women, what ought you to do? Again, in showing Timothy why he has ordered this, he explains that women are gossips and speak when they should not.[2] So, to provide a remedy for so great a plague, let us subdue the tongue by perpetual silence, at least in these places or times: at prayer, in the cloister, the dormitory, refectory, and during all eating and cooking, and from Compline onwards let this be specially observed by all. If necessary in these places or times let us use signs instead of words. Careful attention must be paid to teaching and learning these signs, and if words are also needed for this, the speaker must be asked to speak in a suitable place chosen for the purpose. Once the necessary words are briefly said, she should return to her former duties or the next suitable task.

Any excess of words or signs must be firmly corrected, words especially, in which lies the greater danger – a frequent and serious danger which St Gregory was most anxious to forestall when he instructs us in the seventh book of his *Morals*:[3]

> When we are careless about guarding against idle words, we come on to harmful ones. By these provocation is sown, quarrels arise, the torches of hatred are set alight and the whole peace of the heart is destroyed. And so it is well said through Solomon 'Letting out water starts quarrels.' To let out water is to let loose the tongue in a flood of eloquence. On the other hand he says approvingly that 'Man's utterance is like water which runs deep.' So he who lets out water is a source of quarrels because he does not bridle his tongue and breaks up concord. Thus it is written that 'He who makes a fool keep silence softens anger.'[4]

This is a clear warning that we should employ the strictest

1. 1 Timothy ii, 11–12. 2. 1 Timothy iv, 13. 3. *Moralia*, 7. 37.
4. Proverbs xvii, 14; xviii, 4.

censure to correct this vice above all, lest its punishment be deferred and religion thereby greatly endangered. From this spring slander, litigation and abuse, and often conspiracies and plots which do not so much undermine the whole structure of religion as overthrow it. Once this vice has been cut out, evil thoughts may not perhaps be wholly extinguished but they will cease to corrupt others. Abba Macharius told his brethren to shun this one vice as though he thought that was sufficient for their religion, as it is written in these words:[1]

> Abba Macharius the elder in Scythia said to his brethren 'After Mass, brothers, flee from the churches.' One of them said to him, 'Father, where can we flee further than this wilderness?' He put his finger on his lips and answered 'That is what I say you are to flee.' So saying he went into his cell, shut the door, and sat down alone.

This virtue of silence which, as James says, makes a man perfect,[2] and of which Isaiah prophesied that 'The harvest of righteousness is quietness,' was seized on so eagerly by the holy Fathers that (it is written)[3] abba Agatho carried a stone in his mouth for three years until he should learn to keep silence.

Although a place cannot bring salvation, it still provides many opportunities for easier observance and safeguarding of religion, and many aids or impediments to religion depend on the place. And so the sons of the prophets, whom, as Jerome says,[4] we read of as monks in the Old Testament, removed themselves to the secret places of the wilderness and set up huts by the waters of the Jordan. John also and his disciples, whom we regard as the first of our calling, and after them Paul, Antony, Macharius and all those who have been pre-eminent among us, fled from the tumult of their times and the world full of temptations, and carried the bed of their contemplation to the peace of the wilderness, so that they could devote themselves to God more sincerely. The Lord himself also, whom no stirrings of temptation could ever

1. *Vitae patrum*, V, 4. 27.
2. Cf. James iii, 2; Isaiah xxxii, 17.
3. *Vitae patrum*, V, 4. 7.
4. *Epistulae* lviii, 5. Cf. *Historia calamitatum*, p. 90.

have touched, teaches us by his example, for he sought hidden places particularly and avoided the clamour of the crowd whenever he had something special to do. Thus he consecrated the desert for us by his forty days' fasting, refreshed the crowds in the desert, and for purity of prayer withdrew not only from the crowds of people but even from the apostles. The apostles too he set apart on a mountain to receive instruction and appointment; he honoured the wilderness by the glory of his transfiguration and gladdened the apostles assembled on a mountain by the revelation of his resurrection; he ascended from a mountain into heaven, and all his miracles were performed either in lonely or in hidden places.[1] He also appeared to Moses or the patriarchs of old in the wilderness, and through the wilderness he led his people to the promised land; there too he delivered the Law to the people long held captive, rained manna, brought out water from a rock, and comforted them with frequent apparitions and the miracles he worked. In this he plainly taught them how much his wish to be alone desires a lonely place for us, where we can more purely devote ourselves to him.

He also takes pains to describe symbolically the freedom of the wild ass which loves the wilderness, and warmly approves of it, saying to holy Job:[2] 'Who has let the wild ass of Syria range at will and given the wild ass of Arabia its freedom? – whose home I have made in the wilderness and its lair in the saltings. It disdains the noise of the city and is deaf to the driver's shouting; it roams the hills as its pasture and searches for anything green.' It is as though he says openly 'Who has done this, if not I?' Now the wild ass, which we call the ass of the woods, is the monk, who is freed from the chains of worldly things and has taken himself off to the peace and freedom of the solitary life; he has fled from the world and not remained in it. And so he 'lives in the saltings of the land' and his members through abstinence are parched and dry. He is deaf to the driver's shouting but hears his voice, because he provides for his stomach not what is superfluous

1. Matthew iv, 2; v, 1; xvii, 1; xxviii, 16; Acts i, 9.
2. Job xxxix, 5–8.

but what is needed; for who is so demanding and unremitting a driver as the stomach? It shouts when it makes its immoderate demands for superfluous foods and delicacies, and this is when it should least be heard. The hills for his pasture are the lives and teachings of the sublime Fathers, by reading and meditating on which we are refreshed. By 'anything green' is meant the entire Scriptures on the heavenly and unfading life.

In specially exhorting us on this St Jerome writes as follows to the monk Heliodorus:[1] 'Consider the meaning of the word "monk", your name. What are you doing in a crowd, when you are a solitary?' And in drawing the distinction between our life and that of the clergy, he also writes to the priest Paul:[2]

> If you want to perform the duties of a priest, if the work – or burden – of the episcopate happens to please you, then live in cities and towns and make the salvation of others a profit to your soul. If you desire to be, as you say, a monk, that is, a solitary, what are you doing in cities, the homes not of solitaries but of crowds? Every calling has its leaders, and to come to our own way of life, bishops and priests should take as their example the apostles and apostolic men, whose positions they occupy and to whose merit they should try to attain. For us, the leaders of our calling should be the Pauls, Antonies, Hilaries and Macharius, and, to return to the Scriptures, let our leaders be Elijah and Elisha, the chief of the prophets, who lived in fields and the wilderness and made themselves huts by the river Jordan.[3] Amongst these too are the sons of Rechab who drank neither wine nor cider, who lived in tents and are praised by the voice of God through Jeremiah saying that they shall not lack a descendant to stand before the Lord.[4]

Let us therefore set up huts for ourselves in the wilderness, so that we may be better able to stand before the Lord and, being prepared, take part in serving him, and so that the society of men will not jolt the bed of our repose, disturb our rest, breed temptations, and distract our minds from our holy calling.

1. *Epistulae* xiv, 5. 2. *Epistulae* lviii, 5. 3. 2 Samuel vi, 4. 4. Jeremiah xxxv, 19.

When the Lord directed holy Arsenius to this freedom and peace in life we were all given a clear example in this one man. It is written that:[1]

When abba Arsenius was still in the palace he prayed to the Lord, saying 'Lord, guide me to salvation.' And a voice came to him, saying 'Arsenius, flee from men and you will be saved.' He retired to the monastic life and prayed again, in the same words, 'Lord, guide me to salvation.' He heard a voice say to him 'Arsenius, flee, be silent, be at peace, for these are the roots of not sinning.' And so, acting on this one rule of the divine command, he not only fled from men but even drove them from him. One day his archbishop came to him, along with a certain judge, and asked him for a sermon of edification. 'If I give you one,' said Arsenius, 'will you follow it?' They promised that they would. Then he said to them, 'Wherever you hear of Arsenius, do not go there.' On another occasion the archbishop was visiting him and sent first to see if he would open his door. He sent back word: 'If you come, I will open to you, but if I open to you I am opening to all, and then I can stay here no longer.' Hearing this, the archbishop said: 'If my coming will persecute him I will never go to this holy man.' To a certain Roman matron who came to visit his holiness, Arsenius said: 'Why have you presumed to undertake such a voyage? You must know you are a woman and should not travel at all. Or do you intend to return to Rome and tell other women that you have seen Arsenius, so that they will make the sea a highway for women coming to see me?' 'If the Lord wishes me to return to Rome,' she replied, 'I shall not allow anyone to come here. Only pray for me, and remember me always.' But he answered: 'I pray God to wipe out the memory of you from my heart.' Hearing this she went away dismayed.

It is also recorded that when Arsenius was asked by abba Mark why he fled from men, he replied:[2] 'God knows that I love men, but I cannot be equally with men and with God.'

The holy Fathers did indeed so shun the conversation and attention of men that many of them feigned madness, in order to drive men from them, and, remarkable to relate, even professed to be heretics. Anyone who likes may read in

1. *Vitae patrum*, V, 2. 3ff. 2. *Vitae patrum*, V, 17. 5.

the *Lives of the Fathers* about abba Simon,[1] and how he prepared himself for a visit from the judge of the province; he covered himself with a sack and, holding bread and cheese in his hand, sat at the door of his cell and started eating. He may read too of the hermit[2] who, when he saw people coming towards him with lanterns, pulled off his clothes, threw them into the river, and standing there naked began to wash them. His acolyte blushed for shame at the sight and asked the men to go away, saying 'Our old man has lost his senses.' Then he went to him, and said: 'Why did you do this, father? All who saw you said that "The old man is possessed." ' 'That is what I wanted to hear,' he replied. Let him read also of abba Moses,[3] who in order to keep a judge of the province well away from him, got up and fled into a marsh. The judge and his followers came along and called, 'Tell us, old man, where is the cell of abba Moses?' 'Why do you want to look for him?' he replied. 'The man is crazy and a heretic.' And what of abba Pastor,[4] who even refused to be seen by the judge of the province in order to free from prison the son of his own sister, in answer to her plea?

You see then how the presence of the saints is sought by the powerful in the world with great veneration and devotion, while their aim is to keep people at a distance, even at the loss of their own dignity.

Now, so that you may know the virtue of your own sex in this matter, could anyone adequately tell of that virgin who refused a visit even from the holy saint Martin, so that she could devote herself to contemplation? Jerome writes of this to the monk Oceanus:[5]

In the *Life of St Martin*, we read that Sulpicius relates how St Martin when travelling wished to call on a certain virgin who was outstanding for her morals and chastity. She refused, but sent him a gift, and looking from her window said to the holy man: 'Offer prayer where you are, father, for I have never been visited by a man.' Hearing this St Martin thanked God that a woman of such

1. V, 8. 18. 2. V, 12. 7. 3. V, 8. 10. 4. V, 8. 13.
5. Not traced.

morals had kept her desire for chastity. He blessed her and departed, filled with joy.

This woman in fact disdained or feared to rise from the bed of her contemplation, and was prepared to say to a friend knocking at her door: 'I have washed my feet, how shall I defile them?'[1]

O what an insult to themselves would the bishops or priests of our day consider it, if they received such a rebuff from Arsenius or this virgin! If any monks still remain in solitude, let them blush for such things, whenever they delight in the society of bishops and build them special houses for their entertainment, when they do not shun worldly potentates whom a crowd accompanies or gathers round but rather invite them, and by multiplying their buildings on the pretext of hospitality, change the solitary place they sought into a city. Indeed, by the craft and cunning of the old tempter, nearly all the monasteries of today which were formerly founded in solitude so that men could be avoided, now that religious fervour has subsided, have subsequently invited men to them, have assembled manservants and maidservants and built great villages on monastic sites; and thus they have returned to the world, or rather, have brought the world to them. By involving themselves in such great inconvenience and binding themselves in total slavery both to ecclesiastical and secular powers, while they seek to live at ease and enjoy the fruits of another's labour, they have lost the very name of monk, that is, of solitary, as well as their monastic life. They also often fall a victim to other misfortunes: while struggling to protect the persons and possessions of their followers they lose their own, and in the frequent fires which break out in adjoining buildings the monasteries are burned down as well. Yet not even this checks their ambition.

There are those too who will not submit to monastic restriction of any kind, but are scattered in twos and threes amongst the villages, towns and cities, or even live alone, without observance of a rule, and are thereby worse than men

1. Canticles v, 3.

of the world the more they fall away from their profession. They also make misuse of the places where their people dwell as much they do their own, calling these Obedientaries,[1] though no rule is kept there and no obedience shown except to the belly and the flesh, and there they live with relatives and friends, behaving as freely as they wish, as they have so little to fear from their own consciences. There can be no doubt that in shameless apostates such as these, excesses are criminal which in other men are venial. You should not permit yourselves to take example from such lives nor even to hear of them.

Solitude is indeed all the more necessary for your woman's frailty, inasmuch as for our part we are less attacked by the conflicts of carnal temptations and less likely to stray towards bodily things through the senses. Hence St Antony says:[2] 'Whoever sits in solitude and is at peace is rescued from three wars, that is, wars of hearing, speech and sight; he shall have only one thing to fight against, the heart.' These and all the other advantages of the desert the famous Doctor of the Church Jerome has particularly in mind in giving urgent counsel to the monk Heliodorus:[3] 'O desert rejoicing in the presence of God! What are you doing in the world, brother, when you are greater than the world?'

Now that we have discussed where monasteries should be set up, let us show what the lay-out of the site should be. In planning the site of the actual monastery, also in accordance with St Benedict's Rule,[4] provision should be made if possible for those things which are particularly necessary for monasteries to be contained within its precincts, that is, a garden, water, a mill, a bakehouse with oven, and places where the sisters may carry out their daily tasks without any need for straying outside.

As in the army camps of the world, so in the camp of the Lord, that is, in monastic communities, people must be

1. Obedientaries: small conventual establishments under the rule of a larger monastery.

2. *Vitae patrum*, V, 2. 3.

3. *Epistulae* iv, 10.

4. *Regula*, chapter 66.

appointed to be in authority over the rest. In an army there is one commander over all, at whose bidding everything is carried out, but because of the size of his army and complexity of his duties he shares his burdens with several others, and appoints subordinate officers to be responsible for various duties or companies of men. Similarly in convents it is also necessary for one matron to preside over all; the others must do everything in accordance with her decision and judgement, and no one must presume to oppose her in anything or even to grumble at any of her instructions. No community of people nor even a small household in a single house can continue as a whole unless unity is preserved in it, and complete control rests on the authority of a single person. And so the Ark, as a model for the Church, was many cubits long and wide but rose to a single point. It is written in Proverbs that[1] 'For its sins a land has many rulers,' and on the death of Alexander, when kings were multiplied, evils were multiplied too. Rome could not maintain concord when authority was shared amongst many rulers. Lucan reminds us in his first book:[2]

> You, Rome, have been the cause of your own ills,
> Shared in three masters' hands; the pacts spell death
> Of power that never should devolve on many.

A little later he says:

> So long as earth supports the sea and is itself
> Poised in the air, the sun rolls on its course,
> Night follows day throughout the zodiac's signs,
> No trust binds fellow-rulers, every power
> Rejects a partner ...

Such, surely, were those disciples of the abbot St Frontonius,[3] whom he had assembled to the number of seventy in the city where he was born. He had won great favour there in the eyes of God and men, but then he left the monastery in the city, and with their portable goods took them naked

1. Proverbs xxviii, 2. 2. Lucan, *Pharsalia*, I. 84–6; 89–93.
3. *Vita Frontonii* in *Vitae patrum*, I.

with him into the desert. After a while, like the Israelites complaining against Moses because he had led them out of Egypt into the wilderness, abandoning their fleshpots and wealth in the land, they started grumbling foolishly. 'Is chastity only to be found in the desert and not in town?' they asked. 'Why can't we go back to the city we have left? Will God hear our prayers only in the desert? Who can live by the bread of angels? Who wants to have cattle and wild beasts for company? Why do we have to stay here? Why can't we return and bless the Lord in the place where we were born?'

Hence the apostle James gives warning:[1] 'My brothers, not many of you should try to teach others; be sure that if you do, you will be judged with greater severity.' Similarly, Jerome in writing to the monk Rusticus on the conduct of his life says:[2]

> No skill is learned without a teacher. Even dumb animals and herds of wild beasts follow their leaders; amongst bees, one goes first and the rest follow, and cranes follow one of their number in regular order. There is one emperor, one judge of a province. When Rome was founded there could not be two brothers as kings at the same time, and this was settled by fratricide. Esau and Jacob fought in Rebecca's womb. The churches each have one bishop, one dean, and one archdeacon, and every order in the Church depends on its rulers. In a ship there is one helmsman, in a house one master; in an army, however large, men look to the standard of one man. By all these examples my discourse aims at teaching you that you must not be left to your own will, but must live in a monastery under the discipline of one Father and in the company of many of your fellows.

So that concord may therefore be maintained in all things, it is proper for one sister to be over all, and all to obey her in everything. Several other sisters should also be appointed, as she herself decides, to serve under her, like officers. They shall preside over the duties she has ordered and as far as she wishes, as though they were dukes or counts serving in their lord's army, while all the rest are the soldiers or infantry

1. James iii, 1.

2. *Epistulae* cxxv, 15.

who are under the direction of the others and shall fight freely against the evil one and his hordes.

Seven persons only out of your number I think are all that are needed for the entire administration of the convent: portress, cellaress, wardrober, infirmarian, chantress, sacristan and lastly the deaconess, who is now called the abbess.[1] And so in this camp, and in this kind of service in the Lord's army, as it is written that[2] 'Man's life on earth is like service,' and elsewhere, 'Awesome as a regimented army,' the abbess takes the place of the commander who is obeyed by all in everything. The six under her, the officers as we call them, hold the position of duke or count; while all the other nuns, whom we call the cloistral sisters, perform their service for God promptly, like soldiers, and the lay sisters, who have renounced the world and dedicated themselves to serving the nuns, wear a kind of religious (though not a monastic) habit and, like infantry, hold a lower rank.

Now, under the Lord's inspiration, it remains to marshal the several ranks of this army so it may truly be what is called 'a regimented army' to meet the assaults of demons. And so, starting at the head of this institution, the abbess, let us first dispose of her through whom all must be disposed. First of all, her sanctity: as I said in my preceding letter, St Paul in writing to Timothy describes in detail how outstanding and proved this must be:[3]

> A widow should not be put on the roll under sixty years of age. She must have been faithful in marriage to one man, and must produce evidence of good deeds performed, showing whether she has had the care of children, or given hospitality, or washed the feet of God's people, or supported those in distress – in short, whether she has taken every opportunity of doing good. Avoid younger widows, etc.

And earlier on, when he was laying down rules for the life

1. Abelard often refers to the deaconess as a woman serving in the early Church; cf. Letter 6. He means here that an abbess ('mother') must perform the same duties in the convent. He continues to use the term *diaconessa*, here translated as 'abbess' throughout.

2. Job vii, 1; Canticles vi, 9 (Vulgate).

3. 1 Timothy v, 9–11.

of deacons, he says about deaconesses:[1] 'Their wives, equally, must be high-principled, not given to talking scandal, sober and trustworthy in every way.' I have said enough in my last letter to show how highly I value the meaning and reasoning behind all these words, especially the reason why the Apostle wishes her to be the wife of one husband alone and to be advanced in age.

And so I am much surprised that the pernicious practice has arisen in the Church of appointing virgins to this office rather than women who have known men, and often of putting younger over older women. Yet Ecclesiastes says[2] 'Woe betide the land where a boy is king,' and we all approve the saying of holy Job:[3] 'There is wisdom in age and long life brings understanding.' It is also written in Proverbs:[4] 'Grey hair is a crown of glory if it shall be won by a virtuous life,' and in Ecclesiasticus:[5]

> How beautiful is the judgement of grey hairs and counsel taken from the old! How beautiful the wisdom of the aged, how glorious their understanding and counsel! Long experience is the old man's crown and his pride is the fear of the Lord.

Again:[6]

> Speak, if you are old, for it is your privilege . . . If you are young, speak in your own case, but not much. If you are asked twice, let your reply be brief . . . For the most part be like a man who knows and can keep silence while making enquiries . . . Do not be familiar among the great, nor talk much before your elders.

So the presbyters who have authority over the people in the Church are understood to be Elders, so that their very name may teach what they ought to be. And the men who wrote the *Lives of the Saints* gave the name of Elder to those whom we now call abbas or Fathers.[7]

1. 1 Timothy iii, 11. 2. Ecclesiastes, x, 16 (Vulgate).
3. Job xii, 12. 4. Proverbs xvi, 31.
5. Ecclesiasticus xxv, 4–6.
6. Ecclesiasticus xxxii, 4 and 7–9.
7. Some of the early books of the *Vitae patrum* are called *Verba seniorum*.

Thus in every way care must be taken when electing or consecrating an abbess to follow the advice of the Apostle,[1] and to elect one who must be above all the rest in her life and learning, and of an age to promise maturity in conduct; by obedience she should be worthy of giving orders, and through practising the Rule rather than hearing it she should have learned it and know it well. If she is not lettered let her know that she should accustom herself not to philosophic studies nor dialectical disputations but to teaching of life and performance of works: as it is written of the Lord,[2] he 'set out to do and teach', that is, he taught afterwards what he did first, for teaching through works rather than speech, the deed before the word, is better and more thorough. Let us pay careful heed to what abba Ipitius is recorded to have said:[3] 'He is truly wise who teaches others by deed, not by words.' He gives us no little comfort and encouragement thereby.

We should listen too to the argument of St Antony which confounded the wordy philosophers who laughed at his authority as being that of a foolish and illiterate man:[4] 'Tell me,' he said, 'which comes first, understanding or letters? Which is the beginning of the other – does understanding come from letters or letters from understanding?' When they declared that understanding was the author and inventor of letters, he said: 'So if a man's understanding is sound, he has no need of letters.' He should hear too the words of the Apostle, and be strengthened in the Lord:[5] 'Has not God made the wisdom of this world look foolish?' And again, 'To shame the wise, God has chosen what the world counts weakness. God has chosen the base and contemptible things of the world so as to bring to nothing what is now in being; then no human pride may boast in his presence.' For the kingdom of God, as he says later, is not a matter of talk but of power.

But if to gain better understanding of some things the abbess thinks she should have recourse to the Scriptures, she should not be ashamed to ask and learn from the lettered, nor despise the evidence of their education in these matters, but accept

1. 1 Timothy v. 2. Acts i, 1. 3. *Vitae patrum*, V, 10. 75.
4. *Vitae patrum*, I, 45. 5. 1 Corinthians i, 20; 27–9.

it devoutly and thoughtfully, just as the foremost himself of the apostles thoughtfully accepted public correction from his fellow-apostle Paul.[1] For, as St Benedict also remarks, the Lord often reveals what is better to the lesser man.[2]

So that we may better follow the Lord's injunction which the Apostle recorded above, we should never let this election be made from the nobility or the powerful in the world except under pressure of great necessity and for sound reason. Such women, from their easy confidence in their breeding, become boastful or presumptuous or proud, and especially when they are native to the district, their authority becomes damaging to the convent. Precautions must be taken against the abbess becoming presumptuous because of the proximity of her kindred, and the convent's being burdened or disturbed by their numbers, so that religion suffers harm through her people and she comes under contempt from others: in accordance with the Truth:[3] 'A prophet will always be held in honour except in his native place.' St Jerome also made provision for this when he wrote to Heliodorus and enumerated several things which stand in the path of monks who stay in their native place. 'The conclusion of these considerations,' he says,[4] 'is that a monk cannot be perfect in his native place; and not to wish to be perfect is a sin.'

But what damage to souls will there be if she who is the authority over religion is lacking in religion herself? For it is sufficient for her subordinates if each of them displays a single virtue, but in her examples of all the virtues should shine out, so that she can be a living example of all she enjoins on the others, and not contradict her precepts by her morals, nor destroy by her own deeds what she builds in words; in order that the word of correction may not fall away from her lips when she is ashamed to correct in others the errors she is known to commit herself. The Psalmist prays to the Lord lest this happens to him: 'Rob not my mouth of the

1. Galatians ii, 11.

2. *Regula*, chapter 3, reading *minori*. The alternative reading is *iuniori*, 'younger'.

3. Matthew xiii, 57. 4. *Epistulae* xiv, 7.

power to tell the truth,' he says,[1] for he was expecting that stern rebuke of the Lord to which he refers elsewhere.[2] 'God's word to the wicked man is this: What right have you to recite my laws and make so free with the words of my covenant, you who hate correction and turn your back when I am speaking?' The Apostle too was careful to provide against this: 'I punish my own body,' he says,[3] 'and make it know its master, for fear that after preaching to others I should find myself rejected.' For anyone whose life is despised must see his preaching or teaching condemned as well, and a man who should heal another but suffers from the same infirmity is rightly reproached by the sick man: 'Physician, heal yourself.'[4]

Whoever is seen to have authority in the Church must think carefully what ruin his own fall will bring about when he takes his subjects along with him to the precipice. 'If any man,' says the Truth[5], 'breaks even the lowest of the Lord's commandments and teaches others to do the same, he will be the least in the kingdom of Heaven.' He breaks a commandment who infringes it by acting against it, and if he corrupts others by his example he sits in his chair as a teacher of pestilence. But if anyone acting thus is to be called the least in the kingdom of Heaven, that is in the Church here on earth, what are we to call a superior who is utterly vile, and because of whose negligence the Lord demands the life-blood not only of his own soul but of all the souls subject to him? And so the Book of Wisdom rightly curses such men:[6]

> It is the Lord who gave you your authority, and your power comes from the Most High. He will put your actions to the test and scrutinize your intentions. Though you are viceroys of his kingly power, you have not been upright judges; you do not stand up for the law of justice. Swiftly and terribly will he descend on you, for judgement falls relentlessly on those in high places. The small man may find pardon, but the powerful will be powerfully tormented, and a cruel trial awaits the mighty.

1. Psalm cxix, 43.
2. Psalm l, 16–17.
3. 1 Corinthians ix, 27.
4. Luke iv, 23.
5. Matthew v, 19.
6. Wisdom vi, 4–7.

It is sufficient for each of the subject souls to provide for itself against its own misdeed, but death hangs over those who also have responsibility for the sins of others for, when gifts are increased, the reasons for gifts are also multiplied, and more is expected of him to whom more is committed. We are warned in Proverbs to guard against so great a danger, when it says:[1] 'My son, if you pledge yourself to a friend and stand surety for a stranger, if you are caught by your promise, trapped by some words you have said, do what I now tell you and save yourself, my son, when you fall into another man's power. Run, hurry, rouse your friend, let not your eyes sleep nor your eyelids slumber.' For we pledge ourselves to a friend when our charity admits someone into the life of our community; we promise him the care of our supervision, as he promises his obedience to us. So too we stand surety for him by joining hands when we confirm our willingness to work on his behalf; and we fall into his power because unless we make provision for ourselves against him, we shall find that he is the slayer of our soul. It is against this danger that the advice is given 'Go, hurry etc.'

And so now here, now there, like a watchful and tireless captain, let our abbess go carefully round her camp and watch lest through any negligence a way is opened to him who, like a roaring lion, prowls around looking for someone to devour.[2] She must be the first to know all the evils of her house, so that she may correct them before they are known to the rest and taken as a precedent. Let her beware too of the charge St Jerome lays against the foolish or negligent:[3] 'We are always the last to learn of the evils of our own home, and are ignorant of the faults of our wives and children when they are the talk of the neighbourhood.'

She who thus presides must remember that she has taken on the care of bodies as well as of souls, and concerning the former there is advice for her in the words of Ecclesiasticus:[4]

1. Proverbs vi, 1–4.
2. 1 Peter v, 8.
3. *Epistulae* cxlvii, 10. Cf. *Historia calamitatum*, p. 68.
4. Ecclesiasticus vii, 24; 42; 9.

'Have you daughters? See that they are chaste, and do not be too lenient with them.' Again, 'A daughter is a secret anxiety to her father, and the worry of her takes away his sleep for fear she may be defiled.' But we defile our bodies not only by fornication but by doing anything improper with them, as much by the tongue as by any other member, or by abusing the bodily senses in any member for some idle whim. So it is written,[1] 'Death comes in through our windows,' that is, sin enters the soul by means of the five senses.

What death is more grievous or care more perilous than that of souls? 'Do not fear those who kill the body but cannot kill the soul,' says the Truth.[2] But if anyone hears this, does he not still fear the death of the body rather than of the soul? Who would not avoid a sword rather than a lie? And yet it is written that 'A lying tongue is death to the soul.'[3] What can be destroyed so easily as the soul? What arrow can be fashioned so speedily as a lie? Who can safeguard himself, if only against a thought? Who is able to watch out for his own sins but not those of others? What shepherd in the flesh has the power to protect spiritual sheep from spiritual wolves, both alike invisible? Who would not fear the robber who never ceases to lie in wait, whom no wall can shut out, no sword can kill or wound? He is forever plotting and persecuting, with the religious as his chosen victims, for, in the words of Habakkuk, they 'enjoy rich fare',[4] and it is against him that the apostle Peter urges us to be on our guard, saying:[5] 'Your enemy the devil, like a roaring lion, prowls around looking for someone to devour.' How confident he is of devouring us the Lord himself says to holy Job:[6] 'The flooded river he drinks unconcerned: he is confident he can draw up Jordan into his mouth.' For what would he not be bold enough to try, when he tried to test the Lord himself? It was he who took our first parents straight from Paradise to captivity, and even snatched an apostle whom the Lord had chosen from the apostles' company. What place is safe from him, what doors

1. Jeremiah ix, 21.
2. Matthew x, 28.
3. Wisdom i, 11.
4. Cf. Habakkuk i, 16.
5. 1 Peter v, 8.
6. Job xl, 18 (Vulgate).

are not unbarred to him? Who can take action against his plots or stand up to his strength? It was he who struck with a single stroke the four corners of the house of holy Job, and crushed and killed his innocent sons and daughters.[1]

What then can the weaker sex do against him? Who but women have his seductive ways so much to fear? It was a woman he first seduced, and through her her husband too, and so made captive all their descendants. His desire for a greater good robbed her of her possession of a lesser good, and by the same wiles he can still easily seduce a woman when her desire is for authority, not for service, and she is brought to this through her ambition for wealth or status. Which of the two mattered more to her, the sequel will show. For if she lives more luxuriously when in authority than she did as a subordinate, or claims any special privilege for herself beyond what is necessary, there can be no doubt that she coveted this. If she seeks more costly ornaments after than before, it is certain that she is swollen with vainglory. What she was before will afterwards appear, and her office will reveal whether what she displayed before was true virtue or pretence.

She should be brought to office, not come to it herself, in accordance with the Lord's words:[2] 'Those who have come of themselves are all thieves and robbers,' on which Jerome comments ' "Who have come", not "who were sent." ' She should be raised to the honour, not take it on herself, for 'Nobody,' as the Apostle says,[3] 'takes the honour on himself; he is called by God, as Aaron was.' If called she should mourn as though led to her death; if rejected, rejoice as though delivered from death. When we are said to be better than the rest we blush to hear the words, but when this is proved by the fact of our election, we shamelessly lose all shame. For who does not know that the better are preferable to the rest? So in the twenty-fourth book of *Morals*[4] it is said that 'No one should undertake the leadership of men if he does not know how to rebuke men properly by admonition. Nor

1. Cf. Job i, 19. 2. John x, 8. 3. Hebrews v, 4.
4. St Gregory, *Moralia*, 24. 25.

should the one chosen for this purpose of correcting the faults of others commit himself what ought to have been rooted out.' But if in this election we try to avoid this shamelessness by some light verbal refusal, and only to the ear reject the position offered us, we immediately incur the charge of trying to appear more righteous and worthy than we are.

How many have we seen at their election weeping with their eyes while laughing in their hearts, accusing themselves of unworthiness and thereby courting more approval and human support for themselves! They had in mind the words:[1] 'The just man is the first to accuse himself,' but afterwards when they were blamed and given a chance to retire they were completely shameless and persistent in their efforts to defend the position which they had declared themselves unwilling to accept, with feigned tears and well-founded accusations of themselves. In how many churches have we seen canons resisting their bishops when compelled by them to take holy orders, professing themselves unworthy of such priestly offices and quite unwilling to comply! Yet should the clergy subsequently elect them to the episcopate they are given only a frivolous refusal or none at all. And those who yesterday were avoiding a diaconate to escape endangering their souls, so they said, apparently find justification overnight, and have no fears of downfall from a higher office. In the same book of Proverbs it is written of such people:[2] 'A foolish man applauds when he stands as surety for a friend'; for the poor wretch rejoices though he should rather mourn when he assumed authority over others, and binds himself by his own declaration to caring for his subordinates, by whom he ought to be loved rather than feared.

We can provide against this evil as far as we can by absolutely forbidding the abbess to live in greater luxury and comfort than her subordinates. She must not have private apartments for eating or sleeping, but should do everything along with the flock entrusted to her, and be better able to make provision for them the more she is present in their midst. We know of course that St Benedict was greatly concerned about pilgrims

1. Cf. Letter 4, note 1, p. 143. 2. Cf. Proverbs xvii, 16.

and guests and set a table apart for the abbot to entertain them.[1] Though this was a pious provision at the time, it was afterwards amended by a dispensation which is highly beneficial to monasteries, whereby the abbot does not leave the monks but provides a faithful steward for the pilgrims; for it is easy for discipline to be relaxed at table, and that is the time when it should be more strictly observed. There are many too who use hospitality as an opportunity to think of themselves rather than of their guests, so that those who are not present are troubled by the gravest suspicions and make complaints. The authority of a superior is weakened the less his way of life is known to his people; moreover, any shortage there may be can be more easily accepted by all when it is shared by all, and especially by superiors. This we have learned from the example of Cato, who, it is written,[2] 'when the people with him were thirsty', rejected and poured away the few drops of water offered him 'so that all were satisfied'.

Since therefore sobriety is so necessary for those in authority, they must live sparingly, and the more so as provision for the others rests with them. And lest they turn the gift of God, that is, the authority conferred on them, into pride, and so show themselves insolent to their subjects, let them hear what is written:[3] 'Do not play the lion in your house, upsetting your household and oppressing your servants ... Pride is hateful to God and man.' The beginning of pride in man is renunciation of God, since the heart withdraws from God who made him, just as pride in any form is the beginning of sin. 'The Lord has overturned the seats of proud princes and enthroned the gentle in their place ... Have they chosen you to preside? Do not put on airs; behave to them as one of themselves.'[4] And the Apostle in giving instructions to Timothy about his subordinates says:[5] 'Never be harsh to an elder; appeal to him as though he were your father. Treat

1. Cf. *Regula*, chapters 53, 56.
2. Cf. Lucan, *Pharsalia*, 9, 498 ff.
3. Ecclesiasticus iv, 35; x, 7.
4. Ecclesiasticus x, 17; xxxii, 1.
5. 1 Timothy v, 1.

the younger men as brothers, the older women as mothers and the young as your sisters.' 'You did not choose me,' says the Lord, 'I chose you.'[1] All others in authority are elected by their subjects and are created and set up by them, because they are chosen not to lord over men but to serve them. God alone is truly Lord and has the power to choose his subjects for his service. Yet he did not show himself as a lord but as a servant, and when his disciples were already aspiring to high seats of power he rebuked them by his own example, saying[2] 'You know that in the world rulers lord it over their subjects, and those in authority are called benefactors; but it shall not be so with you.' Whoever seeks dominion over his subjects rather than service to them, who works to be feared, not loved, and being swollen with pride in his authority likes to have[3] 'places of honour at feasts and the chief seats in the synagogue, to be greeted respectfully in the street and to be addressed as "Rabbi" ', imitates the princes of the world. As for the honour of this title, we should not take pride in names but look to humility in everything. 'But you,' says the Lord, 'must not be called "Rabbi" and do not call any man on earth "father".' And afterwards he forbade self-glorification altogether, saying 'Whoever exalts himself shall be humbled.'

We must also make sure that the flock is not imperilled by the absence of its shepherds, and discipline slacken within when authority strays from its duties. And so we rule that the abbess, whose care is for spiritual rather than material matters, must not leave her convent for any external concern, but be the more solicitous for her subordinates the more active she is. Thus her appearances in public will be more highly valued for their rarity, as it is written:[4] 'If a great man invites you, keep away, and he will be the more pressing in his invitation.' But if the convent needs emissaries, the monks or their lay monks[5] should supply them, for it is always men's

1. John xv, 16. 2. Luke xxii, 25. 3. Matthew xxiii, 8–9; 12.
4. Ecclesiasticus xiii, 9.
5. *Conversi*. In a Benedictine house, lay-monks, i.e. monks who had come late to monastic life and were not brought up in the cloister.

duty to provide for women's needs, and the greater the religious devotion of the nuns, the more they give themselves up to God and have need of men's protection. And so Joseph was bidden by the angel to care for the mother of the Lord, though he was not allowed to sleep with her.[1] The Lord himself at his death chose for his mother a second son who should take care of her in material things.[2] There is no doubt either, as I have said elsewhere, that the apostles paid great attention to devout women and appointed the seven deacons for their service.[3] We too then, acting on this authority and in accordance with the demands of the situation, have decided that monks and lay monks, like the apostles and deacons, shall perform for convents of women such duties as call for outside assistance; the monks are necessary especially to celebrate Mass, the lay monks for other services.

It is therefore essential, as we read was the practice in Alexandria under Mark the Evangelist in the early days of the infant church, that monasteries of men should be near at hand for convents of women, and that all external affairs should be conducted for the women through men of the same religious life. And indeed we believe that convents then maintain the religion of their calling more firmly, if they are ruled by the guidance of spiritual men, and the same shepherd is set over the ewes as well as the rams: that is, that women shall come under the same authority as men, and always, as the Apostle ruled,[4] 'Woman's head is man, as man's head is Christ and Christ's is God'. And so the convent of St Scholastica which was situated on land belonging to a monastery was also under the supervision of one of the brothers, and took both instruction and comfort from frequent visits by him or the other brothers. The Rule of St Basil also instructs us on this kind of supervision, in the following passage:[5]

QUESTION: Shall the brother who presides, apart from the sister who presides over the nuns, say anything for their instruction?

1. Cf. Matthew i, 19.
2. Cf. John xix, 26.
3. Acts vi, 5.
4. 1 Corinthians xi, 3.
5. Cf. P.L. 103, 551.

ANSWER: How else shall the precept of the Apostle be observed, which says[1] 'Let all be done decently and in order'?

QUESTION: Is it seemly for him who presides to converse frequently with her who presides over the sisters, especially if some of the brethren are offended by this?

ANSWER: Although the Apostle asks[2] 'Is my freedom to be called in question by another man's conscience?', it is good to follow him when he says 'But I have availed myself of no such right, lest I should offer any hindrance to the gospel of Christ.' As far as possible the sisters should be seldom seen and preaching kept brief.

On this there is also the decision of the Council of Seville:

By common consent we have decreed that the convents of nuns in the Baetic province shall be ruled through the ministration and authority of monks. For we can best provide what is salutary for virgins dedicated to Christ by choosing for them spiritual fathers whose guidance can give them protection and whose teaching provide edification. But proper precautions must be taken so that the monks do not intrude on the privacy of the nuns, nor have general permission even to approach the vestibule. Neither the abbot nor anyone in authority over them shall be permitted, apart from their superior, to say anything to the virgins of Christ concerning regulations for their moral life; nor should he speak often with the superior alone, but in the presence of two or three sisters. Access should be rare and speech brief. God forbid the unmentionable – that we should wish the monks to be familiar with the virgins of Christ; they must be kept separate and far apart, as the statutes of the Rule and the canons lay down. We commit the nuns to their charge in the sense that one man, the best proved of the monks, shall be chosen to take over the management of their lands in the country, or town, and also the erection of buildings, or provision of whatever else is needed by the convent, so that the handmaids of Christ may be concerned only with the welfare of their souls, may live only for divine worship and performance of their own works. Of course the one proposed by his abbot must have the approval of his bishop. The sisters for their part should make clothing for the monasteries to which they look for guidance, since they will receive in return, as I said, the fruits of the monks' labour and support of their protection.

1. 1 Corinthians xiv, 40. 2. 1 Corinthians x, 29; ix, 12.

In accordance with this provision, then, we want convents of women always to be subject to monasteries of men, so that the brothers may take care of the sisters and one man preside over both like a father whose authority each community shall recognize, and thus for both in the Lord 'there will be one flock and one shepherd'.[1] Such a society of spiritual brotherhood should be the more pleasing to God as it is to man, the more perfectly it is able to meet the needs of either sex coming for conversion, the monks taking in the men and the nuns the women, so that it can provide for every soul seeking its own salvation. And whoever wishes to be converted along with a mother, sister, daughter or any other woman for whom he is responsible will be able to find complete fulfilment there, and the two monasteries should be joined by a greater mutual affection and feel a warmer concern for each other the more closely their inmates are united by some kinship or connection.

The Superior of the monks, whom they call Abbot, we want to preside over the nuns too in such a way that he regards those who are the brides of the Lord whose servant he is as his own mistresses, and so be glad to serve rather than rule them. He should be like a steward in a king's palace who does not oppress the queen by his powers but treats her wisely, so that he obeys her at once in necessary matters but pays no heed to what might be harmful, and performs all his services outside the bedchamber without ever penetrating its privacy unbidden. In this way, then, we want the servant of Christ to provide for the brides of Christ, to take charge of them faithfully for Christ, and to discuss everything necessary with the abbess, so that he makes no decisions about the handmaids of Christ and their concerns without consulting her, and issues no instructions or presumes to speak to any of them except through her. But whenever the abbess summons him he should be prompt to come, and not delay carrying out as far as he is able whatever she advises him about the needs of herself or her subordinates. When summoned by her he should speak to her openly, in the presence of approved per-

1. John x, 16.

sons, and not approach too near nor detain her with prolonged talk.

Anything to do with food or clothing, and money too, if there is any, shall be collected amongst the handmaids of Christ, or set aside so that what is surplus to the sisters' requirements can be made over to the brothers. And so the brothers shall attend to everything outside the buildings, and sisters confine themselves to what can suitably be done indoors by women, such as making clothes for themselves and the brothers, doing the washing, kneading bread and putting it to bake, and handling it when baked. They shall also take charge of the milk and its products, and of feeding hens or geese, and whatever women can do more conveniently than men.

The abbot himself on his appointment shall swear in the presence of the bishop and the sisters that he will be to them a faithful steward in the Lord, and will carefully keep their bodies from carnal contamination. If by chance (which God forbid) the bishop finds him negligent in this, he must depose him at once as guilty of perjury. All the brothers too, in making their profession, shall bind themselves by oath to the sisters not to consent to their oppression in any form, and to guarantee their bodily purity as far as they can. None of the men, therefore, except with the abbot's permission, shall have access to the sisters, nor receive anything sent by them except through the hands of the abbot. None of the sisters shall ever leave the precincts of the convent, but everything outside, as was said above, shall be the brothers' concern, for men should sweat over men's work. None of the brothers shall ever enter these precincts, unless he has obtained leave from the abbot and abbess for some necessary or worthy reason. If anyone ventures to do so, he shall be expelled from the monastery immediately.

But so that the men, being stronger than the women, shall not make too heavy demands on them, we make it a rule that they shall impose nothing against the will of the abbess, but do everything at her bidding and, all alike, men and women, shall make profession to her and promise obedience;

for peace will be more soundly based and harmony better preserved the less freedom is allowed to the stronger, while the men will be less burdened by obedience to the weaker women the less they have to fear violence from them. The more a man has humbled himself before God, the higher he will certainly be exalted. Let this be enough for the moment about the abbess. Now let us write of the officers under her.

The Sacristan, who is also the Treasurer, shall provide for the whole oratory; and she herself must keep all the keys that belong to it and everything necessary to it. If there are any offerings she shall receive them, and she shall have charge of making or remaking whatever is needed in the oratory and caring for all its furnishings. It is her duty too to see to the hosts, the vessels, the books for the altar and all its fittings, the relics, incense, lights, clock and striking of the bells. If possible the nuns should prepare the hosts themselves and purify the flour they are made from, and wash the altar-cloths. But neither the sacristan nor any of the sisters shall ever be allowed to touch the relics or the altar-vessels, nor even the altar-cloths except when these are given them to be washed. They must summon the monks or the lay-monks for this and await their coming. If necessary, some of them may be appointed to serve under the sacristan for this duty, who shall be thought fit to touch these things when the need arises, and take them out or replace them when she has unlocked the chests. The sister in charge of the sanctuary must be outstanding in purity of life, whole in mind as in body, if possible, and her abstinence and continence must be proved. She must be particularly well taught to calculate the phases of the moon, so that she can provide for the oratory according to the order of the seasons.

The Chantress shall be responsible for the whole choir, and shall arrange the divine offices and direct the teaching of singing and reading, and of everything to do with writing or composition. She shall also take charge of the book-cupboard, shall hand books out from it and receive them back, undertake the task of copying or binding them, or see that this is done. She shall decide how the sisters are to sit in choir and assign the seats, arrange who are to read or sing, and shall draw up the list, to be recited on Saturdays in Chapter, in which all the duties of the week are set out. Hence it is most important for her to be lettered, and especially to have some knowledge of music. She shall also see to all matters of discipline after the abbess, and if she happens to be busy with other affairs, the infirmarian shall take her place.[1]

The Infirmarian shall take care of the sick, and shall protect them from sin as well as from want. Whatever their sickness requires, baths, food or anything else, is to be allowed them; for there is a well-known saying, 'The law was not made for the sick.' Meat is not to be denied them on any account, except on the sixth day of the week or on the chief vigils or the fasts of the Ember Days or of Lent. But they should all the more be restrained from sin the more it is incumbent on them to think of their departure. That is the time when they should most observe silence, as they are very near their end, and concentrate on prayer, as it is written:[2] 'My son, if you have an illness, do not neglect it but pray to the Lord, and he will heal you. Renounce your sin, amend your ways, and cleanse your heart from all sin.' There must also be a watchful nurse always with the sick to answer their call at once when needed, and the infirmary must be equipped with everything necessary for their illness. Medicaments too must be provided, according to the resources of the convent, and this can more easily be done if the sister in charge of the sick has some knowledge of medicine. Those who have a period of bleeding shall also be in her care. And there should be someone with experience of blood-letting, or it would be necessary for a man to come in amongst the women for this purpose. Provision must also be made for the sick not to miss the offices of the Hours and communion; on the Lord's Day at least they should communicate, as far as possible always after confession and penance. For the anointing of the sick,

1. McLaughlin's text, adding *infirmaria* from the single MS. containing this letter in full. The alternative reading means, 'if the abbess happens to be busy . . . the chantress shall take her place'.

2. Ecclesiasticus xxxix, 9–10.

the precept of St James the apostle[1] is to be carefully observed, and in order to perform this, especially when the sick woman's life is despaired of, two of the older priests with a deacon must be brought in from the monks, bringing with them the holy oil; then they must administer the sacrament in the presence of the whole convent, though divided off by a screen. Communion shall be celebrated when needed in the same way. It is therefore essential for the infirmary to be so arranged that the monks can easily come and go to perform these sacraments without seeing the sisters or being seen by them.

Once at least every day the abbess and the cellaress should visit the sick woman as if she were Christ, so that they may carefully provide for her bodily as well as her spiritual needs, and show themselves worthy to hear the words of the Lord:[2] 'I was sick and you visited me.' But if the sick woman is near her end and has reached her death-agony, someone who is with her must run at once through the convent beating on a wooden board to give warning of the sister's departure. The whole convent, whatever the hour of day or night, must then hurry to the dying, unless prevented by the offices of the Church. Should this happen, as nothing must come before the work of God, it is enough if the abbess and a few others she has chosen shall go there quickly and the convent follow later. Whoever come running at the beating of the board should start at once on the Litany, until the invocation of the saints, male and female, is completed, and then the psalms should follow or the other offices of the dead. How salutary it is to go to the sick or the dead Ecclesiastes points out, when he says:[3] 'It is better to visit the house of mourning than the house of feasting; for to be mourned is the lot of every man, and the living should take this to heart.' Similarly, 'The wise man's heart is where there is grief, and the fool's heart where there is joy.'

The body of the dead woman must then be washed at once by the sisters, clad in some cheap but clean garment and stockings, and laid on a bier, the head covered by the veil.

1. James v, 14.
2. Matthew xxv, 36.
3. Ecclesiastes vii, 2; 4.

These coverings must be firmly stitched or bound to the body and not afterwards removed. The body shall be carried into the church by the sisters for the monks to give it proper burial, and the sisters meanwhile shall devote themselves to psalm-singing and prayer in the oratory. The burial of an abbess shall have only one feature to distinguish it from that of others: her entire body shall be wrapped only in a hair-shirt and sewn up in this as in a sack.

The Wardrober shall be in charge of everything to do with clothing, and this includes shoes. She shall have the sheep shorn and receive the hides for shoes, spin and card flax or wool, take entire charge of weaving, and supply everyone with needle, thread and scissors. She shall also be personally responsible for the dormitory and provide bedding for all, and also for tablecloths, towels and cloths of every kind, and shall see to cutting and sewing and also washing them. To her especially the words apply:[1] 'She seeks wool and flax and works by the skill of her hands . . . She sets her hand to the distaff and her fingers grasp the spindle . . . She will have no fear for her household when it snows, for all her servants are wrapped in two cloaks and she can laugh at to-morrow. She keeps her eye on the ways of her household and does not eat the bread of idleness. Her sons rise up and call her blessed.' She shall keep the tools necessary for her work, and shall arrange what part of it to assign to which of the sisters, for she will have charge of the novices until they are admitted into the community.

The Cellaress shall be responsible for everything connected with food, for the cellar, refectory, kitchen, mill, bakehouse and its oven, and also the gardens, woods and entire cultivation of the fields. She shall also take charge of bees, herds and flocks, and all necessary poultry. She shall be expected to provide all essentials to do with food, and it is most important that she should not be grudging but ready and willing to provide everything required, 'For God loves a cheerful giver.'[2] We absolutely forbid her to favour herself above the others in dispensing her stores; she must neither prepare

1. Proverbs xxxi, 13; 19 ff.
2. 2 Corinthians ix, 7.

private dishes for herself nor keep anything for herself by defrauding the others of it. 'The best steward', says Jerome, 'is one who keeps nothing for himself.' Judas abused his office of steward when he had charge of the common purse and left the company of the apostles. Ananias too and Sapphira his wife were condemned to death for keeping money back.[1]

The Portress or Doorkeeper (which means the same) has the duty of receiving guests and all comers, announcing them or bringing them to the proper place, and dispensing hospitality. She should be discreet in years and mind, so that she will know how to receive and give an answer, and to decide who and who not to admit, and in what way. She especially, as if she were the vestibule of the Lord, should be an ornament for the religious life of the convent, since knowledge of it starts with her. She should therefore be gentle of speech and mild in manner, and should try by giving a suitable reason to establish a friendly relationship even with those she has to turn away. For it is written that[2] 'A soft answer turns away anger, but a sharp word makes tempers hot.' And elsewhere: 'Pleasant words win many friends and soothe enemies.' She also, as she sees the poor more regularly and knows them better, should share out what food and clothing there is for distribution; but if she or any of the officials need support or assistance, the abbess should appoint deputies for them, taking these generally from the lay sisters, lest some of the nuns are absent from the divine offices or from Chapter and the refectory.

The portress should have a lodge by the gate, where she or her deputy can always be ready for all comers; they must not sit idle and, as their talk may easily be heard outside, they should be careful to observe silence. Indeed, her duty is not only to deny entrance to people who must be kept out but also to exclude entirely any rumours, so that they are not carelessly allowed into the convent, and she must be called to account for any failure in this matter. But if she hears what ought to be known, she should report it privately to the abbess

1. John xiii, 29; Acts v, 1–12.
2. Proverbs xv, 1; Ecclesiasticus vi, 5.

so that she may think it over if she wishes. As soon as there is any knocking or clamour at the gate the portress must ask the newcomers who they are and what they want and, if necessary, open the gate at once to admit them. Only women shall be entertained inside; men must be directed to the monks. Thus no man may be admitted for any reason, unless the abbess has been previously consulted and has issued instructions, but entrance shall be granted to women at once. The women when admitted, or the men allowed to enter on some occasion, must be made to wait by the portress in her cell, until the abbess or the sisters, if it is necessary or fitting, shall come to them. In the case of poor women whose feet need to be washed, the abbess herself or the sisters shall duly perform this charitable act of hospitality. For the Lord too was called deacon by the apostles chiefly for this service to humanity, as someone has recorded in the *Lives of the Fathers*, saying:[1] 'For you, O men, the Saviour became a deacon, girding himself with a towel and washing the disciples' feet, and telling them to wash their brothers' feet.' And so the Apostle says of the deaconess 'if she has given hospitality and washed the feet of God's people'. And the Lord himself says: 'I was a stranger, and you took me in.'[2]

All the officials (except the Chantress) should be chosen from the sisters who do not study letters, if there are others better fitted to make use of greater freedom for their studies.

The ornaments for the oratory should be necessary, not superfluous, and clean rather than costly. There should be nothing made of gold or silver in it apart from one silver chalice, or more than one if needed. There must be no furnishings of silk, apart from the stoles or maniples, and no carved images. Nothing but a wooden cross shall be set up on the altar there, though if the sisters like to paint the statue of the Saviour, that is not forbidden. But the altars must have no other statues. The convent must be content with a pair of bells. A vessel of holy water should be set outside the en-

1. *Vitae patrum*, VII, 4. 8.
2. 1 Timothy v, 10; Matthew xxv, 35.

trance to the oratory, for the sisters to bless themselves with when they go in in the morning and come out after Compline.

None of the nuns may be absent from the Canonical Hours, but as soon as the bell is rung, everything must be put down and each sister go quickly, with modest gait, to the divine office. As they come into the oratory unobserved, let all who can, say:[1] 'Through thy great love I will come into thy house, and bow low towards thy holy temple in awe of thee.' No book is to be kept in the choir except the one needed for the office at the time. The psalms should be repeated clearly and distinctly so as to be understood, and any chanting or singing must be pitched so that anyone with a weak voice can sustain the note. Nothing may be said or sung in church which is not taken from authentic scripture, and chiefly from the Old or New Testament. These are to be divided amongst the lessons so that they are read in their entirety in the course of the year. But exposition of the Scriptures or sermons of the Doctors of the Church or any other writings of an edifying nature shall be read aloud in the refectory or in Chapter; the reading of all these is permitted where the need is felt. No one must presume to read or sing without previous preparation, and if anyone happens to mispronounce something in the oratory, she must make amends on the spot by prayer in the presence of all, saying softly to herself: 'Yet again, Lord, forgive my carelessness.'

They must rise at midnight for the Night Office as the prophet enjoins, and so they must retire to bed early, so that their weak nature can sustain these vigils, and all the matters for the day can be done in daylight as St Benedict also laid down.[2] After the Office they should return to the dormitory until the hour is struck for morning Lauds. If any of the night still remains, sleep should not be denied their weakness, for sleep more than anything refreshes weary nature, makes it able to

1. Psalm v, 7–8.

2. i.e. the Night Office and the seven offices of the day, Lauds, Prime, Terce, Sext, Nones, Vespers and Compline. *Regula*, chapter 16. The prophet is David, in Psalm CXIX, 62.

endure toil, and keeps it equable and alert. However, if any of them feel a need to meditate on the Psalter or the lessons, as St Benedict also says,[1] they must concentrate without disturbing those who are asleep, for in this passage he refers to meditation rather than reading, lest the reading of some disturb the sleep of others. And when he spoke of 'the brothers who feel a need', he was certainly not compelling anyone to meditate in this way. But if there is sometimes also a need for instruction in chanting, this will also have to be met for those for whom it is necessary.

The morning Hour should be celebrated as soon as day dawns and, if it can be arranged, the bell should be rung at sunrise. When it is ended the sisters should return to the dormitory and, if it is summer, and the night is short and the morning long, we are willing for them to sleep a little before Prime, until they are waked by the bell. Such sleep after morning Lauds is mentioned by St Gregory in the second chapter of his *Dialogues* in speaking of the venerable Libertinus: 'But on the second day there was a case to be heard for the benefit of the monastery. And so, after morning hymns had been sung, Libertinus came to the abbot's bedside and humbly sought a prayer for himself ...' This morning sleep shall accordingly be permitted from Easter until the autumn equinox, after which the night begins to exceed the day.

On coming out of the dormitory they must wash and then take books and sit in the cloister reading or chanting until Prime is rung. After Prime they should go to Chapter, and when all are seated there, a lesson from the Martyrology should be read, after the day of the month is given out. After this there should either be some edifying words or some of the Rule should be read and expounded. Then if there are matters to correct or arrange they should go on to these.

But it must be understood that neither a monastery nor some particular house should be called irregular if some irregularities occur there, but only if they are not afterwards carefully corrected. For is there any place which is wholly

1. *Regula*, chapter 8. Note that the nuns must not follow the usual contemporary practice of reading aloud.

faultless? St Augustine took due note of this in a certain passage when he was instructing his clergy.[1]

> However strict the discipline in my house, I am a man and live among men. I would not venture to claim that my house is better than Noah's Ark, where one amongst eight persons was found to be a reprobate, or better than the house of Abraham where it was said 'Drive out this slave-girl and her son,' or better than the house of Isaac of which the Lord said 'I love Jacob, I hate Esau,' or better than the house of Jacob where a son defiled his father's bed, or better than the house of David, where one son slept with his sister and another rebelled against the holy mildness of his father;[2] or better than the company of the apostle Paul, who, had he lived among good men would not have said 'Quarrels all round us, forebodings within.' Nor if he had been living among good men would he have said 'There is no one here who takes a genuine interest in your concerns; they are all bent on their own ends.'[3] It is not better than the company of Christ himself, in which eleven good men had to endure the thief and traitor Judas, nor better, lastly, than heaven from which angels fell.

Augustine also, in pressing us to seek the discipline of the monastery, added: 'I confess before God, from the day on which I began to serve God, I have had difficulty in finding better men than those who have made progress in monasteries, but equally I have found none worse than those in monasteries who have fallen.' Hence, I think, it is written in the Apocalypse,[4] 'Let the good man persevere in his goodness and the filthy man continue in his filth.'

Correction must therefore be rigorous, to the extent that any sister who has seen something to be corrected in another and concealed it shall be subjected to a harsher discipline than the offender. No one then should put off denouncing her own or another's wrongdoing. Whoever anticipates the others in accusing herself, as it is written that 'The just man is

1. *Epistulae* lxxviii, 8.
2. Genesis ix, 22 (Ham); xxi, 10 (Hagar and Ishmael); Malachi i, 3; Genesis xxxv, 22 (Reuben and Bilhar, Jacob's concubine); 2 Samuel xiii, 1 ff. (Amnon and his half-sister Tamar); xv, 1 ff. (Absalom and David).
3. 2 Corinthians vii, 5; Philippians ii, 20–21.
4. Revelations xxii, 11.

the first to accuse himself,'[1] deserves a milder punishment, if her negligence has ceased. But no one shall presume to make excuses for another unless the abbess happens to question her about the truth of a matter which is unknown to the rest. No one shall ever presume to strike another for any fault unless she has been ordered to do so by the abbess. Concerning the discipline of correction, it is written: 'My son, do not spurn the Lord's correction nor be cast down at his reproof; for those whom he loves the Lord reproves, as a father punishes a favourite son.' Again, 'A father who spares the rod hates his son, but one who loves him keeps him in order.' 'Strike a scornful man and a fool will be wiser.' 'Punish a scornful man and the simple will be wiser.' 'A whip for the horse, a halter for the ass and a rod for the back of fools.' 'Who takes a man to task will in the end win more thanks than the man with a flattering tongue.' 'Discipline is never pleasant, at the time it seems painful, but later, for those trained by it, it yields a harvest of peace and goodness.' 'There is shame in being the father of a spoilt son, and the birth of a foolish daughter will bring loss.' 'A man who loves his son will whip him often so that he may have joy in him in the end.' 'An unbroken horse turns out stubborn, and an unchecked son turns out headstrong. Pamper your son and he will shock you; play with him and he will grieve you.'[2]

In a discussion on what counsel to take, it shall be open to anyone to offer her opinion, but whatever everyone else thinks, the abbess's decision must not be swayed, for everything depends on her will, even if (which God forbid) she may be mistaken and decide on a worse course. For as St Augustine says in his *Confessions*,[3] 'He who disobeys his superiors in anything sins greatly, even if he chooses what is better than what is commanded him.' It is indeed far better for us to do well than to do good, and we must think less of what should be done and more of the manner and spirit in

1. Cf. Letter 4, note 1 p. 143, and p. 207 in this letter.

2. Proverbs iii, 11–12; xiii, 24; xix, 25; xxi, 11; xxvi, 23; Hebrews xii, 11; Ecclesiasticus xxii, 3; xxx, 1–2, 8–9.

3. This is not in existing texts of the *Confessions*.

which to do it. A thing is well done which is done obediently, even if it seems the least good thing to have done. And so superiors must be obeyed in everything, whatever the material harm, if there is no apparent danger to the soul. The superior must take care that he orders well since it is sufficient for his subjects to obey well and not to follow their own will but, as they professed, that of their superiors. For we absolutely forbid that custom should ever be set above reason; a practice must never be defended on grounds of custom but only of reason, not because it is usual but because it is good, and it should be more readily accepted the better it is shown to be. Otherwise like the Jews we should set the antiquity of the Law before the Gospel.

On this point St Augustine several times gives proof from the counsel of Cyprian, and says in one passage: 'Whoever despises truth and presumes to follow custom is either ill-disposed and hostile towards his fellow-men, to whom truth is revealed, or he is ungrateful to God on whose inspiration his Church is founded.' Again, 'In the Gospel the Lord says "I am Truth." He did not say "I am custom." And so as truth was made manifest, custom must yield to truth.' Again, 'Since the truth was revealed, error must yield to truth, just as Peter, who was previously circumcised, yielded to Paul who preached truth.' Similarly, in the fourth book *On Baptism* he writes: 'In vain do those who are vanquished by reason plead custom against us, as though custom were greater than truth, or in spiritual matters we should not follow what was revealed for the better by the Holy Spirit. This is clearly true because reason and truth must be set before custom.'[1]

Gregory the Seventh writes to Bishop Wimund: 'And certainly, in the words of St Cyprian, any custom, however long established and widespread, must stand second to truth, and practice which is contrary to truth must be abolished.' And we are told how lovingly we should adhere to the truth in speech by Ecclesiasticus when he says 'Do not be ashamed to speak the truth for your soul's sake,' and 'Do not contradict the truth in any way,' and again, 'A true word should

1. Augustine, *De baptismo*, 3. 5, 6, 7; 4. 5.

come before every enterprise and steady counsel before every deed.'[1] Nothing must be taken as a precedent because it is done by many but because it is approved by the wise and good. As Solomon says,[2] 'The number of fools cannot be counted,' and, in accordance with the assertion of the Truth,[3] 'Many are summoned but few are chosen.' Valuable things are rare, and multiplication of numbers diminishes value. In taking counsel no one should follow the larger number of men but the better men; it is not a man's years which should be considered but his wisdom, and regard paid not to friendship but to truth. Hence also the words of the poet:[4]

Even from a foe it is right to learn.

But whenever there is need for counsel it must not be postponed and, if important matters are to be debated, the whole convent should be assembled. For discussing minor affairs it will be enough for the abbess to meet a few of the senior nuns. It is also written concerning counsel that 'The people fares ill that has no guidance, but safety reigns where counsel abounds.' 'The fool is right in his own eyes, but the wise man listens to counsel.' 'Do nothing, my son, except with counsel, and afterwards you will have no regrets.'[5] If something done without taking counsel happens to have a successful outcome, fortune's kindness does not excuse the doer's presumption. But if after taking counsel men sometimes err, the authority which sought counsel is not held guilty of presumption, and the man who believed his advisers is not so much to be blamed as those with whom he agreed in their error.

On coming out from Chapter the sisters should apply themselves to suitable tasks, reading or chanting or handiwork until Terce. After Terce the Mass shall be said, and to celebrate this one of the monks shall be appointed priest for the week. If numbers are large he must come with a deacon and

1. Ecclesiasticus iv, 24; iv, 30; xxxvii, 16.
2. Ecclesiastes i, 15. 3. Matthew xxii, 14.
4. Ovid, *Metamorphoses*, 4. 428.
5. Proverbs xi, 14; xii, 15; Ecclesiasticus xxxii, 24 (Vulgate).

subdeacon to serve him with what is necessary or to perform their own office. Their coming in and going out must be so arranged as to be unseen by the sisters. If more have been needed, arrangements shall be made for them too and, if possible, provision so that the monks never miss divine offices in their own monastery because of the nuns' masses.

If the sisters are to take communion, one of the older priests must be chosen to administer it to them after Mass, but the deacon and subdeacon must first withdraw, to remove any risk of temptation. Three times at least in the year the whole convent must communicate, at Easter, Pentecost and the Nativity of the Lord, as it was ordained by the Fathers for the laity also. For these communions they must prepare themselves in the following way: three days before they should all make their confession and do suitable penance, and by three days of fasting on bread and water and repeated prayer purify themselves humbly and fearfully, taking to themselves those terrible words of the Apostle:[1]

> It follows that anyone who eats the bread or drinks from the cup of the Lord unworthily will be guilty of desecrating the body and blood of the Lord. A man must test himself before eating his share of the bread and drinking from the cup. For he who eats and drinks unworthily eats and drinks judgement on himself if he does not discern the body of the Lord. That is why many of you are feeble and sick and a number have died. But if we judged ourselves we should not be judged at all.

After Mass they should return again to their work until Sext and not waste any time in idleness; everyone must do what she can and what is right for her. After Sext they should have lunch, unless it is a fast-day, when they must wait until None, and in Lent even until Vespers. But at no time must the convent be without reading, which the abbess may end when she wishes by saying 'Enough', and then they should all rise at once to render thanks to God. In summer they should rest in their dormitory after lunch until None, and after None return to work until Vespers. Immediately after Ves-

1. 1 Corinthians xi, 27–31.

pers they should eat and drink, and then, according to the custom of the season, they should go to Collation:[1] but on Saturday, before Collation, they should be made clean by washing of the feet and hands. The abbess should also participate in this rite along with the sisters on duty for the week in the kitchen. After Collation they are to come at once to Compline, and then retire to sleep.

As regards food and clothing, the opinion of the Apostle must be followed, in which he says,[2] 'As long as we have food and something to wear let us rest content.' That is, necessities should be sufficient and superfluous things not sought. They should be allowed whatever can be bought cheaply or easily obtained and taken without giving offence, for the Apostle avoids only what foods will offend his own or his brother's conscience, knowing that it is not the food which is at fault but the appetite for it.[3]

> The man who eats must not hold in contempt the man who does not, and he who does not eat must not pass judgement on the man who does ... Who are you to pass judgement on someone else's servant? ... He who eats has the Lord in mind when he eats, since he gives thanks to God; and he who abstains has the Lord in mind no less, and he too gives thanks to God ... Let us therefore cease judging one another, but rather make this judgement: that no obstacle or stumbling-block be placed in a brother's way. I know on the authority of the Lord Jesus that nothing is unclean in itself, only if a man considers a particular thing unclean ... The kingdom of God is not eating and drinking but justice, peace, and joy in the Holy Spirit ... Everything is pure in itself, but anything is bad for the man who by his eating causes his brother to fall. It is good to abstain from eating meat or drinking wine, or doing anything which causes your brother's downfall.

And after the offence to his brother he goes on to speak of the offence to himself of a man who eats against his own conscience: 'Happy is the man who does not bring judgement upon himself by what he approves. But a man who has doubts

1. The daily reading from the *Conferences* of John Cassian before Compline, instituted by St Benedict in *Regula*, chapter 42.

2. 1 Timothy vi, 8. 3. Romans xiv, 3 ff.

is guilty if he eats, because his action does not arise from his conviction, and anything which is not from conviction is sin.'

For in all that we do against our conscience and against our beliefs we are sinning; and in what we test by the law which we approve and accept, we judge and condemn ourselves if we eat those foods which we discriminate against or exclude by the law and set apart as unclean. So great is the testimony of our conscience that this more than anything accuses or excuses us before God. And so John writes in his First Letter:[1] 'Dear friends, if our conscience does not condemn us, then we can approach God with confidence, and obtain from him whatever we ask, because we keep his commandments and do what he approves.' It was therefore well said by Paul in the passage above that 'Nothing is unclean in the eyes of Christ, but only for the man who considers a thing unclean,' that is, if he thinks it impure and forbidden to him. (Indeed, we call certain foods unclean which according to the Law are clean, because the Law in forbidding them to its own people may still offer them publicly to those outside the Law. Hence 'common' women are unclean, and common things which are offered publicly are cheap or less dear.) And so the Apostle asserts that no food is 'common' or unclean in the eyes of Christ because the law of Christ forbids nothing except, as is said, to remove offence to one's own conscience or another's. On this he says elsewhere,[2] 'And therefore if food be the downfall of my brother, I will never eat meat any more, for I will not be the cause of my brother's downfall.' 'Am I not a free man? Am I not an apostle?' – as if he were to say, Have I not the freedom which the Lord gave to the apostles, to eat whatever I like or to take alms from others? For when the Lord sent out the apostles, he said in a certain passage:[3] 'Eating and drinking what they have', and thus made no distinction between kinds of food. Noting this, the Apostle is careful to say that any kind of food, even if it is the food of unbelievers and consecrated to

1. 1 John iii, 21–2.
2. 1 Corinthians viii, 13; ix, 1.
3. Luke x, 7.

idols, is permitted to Christians and only the giving of offence in food is to be avoided:[1]

There are no forbidden things, but not everything does good. Nothing is forbidden me, but not everything helps to build the community. Nobody should look to his own interests, but the other man's. You may eat anything sold in the meat-market without raising questions of conscience; for the earth is the Lord's and everything in it. If an unbeliever invites you to a meal and you care to go, eat whatever is put before you without raising questions of conscience. But if someone says to you, "This food has been offered in sacrifice to idols," then, out of consideration for him who told you and for conscience's sake, do not eat it – not your conscience, I mean, but the other man's ... Give no offence to Jews or Greeks or to the Church of God.

From these words of the Apostle it is plain that nothing is forbidden us which we can eat without offence to our own or another's conscience. We eat without offence to our own conscience if we are sure that we are keeping to that course of life whereby we can be saved, and without offence to another's if we are believed to be living in a manner leading to salvation. We shall indeed live in this manner if we permit everything necessary to our nature while avoiding sin, and if we are not over-confident of our strength so as to bind ourselves by profession to a rule of life too heavy for us, under which we may fall: and the higher the degree of our profession, the heavier the fall would be. Such a fall, and such a foolish vow of profession Ecclesiastes forestalls, when he says:[2] 'When you make a vow to God do not be slow to pay it, for he has no use for unbelievers and foolish promises. Pay whatever you owe. Better not vow at all than vow and fail to pay.' On this hazard too the Apostle advises, saying:[3] 'It is my wish that younger widows shall remarry, have children, preside over a home, and give no opponent occasion for slander. For there have already been some who have taken the wrong turning and gone to the devil.' Out of con-

1. 1 Corinthians x, 22 ff.
2. Ecclesiastes v, 4–5.
3. 1 Timothy v, 14–15.

sideration for the nature of youth's frailty, he sets the remedy of a freer way of life against the risk of attempting a better one, and advises us to stay in a lowly position lest we fall from a high one.

Following him St Jerome also instructs the virgin Eustochium:[1] 'But if those who are virgins may not be saved on account of other faults, what shall become of those who have prostituted the members of Christ and turned the temple of the Holy Spirit into a brothel? It would have been better for mankind to undergo matrimony, tread level ground, than to aim at the heights and fall into the depths of hell.' And if we search through all the words of the Apostle we shall never find that he allowed a second marriage except to women. To men he preaches continence. 'If anyone was circumcised before he was called, he should not disguise it.' And again, 'If you are free of a wife, do not seek one.'[2] Moses, on the other hand, was more indulgent to men than to women, and allowed one man several wives at the same time, but not one woman several husbands; and he punished the adulteries of women more severely than those of men. 'A woman,' says the Apostle,[3] 'if her husband dies is free from the law of her husband, so that she does not commit adultery if she consorts with another man.' And elsewhere,[4] 'To the unmarried and to widows I say this: It is a good thing if they stay as I am myself, but if they cannot control themselves, they should marry. Better be married than burn with desire.' Again, 'The wife, if her husband is dead, is free to marry whom she will, as long as it is in the Lord. But she will be happier if she stays in accordance with my advice.' Not only does he allow a second marriage to the weaker sex but he does not venture to set a limit to the number, simply permitting them to take other husbands when theirs are dead. He fixes no limit to their marriages, provided that they are not guilty of fornication. They should marry often rather than fornicate once, and pay the debts of the flesh to many rather than once be prostituted to one: such payment is not wholly free from

1. *Epistulae* xxii, 6.
2. 1 Corinthians vii, 18; 27.
3. Romans vii, 3.
4. 1 Corinthians vii, 8–9; 39–40.

sin, but lesser sins are permitted so that greater may be avoided.

No wonder, then, that what has no sin at all is allowed them lest they commit sin; that is, foods which are necessary and not superfluous. For, as we said, the food is not to blame but the appetite, when pleasure is taken in what is not permitted, and forbidden things are desired and sometimes shamelessly snatched, which causes very serious offence.

But what amongst all the foods of men is so dangerous, injurious and contrary to our religion or to holy quiet as wine? The wisest of men well understood this when he particularly warns us against it, saying:[1]

> Wine is reckless, and strong drink quarrelsome. No one who delights in these will be wise . . . Who will know woe, as his father will, and quarrels, brawls, bruises without cause and bloodshot eyes? Those who linger late over wine, and look for ready-mixed wine. Do not look on wine when it glows and sparkles in the glass. It goes down smoothly, but in the end it will bite like a snake and spread venom like a serpent. Then your eyes will see strange sights, and your mind utter distorted words; you will be like a man sleeping in mid-ocean, like a drowsy helmsman who has lost his rudder, and you will say: 'They struck me and it did not hurt, dragged me off and I felt nothing. When I wake up I shall turn to wine again . . .'

Again:

> Do not give wine to kings, O Lemuel, never to kings; there is no privy counsel where drinking prevails. If they drink they may forget what they have decreed and neglect the pleas of the poor for their sons.

And in Ecclesiasticus it says,[2] 'A drunken workman will never grow rich; carelessness in small things leads little by little to ruin. Wine and women rob the wise of their wits and are a hard test for good sense.'

Isaiah, too, passes over all other foods and mentions only wine as a reason for the captivity of his people. 'Shame on you,' he says,[3] 'who rise in the morning to go in pursuit of liquor and drinking until evening, when you are heated with wine. At your feasts you have harp and lute, tabor and pipe

1. Proverbs xx, 1; xxiii, 29–35; xxxi, 4.
2. Ecclesiasticus xix, 1–2.
3. Isaiah v, 11–12; 22; xxviii, 7–9.

and wine, but have no eyes for the work of the Lord. Shame upon you, mighty drinkers, violent mixers of drinks.' Then he extends his lament from the people to priests and prophets, saying, 'These too are fuddled with wine and bemused with drinking. Priest and prophet are stupid with drinking; they are sodden with wine, bemused with liquor; they do not recognize the true visionary and have forgotten justice. Every table is covered with vomit and filth that leaves no clean spot. Whom shall the prophet teach knowledge? Whom shall he compel to listen and understand?' The Lord says through Joel,[1] 'Wake up, you drunkards, and weep for the sweet wine you drink.' Not that he forbids wine when necessary, for the Apostle recommends it to Timothy 'for the frequent ailments of your stomach'[2] – not ailments only, but frequent ones.

Noah was the first to plant a vineyard, still ignorant perhaps of the evil of drinking and, when drunk, exposed his bare thighs, because with wine comes the shame of lechery. When mocked by his son he put a curse on him and bound him by a sentence of servitude, something we know was never done before. Lot was a holy man, and so his daughters saw that he could never be led into incest except through drunkenness. And the holy widow believed that Holophernes in his pride could never be tricked and brought low except by this device. The angels who visited the patriarchs of old and were hospitably received by them took food, we are told, but not wine. Elijah too, the greatest and first of our leaders, when he had retired to the wilderness was brought bread and meat for food by the ravens morning and evening, but not wine. The children of Israel also, we read, were fed in the desert mainly on the delicate flesh of quails, but neither received wine nor wished for it.[3] And those repasts of loaves and fishes wherewith the people were sustained in the wilderness are nowhere said to have included wine. Only a wedding, where incontinence is permitted, was granted the miracle

1. Joel i, 5. 2. 1 Timothy v, 23.

3. Cf. Genesis ix, 20; xix, 33–4; Judith xii–xiii; Genesis xviii, 1 ff.; 1 Kings xvii, 1 ff.

of the wine which promotes sensuality.[1] But the wilderness, the proper habitation of monks, knew the benefit of meat rather than wine. Again, the cardinal point in the law of the Nazarites whereby they dedicated themselves to God forbade only wine and strong drink.[2] For what strength or virtue remains in the drunken? Thus not only wine, but anything which can intoxicate, we read, was also forbidden to the priests of old. And so Jerome, in writing to Nepotian about the life of the clergy, and highly indignant because the priests of the Law abstain from all strong drink and so surpass our clergy in abstinence, says:[3]

> Never smell of wine, lest you hear said of you those words of the philosopher: 'This is not offering a kiss but proffering a cup.' The Apostle condemns priests who are given to drink and the Old Law equally forbids it: 'Those who serve the altar shall not drink wine and strong drink.' By 'strong drink' in Hebrew is understood any drink which can intoxicate, whether produced by fermentation, or from apple juice, or from honeycomb which has been distilled into a sweet, rough drink, or when the fruit of the date-palm is pressed into liquid, or water is enriched with boiled grain. Whatever intoxicates and upsets the balance of the mind, shun it like wine.

According to the Rule of St Pachomius,[4] no one shall have access to wine and liquor except in the sickroom. Which of you has not heard that wine in any form is not for monks, and was so greatly abhorred by the monks of old that in their stern warnings against it, they called it Satan? And so we read in the *Lives of the Fathers* that:[5]

> Certain people told abba Pastor that a particular monk drank no wine, to which he replied that wine was not for monks.

1. Matthew xv, 32 ff.; John ii, 1 ff.
2. Numbers vi, 3.
3. *Epistulae* lii, 11.
4. St Pachomius (*c.* 286–*c.* 346) was the first monk to organize the hermits of the Egyptian desert into a community with a written Rule. Abelard would know the text of this from the Latin translation by St Jerome (P.L. 23,69). The original version is lost.
5. *Vitae patrum*, V, 4. 31; 36; 37. Heloise quotes the same passages in Letter 5, p. 169.

And further on:

Once there was a celebration of the Mass on the Mount of abba Antony, and a jar of wine was found there. One of the elders took a small vessel, carried a cupful to abba Sisoi and gave it to him. He drank once, and a second time he took it and drank, but when it was offered a third time he refused, saying 'Peace, brother, do you not know it is Satan?'

It is also said of abba Sisoi:

His disciple Abraham then asked, 'If this happens on the Sabbath and the Lord's Day in church, and he drinks three cups, is that too much?' 'If it were not Satan,' the old man replied, 'it would not be much.'

St Benedict had this in mind when he allowed wine to monks by special dispensation, saying:[1]

Although we read that wine is never for monks, in our times it is impossible to persuade monks of this.

It is not surprising, then, that if wine is strictly denied to monks, St Jerome absolutely forbids it to women, whose nature is weaker in itself, though stronger as regards wine. He uses strong words when instructing Eustochium, the Bride of Christ, on the preserving of her virginity:[2]

And so, if there is any counsel in me, if my experience is to be trusted, this is my first warning and testimony. The Bride of Christ must avoid wine like poison. It is the first weapon of demons against youth. Greed does not make her waver nor pride bolster her up nor ambition seduce her in the same way. We can easily forgo the other vices, but this is a foe shut up within us. Wherever we go we carry the enemy with us. Wine and youth are the twin fires of lust. Why throw oil on the flame, why add the fuel of fire to the burning body?

And yet it is well known from the evidence of those who write about physic that wine has much less power over women than men. Macrobius Theodosius, in the seventh book of his *Saturnalia*,[3] gives a reason for this:

1. *Regula*, chapter 40. 2. Epistulae xxii, 8.
3. *Saturnalia* VII, 6.16–17; 18. Cf. Letter 5,. p. 166.

Aristotle says that women are rarely intoxicated, but old men often. Woman has an extremely humid body, as can be known from her smooth and glossy skin, and especially from her regular purgations which rid the body of superfluous humours. So when wine is drunk and merged with so general a humidity, it loses its power and does not easily strike the seat of the brain when its strength is extinguished.

Again:

A woman's body which is destined for frequent purgations is pierced with several holes, so that it opens into channels and provides outlets for the moisture draining away to be dispersed. Through these holes the fumes of wine are quickly released.

On what grounds, then, should monks be allowed what is denied to the weaker sex? What madness it is to permit it to those to whom it can do more harm while denying it to others! Nothing could be more foolish than that religion should not abhor what is so contrary to religion and takes us furthest away from God, nothing more shameless than that the abstinence of Christian perfection should not shun what is forbidden to kings and priests of the Law or, rather, should especially delight in it. For who does not know that today the interests of the clergy in particular, and also of the monks, revolve round the cellars, to see how they can fill them with different varieties of wine, and how to brew with herbs, honey and spices so that the more pleasurably they drink, the more easily they make themselves drunk, and the more they are warmed by wine, the more they incite themselves to lust? What error, or rather, what folly is this, when those who bind themselves most stringently by their profession of continence make less preparation for keeping their vow, and even do what makes it least likely to be kept? Though their bodies are confined to the cloister their hearts are filled with lust and minds on fire for fornication. In writing to Timothy the Apostle says:[1] 'Stop drinking nothing but water; take a little wine for your digestion, for your frequent ailments.' Timothy is allowed a little wine for his ailments

1. 1 Timothy v, 23.

because it is clear that when in good health he would take none.

If we profess the apostolic life and especially vow to follow the way of repentance, if we preach withdrawal from the world, why do we particularly delight in what we see to be wholly contrary to our purpose and more delectable than any food? St Ambrose in his detailed description of repentance condemns nothing in the diet of the penitent except wine.[1] 'Does anyone think,' he asks, 'that repentance exists where there is still ambition for high position, pouring out of wine and conjugal enjoyment of sexual union? Renunciation of the world can more easily be found among those who have kept their innocence than among those who have done fitting penance.' Again, in his book *On Renouncing the World* he says: 'You renounce it well if your eye renounces cups and flagons lest it becomes lustful in lingering over wine.' Wine is the only form of nutriment he mentions in this book, and he says that we renounce the world well if we renounce wine, as if all the pleasures of the world depend on this alone: nor does he say 'if the palate renounces the taste of it' but 'if the eye renounces the sight', lest it be captivated by lust and delight in what it often sees. Hence the words of Solomon which we quoted above: 'Do not look on wine when it glows and sparkles in the glass.' But what, pray, are we to say when we have flavoured it with honey, herbs or different spices so as to enjoy its taste as well as the sight of it, and then want to drink it by flagons?

St Benedict was compelled to grant indulgence for wine, saying,[2] 'Let us agree at least on this, that we should drink temperately, not to satiety, for "wine robs even the wise of their wits".'[3] If only our drinking could stop at satiety and not be carried on to the greater sin of excess! St Augustine, too, in setting up monasteries for clerks and writing a Rule for them, says:[4] 'Only on the Sabbath or on the Lord's Day,

1. *De paenitentia*, ii, 10.
2. *Regula*, chapter 40.
3. Ecclesiasticus xix, 2.
4. From the fifth century *Ordo monasterii*, the attribution of which to St Augustine is doubtful.

as the custom is, those who want to may take wine.' This was out of reverence for the Lord's Day and its vigil, the Sabbath, and also because at that time the brothers scattered amongst the cells were gathered together; as when in the *Lives of the Fathers* St Jerome says, when writing of the place he named The Cells,[1] 'They stay each in his own cell, but on the Sabbath and the Lord's Day they assemble in Church, and there see themselves restored to each other as if in heaven.' This indulgence was therefore surely suitable at a time when they met together and could enjoy some relaxation, and feel as well as say 'How good it is and how pleasant for brothers to live together!'[2]

But if we abstain from meat, what a reproach it is to us if we eat everything else to excess, if we procure varied dishes of fish at vast expense, mingle the flavours of pepper and spices, and when we are drunk on neat wine, go on to cups of herb-flavoured liquor and flagons of spiced drink! All this is to be excused by abstinence from ordinary meat provided that we do not guzzle in public – as if the quality rather than excess of food were to blame, although the Lord forbids us only dissipation and drunkenness,[3] that is, excess in food and drink, not the quality. St Augustine takes note of this, for his fears are all for wine, no other form of nourishment, and he draws no distinction between kinds of food when he says briefly what he believes to be sufficient abstinence:[4] 'Subdue your flesh by fasting and by abstinence from food and drink as far as your health permits.' If I am not mistaken, he had read this passage of St Athanasius in his exhortation to monks: 'Let there be no fixed measure of fasts for the willing, but let these last as long as possible, without being prolonged by effort, and except on the Lord's Day, if vowed they should be solemnly observed.' In other words, if they are undertaken by vow they should be devoutly carried out, except on the Lord's Day. No fasts are fixed in advance but are to last as far as health permits, for it is said that[5] 'He regards solely the

1. P. L. 23, 444. 2. Psalm cxxxiii, 1. 3. Cf. Luke xxi, 34.
4. *Epistulae* ccxi, 8. The work by Athanasius is thought to be spurious.
5. Author unknown.

capacity of nature and lets it set its own limit, knowing that there is failure in nothing if moderation is kept in everything.' And so we should not be relaxed in our pleasures more than is right, like the people nourished on the germ of wheat and the purest wine, of whom it is written, 'He grew fat, he grew bloated and unruly;'[1] nor should we succumb, famished and wholly defeated by excessive fasting, and lose our reward by complaining, or glory in our singularity. This Ecclesiastes foresees when he says:[2] 'The righteous man perishes in his righteousness. Do not be over-righteous nor wiser than is necessary, lest you are bewildered;' that is to say, do not swell with pride in your own singularity.

Let discretion, the mother of all the virtues, preside over zeal and look carefully to see on whom she may lay which burdens, that is, on each according to his capacity, following nature rather than putting pressure on it, and removing not the habit of sufficiency but the abuse of excess, so that vices are rooted out but nature is unharmed. It is enough for the weak if they avoid sin, although they may not rise to the peak of perfection, and sufficient also to dwell in a corner of Paradise if you cannot take your seat with the martyrs. It is safe to vow in moderation so that grace may add more to what we owe; for of this it is written,[3] 'When you have carried out all your orders you should say "We are servants and worthless; we have done only what it was our duty to do."' 'The Law,' says the Apostle,[4] 'can bring only retribution: only where there is no law can there be no breach of law.' And again, 'In the absence of law, sin is dead. There was a time when, in the absence of law, I was alive, but when the commandment came, sin sprang to life and I died. The commandment was meant to lead to life, but in my case it led to death, because sin found its opportunity in the commandment, seduced me, and through the commandment killed me.'

Augustine writes to Simplician: 'By being prohibited

1. Deuteronomy xxxii, 15. The N.E.B. gives 'and unruly' as the meaning of *recalcitravit* ('kicked').
2. Ecclesiastes vii, 17–18.
3. Luke xvii, 10.
4. Romans iv, 15; vii, 8 ff.

desire has increased, it has become sweeter and so deceived me.' Similarly, in the *Book of Questions*, number 83: 'The persuasiveness of pleasure towards sin is more urgent when there is prohibition.' Hence the poet says,[1]

> Always we seek the forbidden and desire what is denied.

Let him pay heed to this with reverence, who wishes to bind himself under the yoke of any rule, as though by obedience to a new law. Let him choose what he can, fear what he cannot. No one is held liable under a law unless he has accepted its authority. Think carefully before you accept it, but once you have done so, keep it. What was voluntary before afterwards becomes compulsory. 'There are many dwelling places,' says the Truth,[2] 'in my Father's house.' So too there are many ways whereby we may come to them. The married are not damned, but the continent are more easily saved. The rulings of the holy Fathers were not given us simply so that we can be saved, but so that we can be saved more easily and be enabled to devote ourselves more purely to God. 'If a virgin marries,' says the Apostle,[3] 'she has done no wrong. But such people will have trouble in the flesh, and my aim is to spare you.' Again:

> The unmarried and virgin woman cares for the Lord's business; her aim is to be holy both in body and spirit. But the married woman cares for worldly things and her aim is to please her husband. In saying this I have no desire to keep you on a tight rein; I am thinking simply of your own good, of what is seemly, and of your freedom to wait upon the Lord without distraction.

The time for this to be most easily done is when we withdraw from the world in body too, and shut ourselves in the cloisters of monasteries lest we are disturbed by the tumult of the world. Not only he who receives but he who makes a law should take care not to multiply transgressions by multiplying restrictions. The Word of God came down to earth and curtailed the word on earth. Moses said many things, and yet, in the words of the Apostle,[4] 'The Law brought nothing

1. Ovid, *Amores*, III, 4. 17.
2. John xiv, 2.
3. 1 Corinthians vii, 28; 34–5.
4. Hebrews vii, 19; Acts xv, 10–11.

to perfection.' He did indeed say many things, which were so burdensome that the apostle Peter declares that no one can endure his precepts: 'Men and brothers, why do you provoke God, laying on the shoulders of these converts a yoke which neither we nor our fathers were able to bear? No, we believe that it is by the grace of the Lord Jesus that we are saved, and so are they.'

Christ chose only a few words to give the apostles moral instruction and teach the holiness of life and the way of perfection. He set aside what was austere and burdensome and taught sweetness and light, which for him was the sum of religion. 'Come to me,' he said,[1] 'all you whose work is hard, whose load is heavy, and I will give you relief. Bend your necks to my yoke, and learn from me, for I am gentle and humble-hearted, and your souls will find rest. For my yoke is pleasant to bear and my load is light.'

We often treat our good works as we do the business of the world, for many in their business labour more and gain less, and many outwardly afflict themselves more but inwardly make less progress in the sight of God, who regards the heart rather than works. The more they are taken up with outward things, the less they can devote themselves to inner ones; and the more they shine out amongst men, who judge by externals, the greater the fame they seek among them, and the more easily they are led astray by pride. The Apostle deals with this error when he firmly belittles works and extols justification by faith:[2] 'For if Abraham was justified by works, then he has a ground for pride, but not before God. For what does Scripture say? "Abraham put his faith in the Lord and that faith was counted as righteousness."' And again: 'Then what are we to say? That Gentiles, who made no effort after righteousness, nevertheless achieved it, a righteousness based on faith; whereas Israel made great efforts after a law of righteousness but never achieved it. Why was this? Because their efforts were not based on faith, but (as they supposed) on works.' They clean the outside of the pot or dish but pay little heed to cleanliness inside,

1. Matthew xi, 28–9. 2. Romans iv, 2; ix, 30–32.

they watch over the flesh more than the soul, and so are fleshly rather than spiritual.

But we who desire Christ to dwell in the inner man by faith, think little of outward things which are common to the sinner and the chosen; we heed the words 'I am bound by vows to thee, O God, and will redeem them with praise of thee.'[1] Moreover, we do not practise that outward abstinence prescribed by the Law, which certainly confers no righteousness. Nor does the Lord forbid us anything in the way of food except dissipation and drunkenness,[2] that is, excess; and he was not ashamed to display in himself what he has allowed to us, although many of those present took offence and sharply rebuked him. With his own lips he says:[3] 'John came neither eating nor drinking, and they say "He is possessed." The Son of Man came eating and drinking, and they say, "Look at him! a glutton and a drinker." ' He also excused his own disciples because they did not fast like the disciples of John, nor when they were about to eat did they bother much about bodily cleanness and hand-washing. 'The children of the bridegroom', he said, 'cannot be expected to mourn when the bridegroom is with them.' And elsewhere, 'A man is not defiled by what goes into his mouth but by what comes out of it. What comes out of the mouth has its origins in the heart, and that is what defiles a man; but to eat without first washing his hands, that cannot defile him.'

Therefore no food defiles the soul, only the appetite for forbidden food. For as the body is not defiled except by bodily filth, so the soul can only be defiled by spiritual filth. We need not fear anything done in the body if the soul is not prevailed on to consent. Nor should we put our trust in the cleanliness of the flesh if the mind is corrupted by the will. Thus the whole life and death of the soul depends on the heart, as Solomon says in Proverbs:[4] 'Guard your heart more than any treasure, for it is the source of all life.' And according to the words of the Truth we have quoted, what defiles a man comes from the heart, since the soul is lost or saved by evil or good desires.

1. Psalm lvi, 12.
2. Cf. Luke xxi, 34.
3. Matthew xi, 18; ix, 15; xv, 11, 18, 20.
4. Proverbs iv, 23.

But since soul and flesh are closely conjoined in one person, special care must be taken lest the pleasure enjoyed by the flesh leads the soul to comply, and when the flesh is over-indulged it grows wanton, resists the spirit, and begins to dominate where it should be subject. However, we can guard against this if we allow all necessities but, as we have often said, cut off completely any excess, and so not deny the weaker sex any use of food while forbidding all abuse of it. Let everything be permitted but nothing consumed beyond measure. 'For everything,' says the Apostle,[1] 'that God created is good, and nothing is to be rejected when it is taken with thanksgiving, since it is hallowed by God's own word and prayer. By offering such advice as this to the brethren you will prove a good servant of Jesus Christ, bred in the precepts of our faith and of the sound instruction which you have followed.'

Let us therefore, with Timothy, follow the teaching of the Apostle, and, in accordance with the words of the Lord, shun nothing in food except dissipation and drunkenness; let us moderate everything so that we sustain weak nature in every way but do not nurture vices. Whatever can do harm by excess must be the more strictly moderated, for it is better and more praiseworthy to eat in moderation than to abstain altogether. Thus St Augustine, in his book *On the Good of Marriage*, when he deals with bodily sustenance, says that 'A man makes no good use of these things unless he can also abstain from them. Many find it easier to abstain and not use at all than to be moderate so as to use well. But no one can use wisely unless he can also restrain himself from using.' St Paul also said of this practice,[2] 'I know both what it is to have plenty and what it is to suffer need.' To suffer need is the lot of all men, but to know how to suffer it is granted only to the great. So too, any man can begin to have plenty, but to know how to have plenty is granted only to those whom plenty does not corrupt.

As regards wine, then, because (as we said) it is a sensual and turbulent thing, and so entirely opposed both to con-

1. 1 Timothy iv, 4–6. 2. Philippians iv, 12.

tinence and to silence, women should either abstain altogether, in God's name, just as the wives of the Gentiles are forbidden it through fear of adultery, or they should mix it with enough water to make it satisfy their thirst and benefit their health while not being strong enough to hurt them. This we believe can be done if at least a quarter of the mixture is water. It is indeed very difficult when drink is set before us to make sure that, as St Benedict ordered,[1] we do not go on drinking to satiety. And so we think it safer not to forbid satiety and run the risk of breaking a rule, for it is not this, as we have often said, which is culpable, but excess. The preparation of wine mixed with herbs for medicinal purposes or even the drinking of neat wine is not to be forbidden, so long as the convent in general never takes these, but they are drunk separately by the sick.

Fine wheat flour we absolutely forbid; whenever the sisters use flour, a third part at least of coarser grain must be mixed with it. And they must never enjoy bread hot from the oven, but eat only what has been baked at least one day before. As for other foods, the abbess must see that, as we said above, what can be cheaply bought or easily obtained shall meet the needs of their weaker nature. For what could be more foolish than to buy extras when our own resources are sufficient, or to look outside for superfluous things when we have everything necessary to hand? We are taught this necessary moderation and discretion not so much by human as by angelic example, or even by that of the Lord himself, and should therefore know that for meeting the needs of this life we should not seek particular kinds of food but rest content with what we have; for the angels fed on meat set before them by Abraham, and the Lord Jesus refreshed a hungry multitude with fishes found in the wilderness.[2] From this we are surely to learn that we are to eat meat or fish without distinguishing between them, and to take especially what is without offence of sin and is freely available, and consequently easier to prepare and less costly.

And so Seneca, the chief exponent of poverty and conti-

1. *Regula*, chapter 40. 2. Genesis xviii, 9; Mark viii, 8.

nence, and of all the philosophers the greatest teacher of morals, says:[1]

> Our motto, as we all know, is to live according to nature. It is against nature for a man to torment his body, to hate simple cleanliness and seek out dirt, to eat food which is not only cheap but disgusting and revolting. Just as a craving for dainties is a token of extravagance, avoidance of what is familiar and cheaply prepared is madness. Philosophy calls for simple living, not a penance, and a simple way of life need not be a rough one. This is the standard I approve.

Gregory too, in the thirtieth book of his *Morals*, when teaching that in forming men's character we should pay attention to the quality of our minds, not of our food, and distinguishing between the temptations of the palate, said: 'One moment it seeks more delicate food, another it desires its chosen dishes to be more scrupulously prepared.' Yet often what it craves is quite humble, but it sins even more by the very heat of its immense desire.

The people led out of Egypt fell in the desert because they despised manna and wanted meat, which they thought a finer food. And Esau lost the birthright of the firstborn because he craved with burning desire for a cheap food, lentils, and proved with what an appetite he longed for it by preferring it to the birthright he sold. Not the food but his appetite is at fault. And so we can often be blameless when we take more delicate foods but eat humbler fare with a guilty conscience. The Esau we spoke of lost his rights as firstborn for a dish of lentils, while Elijah in the desert maintained his bodily strength by eating meat.[2] Thus our old enemy, knowing that it is not food but the desire for food which is the cause of damnation, brought the first man into his power not with meat but by an apple, and he tempted the second not with meat but with bread.[3] Consequently the sin of Adam is often committed when plain and ordinary food is taken, and

1. *Epistulae ad Lucilium*, 5. 4.
2. Cf. Genesis xxv; 1 Kings xvii, 4.
3. The temptation of Jesus by the devil: Matthew iv, 1–4.

those things are to be eaten which the needs of nature require, not those which desire for eating suggests. But we crave with less desire for what we see is not so costly, but more plentiful and cheaper to buy: for example, the ordinary kind of meat which is much more strengthening than fish for a weak nature, and is less expensive and easier to prepare.

The use of meat and wine, like marriage, is considered to lie between good and evil, that is, it is indifferent, although the marriage tie is not wholly free from sin, and wine brings more hazards than any other food. Then if a moderate consumption of wine is not forbidden to religion, what have we to fear from other foods, so long as moderation is maintained? If St Benedict declares that wine is not for monks, and yet is obliged to allow it by special dispensation to the monks of his time when the fervour of the early Christian charity was cooling off, why should we not allow women other things which up to now no vow has forbidden them? If the Pontiffs themselves and the rulers of the Holy Church, if indeed monasteries of clerks are even allowed to eat meat without offence, because they are not bound by any profession of abstinence, who can find fault if women are allowed this too, especially if in other respects they submit to a much stricter discipline? 'It is sufficient for a pupil to be like his master',[1] and it seems over-severe if what is allowed to monasteries of clerks is denied to convents of women.

Nor should it be counted as insignificant if women, who are subject to other monastic restrictions, are not inferior in observance to religious laymen in this one indulgence of meat, especially since, as Chrysostom bears witness:[2] 'Nothing is lawful to the lay clerk which is not also lawful for the monk, with one exception, intercourse with a wife.' St Jerome too, judging the religion of clerks to be not inferior to that of monks, says 'As though whatever is said against monks did not redound on clerks, who are the fathers of monks.' And who does not know that it is against all good sense if the same

1. Matthew x, 24.

2. *Homilia* VII in *Epistolam ad Hebraeos*; Jerome, *Epistulae* 54 *ad Furiam*.

burdens are imposed on the weak as on the strong, if equally strict abstinence is enjoined on women as on men? If anyone demands authority for this beyond the evidence of nature, let him consult St Gregory on this point too. For this great Ruler and Doctor of the Church gives considered instruction to the other Doctors on this matter in the twenty-fourth chapter of his *Pastoral*: 'And so men should be admonished in one way, women in another, for heavy burdens may be laid on men, and great matters exercise them, but lighter burdens on women, who should be gently converted by less exacting means.' What matters little in the strong is thought important in the weak. And although this permission to eat ordinary meat gives less pleasure than eating the flesh of birds or fishes, St Benedict does not forbid us these either;[1] the Apostle also distinguishes between different kinds of flesh, and says, 'All flesh is not the same; there is flesh of men, flesh of beasts, of birds and of fishes, all different.' Now the law of the Lord assigns the flesh of beasts and of birds to sacrifice, but not that of fish, so no one may suppose that eating fish is purer in the eyes of God than eating meat. Fish is indeed more of a hardship to the poor, being dearer, since it is in shorter supply than meat, and less strengthening for weak nature; so that on the one hand it is more of a burden and, on the other, gives less help.

We therefore, considering both the resources and nature of mankind, forbid nothing in the matter of food, as we said, except excess, and we regulate the eating of meat as of everything else in such a way that the nuns can show greater abstinence with everything allowed them than monks do with certain things forbidden. And so we would make it a rule for the eating of meat that the sisters do not take it more than once a day, different dishes must not be prepared for the same person, and no sauces may be added separately; nor may it ever be eaten more than three times a week,[2] on the first,

1. *Regula*, chapter 39, where the flesh of four-footed animals is allowed only to the sick and weak: 1 Corinthians xv, 39.

2. For the question of meat-eating at the Paraclete, see Introduction, p. 31 and McLeod, op. cit., pp. 220–23.

third and fifth days, whatever feast-days intervene. For the more solemn the feast, the more dedicated should be the abstinence which celebrates it; this is warmly recommended to us by the famous doctor Gregory of Nazianzus in Book III *On Lights* or *The Second Epiphany*, where he says: 'Let us celebrate a feast-day not by indulging the belly but exulting in the spirit.' And in Book IV *Of Pentecost and The Holy Spirit*, 'This is our feast-day,' he says, 'let us store away in the soul's treasure-house something perennial and everlasting, not things which perish and melt away. Sufficient for the body is its own evil; it needs no richer matter, nor does the insolent beast need more lavish food to make it more insolent and violent in its demands.'[1] And so the feast-day should rather be kept spiritually, as St Jerome, Gregory's disciple, says in his letter about accepting gifts, where there is this passage:[2] 'Thus we must take special care to celebrate the day of festival with exultation of spirit rather than abundance of food, for it is palpably absurd to honour by over-indulgence a martyr whom we know to have pleased God by his fasting.' Augustine *On the Medicine of Penitence* says: 'Consider all the thousands of martyrs. Why do we take pleasure in celebrating their birthdays with vile banquets and not in following the example of their lives in honest ways?'

Whenever the convent has a meatless day, the nuns are to be allowed two dishes of vegetables, to which we are willing for fish to be added. But no costly condiments may be used in the food in the convent, and the sisters must content themselves with the produce of the country where they live. Fruit, however, they should eat only for supper. But as medicine for those who need it, we never forbid herbs or root vegetables, or any fruits or other similar things to appear on the table. If there happens to be any pilgrim nun staying as a guest and present at a meal, she should be shown the courtesy of charity by being offered an extra dish and, if she wishes to

1. Cf. *Patrologia Graeca* 36, 358 and 430: the works Abelard loosely names and quotes are *Orationes* 39 and 46. 'Books' must refer to the folios he used.

2. *Epistulae* 31 *ad Eustochium*.

share this, she may. She and any other guests should sit at the high table and be served by the abbess, who will then eat later with those who wait at table. If any of the sisters wishes to mortify the flesh by a stricter diet, on no account may she do so except by way of obedience, but on no account shall this be refused her if her reason for wanting it seems sound and not frivolous, and her strength is sufficient to bear it. But no one must ever be permitted to go out of the convent for this reason, nor spend a whole day without food.

They must never use fat for flavouring on the sixth day of the week, but be content with Lenten food, and by their abstinence share the suffering of their bridegroom on that day. But one practice, common in many monasteries, is not only to be forbidden but strictly abhorred, that is, the habit of cleaning and wiping the hands and knives on some of the bread which is left uneaten and kept for the poor, so that in wishing to spare the tablecloths they pollute the bread of the poor, or indeed, the bread of him who treats himself as one of the poor when he says:[1] 'Anything you did for one of my brothers here, however humble, you did for me.'

As regards abstinence at fasts: the general ruling of the Church should be sufficient for them. We do not venture to burden them in this beyond the observance of religious laymen, nor dare to set their weakness above the strength of men. But from the autumn equinox until Easter, when the days are short, we believe one meal a day should be enough and, as the reason for this is not religious abstinence but seasonal shortness, here we make no distinction between kinds of food.

Costly clothes, which Scripture utterly condemns, must be absolutely banned. The Lord warns us especially against them, and condemns the pride in them of the rich man who was damned, while by contrast he commends the humility of John. St Gregory draws attention to this in his Sixth Homily on the Gospels:

> What does it mean to say 'Those who wear fine clothes are to be

1. Matthew xxv, 40.

found in palaces'[1] unless to state in plain words that those men who refuse to endure hardships fight not for a heavenly but an earthly kingdom, and by devoting themselves only to outward show, seek the softness and pleasure of this present life?

And in his Fortieth Homily he says:

There are some who do not think that the fashion of fine and costly garments is a sin. But surely if it were not blameworthy, the Word of God would never say so explicitly that the rich man who was tormented in hell had been clothed in satin and purple. For no one seeks special garments except for vainglory, in order to appear more worthy of esteem than his fellows; from vainglory alone is costly clothing sought. This is proved by the fact that no one cares to wear costly clothes where others cannot see him.

The First Letter of Peter warns lay and married women against the same thing:[2]

In the same way you women must accept the authority of your husbands, so that if there are any of them who disbelieve the Gospel they may be won over, without a word being said, by observing the chaste and reverent behaviour of their wives. Your beauty should reside, not in outward adornment – the braiding of the hair, or jewellery, or dress – but in the inmost centre of your being, the ornament of a gentle, quiet spirit, which is of value in the sight of God.

And he rightly thought that women rather than men should be warned against this vanity, for their weak minds desire more strongly what enables extravagance to find fuller expression in them and through them. But if lay women are to be forbidden these things, what care must be taken by women dedicated to Christ? Their fashion in dress is that they have no fashion and, whoever wants fashion, or does not refuse it if offered, loses the proof of her chastity. Any such person would be thought to be preparing herself not for religion but for fornication, and be judged not a nun but a whore. Moreover, fashion itself is the badge of the pimp and

1. Matthew xi, 8 2. 1. Peter iii, 1–4.

betrays his lewd mind, as it is written:[1] 'A man's clothes and the way he laughs and his gait reveal his character.'

We read that the Lord, as we said above, praised and commended the cheapness and roughness of John's clothing rather than of his food. 'What did you go out to see in the wilderness?' he asked, 'A man clad in fine clothes?'[2] For there are times when the serving of costly food can usefully be conceded, but none for the wearing of costly clothing. Indeed, the more costly such clothing is, the more carefully it is preserved and the less useful it is – it is more of a burden to its purchaser, and being so fine it is more easily damaged and provides less warmth for the body. Black clothes are most fitting of all for the mournful garb of penitence, and lambs' wool the most suitable for the brides of Christ, so that even in their habits they can be seen to wear, or be told to wear, the wool of the Lamb, the bridegroom of virgins.

Their veils should not be made of silk but of dyed linen cloth, and we would have two sorts of veil, one for the virgins already consecrated by the bishop, the other for those not to be consecrated. The veils of the former should have the sign of the Cross marked on them, so that their wearers shall be shown by this to belong particularly to Christ in the integrity of their virginity, and as they are set apart from the others by their consecration, they should also be distinguished by this marking on their habit which shall act as a deterrent to any of the faithful against burning with desire for them. This sign of virginal purity the nun shall wear on the top of her head, marked in white thread, and she shall not presume to wear it before she is consecrated by the bishop. No other veils shall bear this mark.

They should wear clean undergarments next to the skin, and always sleep in them; nor do we deny their weak nature the use of soft mattresses and sheets. But each one must sleep and eat alone. No one should dare to be indignant if the clothing or anything else passed on to her by someone else is made over to another sister who has greater need of them; but she should look on it as an occasion for rejoicing when

1. Ecclesiasticus xix, 30. 2. Matthew xi, 8.

she enjoys the benefit of having given something as an act of charity, or sees herself as living for others and not only for herself. Otherwise she does not belong to the sisterhood of the holy society, and is not free of the sacrilege of having possessions.

It should be sufficient, we think, for them to wear an undergarment and woollen gown, with a cloak on top when the cold is very severe. This they can also use as a coverlet when lying in bed. To prevent infestation by vermin and allow accumulation of dirt to be washed away, all these garments will have to be in pairs, precisely as Solomon says in praise of the capable and provident housewife,[1] 'She has no fear for her household when it snows, for all her servants are wrapped in two cloaks.' These cloaks must not be made so long as to hang down below the ankles and stir up dust, and the sleeves must not extend beyond the length of the arms and hands. Their feet and legs must be protected by shoes and stockings, and they are never to go barefoot on account of religion. On their beds a single mattress, bolster, pillow, blanket and sheet should suffice. They should wear a white band on their heads with the black veil over it, and because of their close-cropped hair a cap of lambs' wool may be worn if needed.

Excess must be avoided not only in diet and clothing but also in buildings or any possessions. In buildings excess is plain to see when they are made larger or finer than necessary, or if we adorn them with sculpture or paintings so as to set up palaces fit for kings instead of dwelling-places for the poor. 'The Son of Man,' says Jerome,[2] 'has nowhere to lay his head, but you are measuring out vast porches and spacious roofs.' When we take pleasure in costly or beautiful equipment the emptiness of pride is displayed as well as excess; and when we multiply herds of animals or earthly possessions, mounting ambition extends to outward things, and the more possessions we have on earth, the more we are obliged to think of these and are called away from contemplation of heavenly things. And although we may be enclosed in cloisters in the body,

1. Proverbs xxxi, 21 (Vulgate).
2. Matthew viii, 20: Jerome, *Epistulae* 14 *ad Heliodorum*.

the mind still loves things outside, has an urge to pursue them, and dissipates itself in all directions with them. The more we possess which can be lost, the greater the fear which torments us, and the more costly these are, the more they are loved and ensnare the wretched mind with ambition to have them.

And so every care must be taken to set a firm limit to our household and our expenditure, and beyond what is necessary not to desire anything, receive any offering or keep what we have accepted. Whatever is over and above our needs we possess by robbery, and are guilty of the deaths of all the poor whom we could have helped from the surplus. Every year then, when the produce has been gathered in, sufficient provision must be made for the year, and anything left over must be given, or rather, given back to the poor.

There are some who lack foresight, and though their harvest is poor are pleased to think they have a large household, but when harassed by the responsibility to provide for it, they go begging without shame, or extort forcibly from others what they do not have themselves. Several abbots of monasteries we see to be like this. They boast of the numbers in their community and care more about having many sons than about having good ones; and they stand high in their own eyes if they are held to be higher than many. To draw these numbers under their rule they make smooth promises when they should preach harsh words, and easily lose as backsliders those whom they take in indiscriminately with no previous test of faith. Such men, I think, the Truth rebuked in the words:[1] 'Alas for you, for you travel over sea and land to win one convert; but when you have won him, you make him twice as fit for hell as yourselves.' They would surely boast less of their numbers if they sought to save souls instead of counting them, and presumed less on their strength when giving an account of their rule.

The Lord chose only a few apostles, and one of those he chose fell so far away that the Lord said of him:[2] 'Have I not chosen you twelve? Yet one of you is a devil.' And as Judas was lost to the apostles, so was Nicholas to the deacons; then

1. Matthew xxiii, 15. 2. John vi, 21.

when the apostles had gathered together no more than a few, Ananias and Sapphira his wife earned sentence of death.[1] Indeed, many of his disciples had previously fallen away from the Lord himself, and few stayed with him. The road which leads to life is narrow, and few set foot on it, but by contrast the road that leads to death is wide, with plenty of room, and many choose to go that way. For as the Lord testifies elsewhere,[2] 'Many are invited but few are chosen,' and according to Solomon,[3] 'The number of fools cannot be counted.' And so whoever rejoices in the large numbers of those beneath him should fear lest, in the words of the Lord, few are to be found chosen, and he himself by unduly increasing the numbers of his flock shall be less capable of watching over them; so that the words of the Prophet may rightly be applied to him:[4] 'You increased their numbers but gave them no joy of it.' Such men as boast of numbers, and are often obliged to meet their own needs and those of their people by going out and returning to the world to run round begging, involve themselves in bodily rather than spiritual cares, and incur disgrace instead of winning glory.

This is indeed all the more shameful in the case of women, for whom it seems less safe to be out in the world. And so whoever desires to live quietly and virtuously, to devote himself to the divine offices and be held as dear to God as to the world, should hesitate to gather together those for whom he cannot provide; for his own expenses he should not rely on other men's purses, and he should watch over the giving, not the seeking of alms. The Apostle and great preacher of the Gospel had authority from the Gospel to accept gifts for his expenses, but he worked with his hands so that he would not appear to be a burden to anyone nor detract from his glory.[5] How bold and shameless then are we, whose business is not preaching but lamenting our sins, if we go begging! How are we to support those whom we have thoughtlessly brought

1. Acts vi, 5; v, 1 ff.
2. Matthew vii, 13; xxii, 14.
3. Cf. Ecclesiastes i, 15 (Vulgate).
4. Isaiah ix, 3 (Vulgate: the negative is in doubt).
5. Cf. 1 Corinthians ix, 14–15.

together? We also often break out into such madness that being ignorant of preaching ourselves, we hire preachers and lead around with us these false apostles, carrying crosses and phylacteries of relics to sell these or other such figments of the devil to guileless and foolish Christians, and we promise them whatever we believe will enable us to extort money. How far our Order and the very preaching of the divine Word is debased by such shameless cupidity, which seeks what is its own and not of Jesus Christ, is known, I think, to all.

Consequently abbots themselves or those who appear to have authority in monasteries take themselves off to pester the secular powers and the courts of the world, and have already learned to be courtiers rather than monks. They woo the favour of men by any device, they have grown accustomed to gossiping with men instead of communing with God; they read St Antony's warning often but to no purpose, ignoring it or hearing it without paying heed: 'As fish die, if they linger on land so too do monks, if they linger outside the cell or stay among men of the world and are released from their vow of quiet. So it is necessary for us to hurry back to the cell like fishes to the sea, lest by lingering outside we forget to care for what is within.'[1]

The author of the monastic Rule, St Benedict himself, also paid serious attention to this; he wished abbots to be active inside their monasteries and to keep careful watch over their flock, and he openly taught it in his writings and by his own example. For when he had left his brothers and gone to visit his holy sister, and she wished to keep him for one night at least, he frankly declared that it was quite impossible for him to stay outside his cell. In fact he did not say 'we cannot' but 'I cannot', because the brothers might do so by his leave, but he could not, except by revelation from the Lord, as afterwards came to pass. And so when he came to write the Rule, he made no mention of the abbot's but only of the brothers' going out of the monastery, and he made careful provision for the abbot's continual presence by laying down

1. *Vitae patrum*, V, 2. 1.

that on the vigils of Sundays and feast-days, the Gospel and what follows it[1] should be read by the abbot alone. And when he rules that the abbot's table shall always be shared with pilgrims and guests, and that whenever there are no guests he shall invite to it any of the brothers he likes, leaving only one or two of the other brothers with the rest,[2] he evidently implies that at mealtimes the abbot should never be absent from the monastery, nor leave the ordinary bread of the monastery to his subordinates as if he were one of those accustomed to the delicate fare of princes. Of such men the Truth says:[3] 'They make up packs too heavy to carry and pile them on men's shoulders, but will not raise a finger to lift the load themselves.' And elsewhere, of false preachers, 'Beware of false prophets who come to you ...' They come of themselves, says the Truth, not sent by God, nor waiting to be summoned. John the Baptist, the first of us monks, to whom the priesthood came by inheritance, went out only once from the city to the wilderness, leaving his priestly for a monastic life and the cities for solitude. The people went out to him, he did not go in to the people. When he was so great that he was believed to be Christ and could correct many things in the cities, he was already in that bed from which he was ready to answer to the knocking of the Beloved: 'I have slipped off my dress: must I put it on again? I have washed my feet: must I soil them?'[4]

Whoever therefore wishes to learn the secret of monastic quiet must be glad to have a narrow bed and not a wide one. From the wider bed, as the Truth says,[5] 'one will be taken, and the other left'. But we read that the narrow bed belongs to the bride, that is to the contemplative soul which is more closely joined to Christ, and clings to him with the strongest desire. None, we read, have been left who lay on this, and the bride herself says of it: 'By night on my narrow bed I sought him whom my soul loves.'[6] She also refuses or fears to rise from this bed, but answers, as we said above, to the

1. i.e. the Lesser Litany and Collect. 2. *Regula*, chapter 56.
3. Matthew xxiii, 4; vii, 15. 4. Canticles v, 3.
5. Luke xvii, 34. 6. Canticles iii, 1.

knocking of the Beloved. For she believes that the dirt she fears will soil her feet is only outside it.

Dinah went out to see alien women and was defiled.[1] And as it was foretold by his abbot to Malchus, that captive monk, and he afterwards found out for himself, the sheep which leaves the sheepfold is soon exposed to the bite of the wolf.[2] So let us not assemble a crowd in which we look for an excuse, or rather, a compelling reason for going out and making money for others with detriment to ourselves; like lead which is melted in the furnace so that silver may be saved. We must rather beware lest lead and silver alike are consumed in the burning furnace of temptation. The Truth, men argue, says:[3] 'The man who comes to me I will never turn away.' Nor do we want to turn away those who have been admitted, but to be careful about admitting them, lest when we have taken them in we have to turn ourselves away on their account. For the Lord himself, we read, did not turn away anyone once admitted, but rejected some who offered themselves; to a man who said 'Master, I will follow you wherever you go,' he replied 'The foxes have holes . . .'[4]

He also warns us strictly to consider first the necessary cost when we think of doing something. 'Would any of you think of building a tower without first sitting down and calculating the necessary cost, to see whether he can afford to finish it? Otherwise, if he has laid the foundation and then is unable to finish, all onlookers will laugh at him. "There is the man," they will say, "who started to build and could not finish."'[5] It is a great thing if a man is able to save even himself alone, and dangerous for him to provide for many when he is scarcely able to keep watch over himself. No one is in earnest about keeping watch unless he has been cautious in granting admission, and no one perseveres in an undertaking like the man who takes time and forethought over making a start. In this indeed women show greater fore-

1. Cf. Genesis xxxiv, 1.
2. Cf. Jerome *Vita Malchi*, and *Historia calamitatum* p. 101, note 1.
3. John vi, 37.
4. Matthew viii, 19, 20.
5. Luke xiv, 28–30.

thought, because their weakness is less able to bear heavy burdens, and is most in need of quiet to cherish it.

It is agreed that Holy Scripture is a mirror of the soul, in which anyone who lives by reading and advances by understanding perceives the beauty of his own ways or discovers their ugliness, so that he may work to increase the one and remove the other. Reminding us of this mirror, St Gregory says in the second book of his *Morals*: 'The Holy Scripture is set before the mind's eye as if it were a mirror in which our inward face may be seen reflected. For there we see our beauty or recognize our hideousness, there we perceive how far we have advanced and how distant we are from advancing.' But whoever looks at a Scripture which he does not understand is like a blind man holding a mirror to his eyes in which he is unable to see what sort of man he is; nor does he look for the instruction in Scripture for which alone it was composed. Like an ass before a lyre, he sits idly before the Scripture, and has bread set before him on which he does not break his fast, when he cannot see into the word of God by understanding it himself, nor have it opened to him by another's teaching, and so has no use for the food which does him no good.

Hence the Apostle, in a general exhortation to us to study the Scriptures, says:[1] 'For all the ancient scriptures were written for our instruction, so that from the message of endurance and comfort the scriptures bring us, we may derive hope.' And elsewhere: 'Be filled with the Holy Spirit; speak to yourselves in psalms, hymns and spiritual songs.' For a man speaks to himself or with himself who understands what he is saying, or by his understanding reaps the benefit of his words. To Timothy he says:[2] 'Until I arrive, devote yourself to public reading, to exhortation and to teaching.' And again:

> But for your part, stand by the truths you have learned and are assured of. Remember from whom you learned them; remember

1. Romans xv, 4; Ephesians v, 18–19.
2. 1 Timothy iv, 13; 2 Timothy iii, 14–17.

that from early childhood you have been familiar with the sacred writings which have power to lead you to salvation through faith in Christ Jesus. Every inspired scripture has its use for teaching the truth and refuting error, for correction and instruction in righteousness, so that the man who belongs to God may be perfected and equipped for good work of any kind.

And when he is exhorting the Corinthians to understand Scripture so that they may be able to explain what others say of it, he says:[1]

Make love your aim and spiritual gifts your aspiration and, above all, the gift of prophecy. The man who uses the language of ecstasy is talking to God, not man, but by prophesying he can build up the Church. And so he who speaks in the language of ecstasy must pray for the power to interpret it. I will pray with inspiration, I will pray too with my intelligence: I will sing hymns with inspiration and with intelligence. Otherwise, if you praise God with the language of inspiration, who will take the place of the plain man? How will he say Amen to your thanksgiving when he does not know what you are saying? True enough, you give thanks, but the other's faith is not built up. Thank God I am more gifted in ecstatic utterance than you, but in church I would rather speak five intelligible words for your instruction than ten thousand in the language of ecstasy. Brothers, do not be childish in your thoughts; be as innocent of evil as small children but grown men in your thinking.

A man who 'speaks in the language of ecstasy' is one who forms words with his lips but does not give help with his intelligence by explaining them. But one who prophesies or interprets in the same way as the prophets, who are called 'seers', that is, 'understanders', understands the things he says so that he can explain them. The former prays or sings with inspiration but forms his words only by breathing and pronouncing them, without applying the understanding of his mind. When we pray with inspiration, that is, we form words only by breathing and pronouncing them, and what the mouth speaks is not conceived in the heart, our mind does not benefit as it should by prayer so as to be moved

1. Cf. 1 Corinthians xiv, 1 ff. and 13–20.

and fired towards God by its understanding of the words. And so the Apostle adjures us to seek this maturity in words, so that we may not, like children, only know how to speak them, but may also have a sense of the meaning in them; or else, he argues, our praying and hymn-singing does no good.

Following him, St Benedict says:[1] 'Let us sing the psalms so that mind and voice may be in harmony.' The Psalmist too tells us to 'Sing hymns with understanding', so that the words we speak do not lack the savour and seasoning of meaning, and with him we can truthfully say to the Lord, 'How sweet are thy words in my mouth,' and elsewhere, 'He will take no pleasure in a man's flute,'[2] for the flute gives out sounds for the gratification of pleasure, not for understanding by the mind. And so men are said to sing well to the flute but not to please God in doing so, because they delight in the melody of their singing but nothing can be built on its meaning. And how, asks the Apostle, can Amen be said after thanksgiving in church if no one understands what is prayed for, whether the object of the prayer is good or not?

For we often see in church how many simple and illiterate people pray by mistake for things which will bring them harm rather than benefit; for example, in the words 'that we may so pass through temporal things that we lose not things eternal', many are easily confused by the similarity in sound, so that either they say 'that we lose things eternal' or 'that we admit not things eternal'.[3] The Apostle is well aware of this hazard, when he asks: 'Otherwise, if you praise God with the language of inspiration,' (that is, you form the words of thanksgiving only by breathing their sound and do not instruct the mind of the listener in their meaning)

1. *Regula*, chapter 19.

2. Psalm xlvii, 7; cxix, 103; cxlvii, 10. *Non in tibiis viri beneplacitum erit ei*. This is usually interpreted as 'takes no pleasure in a runner's legs', as the first half-verse refers to the strength of a horse. *Tibia* can mean both leg-bone and flute or pipe.

3. i.e. instead of saying *ut non amittamus aeterna* some say *ut* nos *amittamus aeterna*, others *ut non* admittamus *aeterna*.

'who will take the place of the plain man?' That is, who among the congregation whose duty it is to respond, will be sure of not making a response which an ordinary man cannot or should not make? 'How will he say Amen' when he has no idea whether you are invoking a curse or a blessing? Finally, if the sisters have no understanding of Scripture, how will they be able to instruct each other by word, or even to explain or understand the Rule, or correct false citations from it?

And so we very much wonder what prompting of the enemy brought about the present situation in monasteries, whereby there is no study there on understanding the Scriptures, but only training in singing, which is no more than the forming of words without understanding them: as if the bleating of sheep were more useful than the feeding of them. For the food of the soul and its spiritual refreshment is the God-given understanding of Scripture, and so when the Lord destined the prophet Ezekiel for preaching, he first fed him on a scroll, which immediately 'in his mouth became sweet as honey.'[1] Of such food Jeremiah also writes that 'Young children begged for bread but there was no one to break it for them.' He breaks bread for young children who reveals the meaning of letters to the simple, and these children beg for bread to be broken when they long to feed their souls on understanding the Scripture, as the Lord bears witness elsewhere:[2] 'I will send famine on the land, not hunger for bread nor thirst for water, but for hearing the word of the Lord.'

On the other hand, the old enemy has implanted in cloisters of monasteries a hunger and thirst for hearing the words of men and gossip of the world, so that by giving ourselves up to empty talk we may weary of the word of God, and the more so if we find it tasteless because it lacks the sweetness and savour of meaning. Hence the Psalmist, as we said above, cried:[3] 'How sweet are thy words in my mouth, sweeter than honey on my lips,' and what this sweetness was he went

1. Ezekiel iii, 1–3: Lamentations iv, 4. 2. Amos viii, 11.
3. Psalm cxix, 103–104.

on to say at once: 'From thy precepts I got understanding', that is, I gained understanding from God's precepts rather than men's, and was taught and instructed by them. Nor did he omit to state what was to be gained from such understanding, adding 'Therefore I hate every path of wrongdoing.' For many paths of wrongdoing are so plainly seen for what they are that they easily come to be hated and despised by all, but only through the word of God can we know every one of them so as to avoid them all. So it is also written that[1] 'I treasure thy words in my heart, so that I may not sin against thee.' They are treasured in the heart rather than sounded on the lips when we meditate and retain understanding of them, but the less we care about understanding, the less we recognize and shun these paths of wrongdoing, and the less we can guard ourselves against sin.

Such negligence is all the more reprehensible in monks who aspire to perfection, the more opportunities they have for being taught, when they have abundance of sacred books and enjoy the peace of quiet. Those monks who boast about the numbers of their books but find no time to read them are sharply rebuked by that elder in the *Lives of the Fathers*, who says:[2] 'The prophets wrote books: and your forebears came after and did much work on them. Then their successors committed them to memory. But now comes the present generation, which has copied them on paper and parchment and put them back to stand idle on the shelves.' So too, abba Palladius in exhorting us to learn and also to teach, says: 'It behoves the soul which professes to live in accordance with the will of Christ either to learn faithfully what it does not know or to teach plainly what it knows.' But if it is unwilling to do either, though well able, it suffers from the disease of madness. For boredom with learning is the

1. Psalm cxix, 11.

2. *Vitae patrum* V, 10. 114; V, 10. 67. *Fenestrae*, 'shelves', or rather alcoves like blind windows in walls. A twelfth century example from an Augustinian abbey of Lilleshall, Shropshire, is shown in C. Brooke, *The Twelfth Century Renaissance*, Fig. 14.

beginning of a withdrawal from God, and how can a man love God when he does not seek that for which the soul always hungers? St Athanasius too, in his *Exhortation to Monks*, recommends the practice of learning or reading so highly that he even allows prayers to be interrupted for this. 'Let me trace the course of our life,' he says. 'First must come care for abstinence, endurance of fasting, perseverance in prayer and desire to read or, if there be any who are still illiterate, to listen in eagerness to learn. For these are the first cradle-songs, as it were, of suckling infants, in knowledge of God.' And a little later, after saying that 'Your prayers should be so assiduous that scarcely any interval should come between them', he then adds: 'If possible, they should be interrupted only by intervals for reading.'

Nor would the apostle Peter give different advice. 'Be always ready to give an answer to all who ask you to account for your faith and hope.'[1] And the Apostle says:[2] 'We have not ceased to pray for you, that you may be filled with knowledge of God's will in all wisdom and spiritual understanding.' And again, 'Let the message of Christ dwell in you in all richness and wisdom.' In the Old Testament, too, the Word implanted in men a similar care for holy teaching. Thus David says,[3] 'Happy is the man who does not take the wicked for his guide ... but his heart is set on the law of the Lord.' And to Joshua God says, 'This book of the law shall never leave your hands and you must ponder over it day and night.'

Moreover, amongst these occupations the hazards of wrong-thinking often insinuate themselves, and although constant application may keep the mind intent on God, the gnawing anxiety of the world makes it restless. If one who is dedicated to the toil of the religious life must suffer this, frequently and painfully, the idle man is surely never free of it. St Gregory the Pope, in the nineteenth book of his *Morals*, says:

1. 1 Peter iii, 15. 2. Colossians i, 9; iii, 16.
3. Psalm i, 1; Joshua i, 8.

We deplore that the time has now come when we see many holding office in the Church who are either unwilling to perform what they understand or scorn to understand and recognize the very words of God. They close their ears to the truth and turn away to listen to fables, while 'they are all bent on their own ends, not on the cause of Jesus Christ'.[1] God's Scriptures are everywhere to be found and are set before men's eyes, but they refuse to read them. Scarcely anyone wants to understand what he believes.

And yet both the Rule of their own profession and the example of the holy Fathers exhort them to do so. Benedict in fact says nothing about the teaching and study of chanting, though he gives many instructions about reading, and expressly assigns times for this as he does for manual work.[2] In his provision for teaching composition or writing, amongst the essentials for which the monks must look to the abbot, he includes tablets and pens. And when amongst other things he orders that 'At the beginning of Lent all the monks shall receive a book each from the library, which they shall read through consecutively,' what could be more absurd than for them to give time to reading if they do not take pains to understand? There is a well-known saying of the Sage,[3] 'To read without understanding is to mis-read'; and to such a reader the philosopher's reproach about the ass and the lyre is rightly applicable, for a reader who holds a book but cannot do what the book was intended for is like an ass sitting before a lyre. Readers such as this would more profitably concentrate on what might be some use to them, instead of idly looking at the written letters and turning the pages, for in them we see the words of Isaiah clearly fulfilled:[4]

All prophetic vision has become for you like the words of a sealed book. Give such a book to one who can read and say 'Read this,' and he will answer, 'I cannot, for it is sealed.' Give it to one who cannot read and say, 'Read it,' and he will answer 'I cannot

1. Philippians ii, 21. 2. *Regula*, chapters 48 and 55.

3. Cato, whose apocryphal sayings were widely quoted in the Middle Ages. The Greek proverb about the ass and the lyre is quoted by St Jerome.

4. Isaiah xxix, 11 ff.

read.' Then the Lord said: 'Because these people approach me with their mouths and honour me with their lips while their hearts are far from me and their fear of me is but a precept of men, learned by rote, therefore yet again I must strike awe into the hearts of these people with some great and resounding miracle. For the wisdom of their wise men shall vanish and the discernment of the discerning shall be lost.'

In the cloister those are said to know letters who have learned to pronounce them; but as far as understanding them is concerned, those who admit they cannot read have a book given to them which is just as much sealed as it is for those whom they call illiterate. The Lord rebukes them, saying that they approach him with their mouths and lips rather than with their hearts because they are able to pronounce words after a fashion but are quite unable to understand them. Lacking knowledge of the Word of God, they follow in their obedience the custom of men, not the benefit of Scripture. Therefore the Lord threatens that even those who are reckoned learned and sit as doctors among them shall be blinded.

Jerome, the greatest doctor of the Church and glory of the monastic profession, in exhorting us to love of letters, says:[1] 'Love knowledge of letters and you will not love the vices of the flesh:' and we have learned from his own testimony how much labour and expense it cost him to learn them. Amongst other things which he writes about his own studies for the purpose of instructing us by his example, he recalls in the following passage, addressed to Pammachius and Oceanus:[2]

When I was a young man I was on fire with a marvellous love of learning. I did not teach myself, as some men are rash enough to do, but I frequently heard Apollinaris at Antioch and sat at his feet for instruction in the Holy Scriptures. My hair was already flecked with grey and I should have been a teacher rather than a pupil, yet I went on to Alexandria and heard Didymus, to whom I am grateful for much, learning from him what I did not know. Men thought I had come to an end of learning, but I returned to

1. *Epistulae* cxxv, 11. 2. *Epistulae* lxxxiv, 3.

Jerusalem and Bethlehem, and there I had Baraninas the Jew as my teacher – with what labour and expense! He taught at night, for he feared the Jews, and to me he was a second Nicodemus.

Surely Jerome had stored away in his memory what he had read in Ecclesiasticus:[1] 'My son, seek learning while you are young, and when your hair is white you will still find wisdom.'

Thus his learning not only from the words of Scripture but also through the example of the holy Fathers, has added to the wealth of tributes paid to the excellent monastery he founded one on its exceptional training in the Holy Scriptures: 'As for meditation on and understanding of the Holy Scriptures and also of sacred learning, never have we seen such a degree of training; you might suppose nearly every one of them to be a professional spokesman for sacred wisdom.'[2]

The Venerable Bede too, who had been received into a monastery as a boy, says in his *History of the English People*,[3] 'From then on I have spent the rest of my life living in the same monastery and devoted myself entirely to studying the Scriptures. While I have observed monastic discipline and sung the daily offices in church, learning and writing have always been my delight.' But those who are educated in monasteries today are so persistent in their stupidity that they are content merely with the sound of letters, pay no attention to understanding them, and care only to instruct the tongue, not the heart. They are openly rebuked in a proverb of Solomon:[4] 'A discerning man seeks knowledge, but the stupid man feeds on folly,' that is, when he takes pleasure in words he does not understand. Such men are the less able to love God and be warmed towards him, the further they keep themselves from understanding him and appreciating the Scripture that teaches us about him.

This situation we believe has arisen in monasteries mainly for two reasons: either because of jealousy on the part of the lay monks, or even of the abbots themselves, or through the

1. Ecclesiasticus vi, 18.
2. Rufinus, *Historia monachorum*, 21.
3. *Historia ecclesiastica gentis Anglorum*, 5. 24.
4. Proverbs xv, 14.

empty chatter of idleness, to which we see present-day monastic cloisters much addicted. Men like this try to attach us along with themselves to earthly rather than spiritual things, and are like the Philistines who persecuted Isaac when he was digging wells, filled them in with heaps of earth and tried to keep water from him.[1] St Gregory explains this in the sixteenth book of his *Morals*: 'Often when we try to concentrate on the word of God we are more seriously troubled by the designs of evil spirits who scatter the dust of earthly thoughts in our minds, so that they may darken the eyes of our concentration and withold the light of inward vision.' This the Psalmist had suffered greatly when he said,[2] 'Go away, you evil-doers, and I will keep the commandments of my God,' for he clearly meant that he could not keep the commandments of God when suffering in mind from the designs of evil spirits.

We understand that the same thing is meant by the wickedness of the Philistines during the work of Isaac, when they heaped earth in the wells he had dug. For we are surely digging wells when we penetrate deeply into the hidden meaning of Holy Scripture, and the Philistines secretly fill these up when they introduce the earthly thoughts of an impure spirit while we are looking towards higher things, and so take away the water of sacred learning which we have found. But no one can overcome these enemies by his own power, as we are told through Eliphaz:[3] 'The Almighty shall be your defence against your enemies, and he will be your silver heaped up.' That is, when the Lord has driven evil spirits away from you by his own power, the talent of the divine Word will shine more brightly in you. St Gregory, if I am not mistaken, had read the *Homilies* of the great Christian philosopher Origen on Genesis, and had drawn from Origen's wells what he now says about these wells. For that zealous digger of spiritual wells strongly urges us not only to drink of them but also to dig our own, as he says in the twelfth homily of his exposition:

1. Cf. Genesis xxvi, 15.
2. Psalm cxix, 115.
3. Job xxii, 25.

Let us try also to do what Wisdom bids us, saying:[1] 'Drink water from your own cistern and running water from your own spring. Let them be yours alone.' Do you then try too, my listener, to have your own well and your own spring, so that you also when you take up a book of the Scriptures may start to show some understanding of it from your own perception and in accordance with what you have learned in church. Try too to drink from the spring of your own spirit. You have within you a source of living water, the open channels and flowing streams of rational perception, so long as they are not clogged with earth and rubbish. Try to dig your ground and clear the filth from your spirit, remove idleness and inertia from your heart. Hear what Scripture says:[2] 'Hurt the eye and tears will flow; hurt the heart and you will make it sensitive.' So clean your spirit and then someday you too may drink from your own springs and draw living water from your wells. For if you have received living water from Jesus and received it with faith, it shall become in you a source of water gushing out towards everlasting life.

In the following homily Origen also says of the wells of Isaac we spoke of:

Those which the Philistines had filled with earth are surely men who close their spiritual understanding, so that they neither drink themselves nor allow others to drink. Hear the word of the Lord:[3] 'Alas for you lawyers and Pharisees! You have taken away the key of knowledge; you did not go in yourselves, and did not permit those who wished to enter.' But let us never cease from digging wells of living water, and by discussing new things as well as old, let us make ourselves like the teacher of the law in the Gospel, of whom the Lord said that he could 'produce from his store both old and new'.[4] Let us return to Isaac and dig with him wells of living water, even if the Philistines obstruct us; even if they use violence, let us carry on with our well-digging, so that to us too it may be said: 'Drink water from your own cisterns and your own wells.' And let us dig until our wells overflow with water in our courtyards, so that our knowledge of the Scriptures is not only sufficient for ourselves but we can teach others and show them how to drink. Let our flocks drink too, as the Prophet also says: 'Man and beast you will save, O Lord.'[5]

1. Proverbs v, 15; 17. 2. Ecclesiasticus xxii, 19.
3. Luke xi, 52. 4. Matthew xiii, 52. 5. Psalm xxxvi, 7.

Later on Origen says:

> He who is a Philistine and knows earthly things, does not know where in the earth to find water, where to find a rational perception. What do you gain by having learning and not knowing how to use it, having speech but being unable to speak? That is like the sons of Isaac who dig wells all over the earth for living water.

You must not be like this, but refrain altogether from idle talk, while those of you who have been given the grace of learning must work to be instructed in the things which are God's, as it is written of the happy man:[1] 'The law of the Lord is his delight, the law his meditation day and night.' And the profit which follows on his diligent application to the law of the Lord is added at once: 'And he will be like a tree planted by a watercourse,' for a dry tree is also unfruitful, because it is not watered by the streams of the words of God. Of these streams it is written that 'Rivers of living water shall flow from his bosom,'[2] and these are the streams of which the bride sings in the Canticles in praise of the bridegroom, describing him thus: 'His eyes are like doves beside brooks of water, bathed by the milky water as they sit by the flooding streams.'[3] You too, then, are bathed in milky water, that is, you are shining with the whiteness of chastity, and must sit like doves by these streams, so that by drawing from them draughts of wisdom you may be able both to learn and also to teach, and be like eyes showing a path to others, and not only seeing the bridegroom but able to describe him to others.

Of his special bride, whose glory it was to conceive him by the ear of the heart, we know it is written, 'But Mary treasured all these words and pondered over them in her heart.'[4] Thus the Mother of the Supreme Word, having his words in her heart rather than on her lips, pondered over them carefully as she considered each one separately and then compared them with each other, seeing how closely all agreed together. She knew that according to the revelation of the Law every animal is called unclean unless it chews the cud and

1. Psalm i, 2–3. 2. John vii, 38. 3. Canticles v, 12.
4. Luke ii, 19.

divides the hoof. And so no soul is clean and pure unless by meditating to the best of its ability it chews the cud of God's teachings and shows understanding in obeying them, so that it not only does good things but does them well, that is, with right intention. For division of the hoof is the mind's ability to distinguish, about which it is written: 'If you offer rightly but do not divide rightly, you have sinned.'[1]

'Anyone who loves me,' says the Truth,[2] 'will heed what I say.' But who can heed the words or precepts of the Lord by obeying them unless he has first understood them? No one will be zealous in obedience unless he has been attentive as a listener, like that blessed woman of whom we read that she put everything else aside and sat at the Lord's feet listening to his words – and listened with the ears of understanding which he himself requires, saying, 'If you have ears to hear, then hear.'[3]

Yet if you are unable to be kindled to such fervour of devotion, you can at least in your love and study of sacred Scriptures model yourselves on those blessed disciples of St Jerome, Paula and Eustochium, for it was mainly at their request that the great doctor wrote so many volumes to bring enlightenment to the Church.[4]

1. Genesis iv, 7.
2. John xiv, 23.
3. Matthew xi, 15. The woman is Mary, sister of Martha, in Luke x, 38–42.
4. The letter breaks off abruptly without the formal ending of Letter 6.

Abelard's Confession of Faith

Heloise my sister, once dear to me in the world, now dearest to me in Christ, logic has made me hated by the world. For the perverted, who seek to pervert and whose wisdom is only for destruction, say that I am supreme as a logician, but am found wanting in my understanding of Paul. They proclaim the brilliance of my intellect but detract from the purity of my Christian faith. As I see it, they have reached this judgement by conjecture rather than weight of evidence. I do not wish to be a philosopher if it means conflicting with Paul, nor to be an Aristotle if it cuts me off from Christ. For there is no other name under heaven whereby I must be saved. I adore Christ who sits on the right hand of the Father. I embrace in the arms of faith him who acts divinely in the glorious flesh of a virgin which he assumed from the Paraclete. And so, to banish fearful anxiety and all uncertainties from the heart within your breast, receive assurance from me, that I have founded my conscience on that rock on which Christ built his Church. What is written on the rock I will testify briefly.

I believe in the Father, the Son and the Holy Spirit; the true God who is one in nature; who comprises the Trinity of persons in such a way as always to preserve Unity in substance. I believe the Son to be co-equal with the Father in all things, in eternity, power, will and operation. I do not hold with Arius, who is driven by perverted intellect or led astray by demoniac influence to introduce grades into the Trinity, laying down that the Father is greater and the Son less great, forgetting the injunction of the Law, 'You shall not mount up to my altar by steps.' He mounts up to the altar of God by steps[1] who assigns first and second place in the Trinity. I bear witness that in everything the Holy Spirit is consubstantial and co-equal with the Father and the Son, and is he who, as my books often declare, is known by the name of Good-

1. Exodus xx, 26.

ness. I condemn Sabellius, who, in holding that the person of the Father is the same as that of the son, asserts that the Passion was suffered by the Father – hence his followers are called *Patripassiani*.

I believe that the Son of God became the Son of Man in such a way that one person is of and in two natures; that after he had completed the mission he had undertaken in becoming man he suffered and died and rose again, and ascended to heaven whence he will come to judge the living and the dead. I also declare that in baptism all offences are remitted, and that we need grace whereby we may begin on good and persevere in it, and that having lapsed we may be restored through penitence. But what need have I to speak of the resurrection of the body? I would pride myself on being a Christian in vain if I did not believe that I would live again.

This then is the faith on which I rest, from which I draw my strength in hope. Safely anchored on it, I do not fear the barking of Scylla, I laugh at the whirlpool of Charybdis, and have no dread of the Sirens' deadly songs.[1] The storm may rage but I am unshaken, though the winds may blow they leave me unmoved; for the rock of my foundation stands firm.[2]

1. Once more Abelard uses classical symbols, here as a means of expressing dilemmas and temptations. Cf. p. 147.

2. This confession, moving in its simplicity and the fact that it is addressed to Heloise, is preserved only in an open letter by one of Abelard's pupils, Berengar of Poitiers, violently attacking St Bernard and all Abelard's detractors at the Council of Sens. It is not known whether it was written shortly before or immediately after the Council, nor how Berengar came by it. He says it is a fragment, but it appears to be complete. The whole of Berengar's *Apologeticus* is printed in Cousin, Vol. II, pp. 771–86 (P.L. 178, 1857–70), and the *Confessio Fidei* alone in Vol. I, pp. 680–81 (P.L. 178, 375c).

Letters of Peter the Venerable and Heloise

Peter the Venerable: Letter (98)[1] *to Pope Innocent II*

To the sovereign Pope Innocent, our special father, brother Peter, humble abbot of Cluny: obedience and love.

Master Peter, well known, I believe to your Holiness, passed by Cluny recently on his way from France. We asked him where he was going. He replied that he was weighed down by the persecutions of those who accused him of heresy, a thing he abhorred, that he had appealed to papal authority and sought protection from it. We praised his intention, and urged him to make his way to that common refuge which we all know. We told him that apostolic justice has never failed anyone, be he stranger or pilgrim, and would not be denied him, and assured him that if he had real need of mercy he would find it with you.

In the meantime the lord abbot of Cîteaux arrived, and spoke with us and with him about a reconciliation between him and the abbot of Clairvaux, the reason for his appeal to you. We too did our best to restore peace, and urged him to go to Clairvaux with the abbot of Cîteaux. We further counselled him, if he had written or said anything offensive to orthodox Christian ears, to take the advice of the abbot of Cîteaux and of other wise and worthy men, curb his language and remove such expressions from his writings. This he did. He went and came back, and on his return told us that through the mediation of the abbot of Cîteaux he had made his peace with the abbot of Clairvaux and that their previous differences were settled. Meanwhile, on our advice, or rather, we believe, inspired by God, he decided to abandon the turmoil of schools and teaching and to remain permanently in your house of Cluny. We thought this a proper decision

1. This, and the following three letters are numbered according to Constable's *The Letters of Peter the Venerable.*

in view of his age and weakness and his religious calling, and believed that his learning, which is not altogether unknown to you, could be of benefit to our large community of brothers; we therefore granted his wish, and on condition that it is agreeable to your Holiness, we have willingly and gladly agreed that he shall remain with us who, as you know, are wholly your own.

And so I, your humble servant, beg you, your devoted community of Cluny begs you, and Peter himself begs this on his own part, through us, through your sons who bring this letter, and through these very words which he asked me to write: permit him to spend the remaining days of his life and old age, which perhaps will not be many, in your house of Cluny, so that no one's intervention shall be able to disturb or remove him from the home the sparrow has reached or the nest the turtle-dove is so happy to have found.[1] For the honour in which you hold all good men and the love you bear him, let the shield of your apostolic protection cover him.[2]

1. Psalm lxxxiv, 3.

2. This letter was written by Peter the Venerable to Pope Innocent the Second probably in July 1140, after Abelard's condemnation by the Council of Sens, but before the papal sentence of 16 July had reached France. It is the only evidence we have for the reconciliation between Abelard and Bernard of Clairvaux, and suggests that Peter the Venerable supported the overtures made by Abbot Rainald of Cîteaux rather than made the first move himself. The request was granted, as the next letter translated shows.

Peter the Venerable: Letter (115) to Heloise

To the venerable and greatly beloved sister in Christ, the abbess Heloise, brother Peter, humble abbot of Cluny: the salvation which God has promised those who love him.

I was happy to receive from your Grace the letter which you sent me recently[1] through my son Theobald, and took it with friendly sentiments towards the sender. I wanted to write back at once to express what was in my heart, but the persistent demands of the duties to which I am obliged to give up most, or rather, all of my time, made it impossible. Now at last there is a day's respite (scarcely that) from turmoil, when I can try to carry out my intention.[2] I thought that I should make haste to repay if only in words the affection for me I discerned in your letter, and previously from the gifts you sent me, and to show you how large a place in my heart is reserved for my love for you in the Lord. For in fact it is not only now that I begin to love you; I can remember having done so for a long time. I had yet not quite passed the bounds of youth and reached early manhood when I knew of your name and your reputation, not yet for religion but for your virtuous and praiseworthy studies. I used to hear at that time of the woman who although still caught up in the obligations of the world, devoted all her application to knowledge of letters, something which is very rare, and to the pursuit of secular learning, and that not even the pleasures of the world, with its frivolities and delights, could distract her from this worthy determination to study the arts. At a time when nearly the whole world is indifferent and deplorably apathetic towards such occupations, and wisdom can scarcely find a foothold not only, I may say, among women who have

1. This letter does not survive.

2. Abelard died on 21 April 1142, but as Peter the Venerable is known to have been travelling to Spain at the time, his reply must have been written in 1143 at the earliest.

banished her completely, but even in the minds of men, you have surpassed all women in carrying out your purpose, and have gone further than almost every man.

Later on when, in the Apostle's words,[1] 'It pleased God who had set you apart since you were in your mother's womb to call you through his grace', you turned your zeal for learning in a far better direction, and as a woman wholly dedicated to philosophy in the true sense, you left logic for the Gospel, Plato for Christ, the academy for the cloister. You removed the spoils from your vanquished foe, crossed the desert of life's pilgrimage with the treasures of Egypt, and set up a precious tabernacle to God in your heart. With Miriam you sang a hymn of praise as Pharaoh sank beneath the waves,[2] like her in days of old, you took up the tambourine of blessed mortification, so that your skill with it sent the strain of new harmonies to the very ears of God. Now you trod underfoot what at the start you wore down by perseverance through the grace of the Almighty – the head of the serpent, the old enemy who always lies in wait for women – and crushed it so that it will never dare to hiss against you again. You make and will continue to make a laughing-stock of the proud prince of the world, and him whom the divine voice, in the words of God himself on the lips of holy Job, calls 'the King of the sons of pride',[3] you will force to groan when he is enchained for you and the handmaids of God who live with you.

Truly a unique miracle, one to be exalted above all marvellous works, for him of whom the prophet says[4] 'No cedar in God's garden overshadowed it, and no firs could equal the height of its boughs' to be overcome by the weaker sex, and the most powerful of archangels to fall before a frail woman! Such a combat brings supreme glory to the Creator, but to the Tempter the greatest ignominy. This contest proves to his shame that it was not only foolish but above all absurd for him to have aspired to equality with the sublime Majesty, when he cannot even sustain a brief conflict with a

1. Galatians i, 15. 2. Exodus xv, 20. 3. Cf. Job xli, 25.
4. Ezekiel xxxi, 8.

woman's weakness; while she, alone victorious, will justly receive for her brow a jewelled crown from the King of heaven, so that though she was weaker in the flesh, in the battle she fought she will appear the more glorious in her everlasting reward.

I say this not to flatter you, my sister, dearest in the Lord, but by way of encouraging you to awareness of the great benefit you have long enjoyed; so that you will be the more eager to preserve it with due care, and the holy women who serve the Lord with you, through God's grace conferred on you, may be fired by your word and example to join eagerly in the same struggle. For you are one of those animals in the vision of the prophet Ezekiel,[1] woman though you are, and must not only burn like coal but glow like a lamp and give light as well. You are indeed the disciple of truth, but in your duty towards those entrusted to you, you are the teacher of humility. For surely the teaching of humility and of all instruction in heavenly matters is a task laid on you by God, and so you must have a care not only for yourself but for the flock in your keeping; and being responsible for all shall receive a higher reward than theirs. Yes, the palm is reserved for you on behalf of the whole community, for, as you must know, all those who, by following your lead, have overcome the world and the prince of the world, will prepare for you as many triumphs and glorious trophies before the eternal King and Judge.

Moreover, it is not altogether exceptional amongst mortals for women to be in command of women, nor entirely unprecedented for them even to take up arms and accompany men to battle. For if there is truth in the saying:

> Even from a foe it is right to learn,[2]

amongst the pagans it is recorded that Penthesilea, queen of the Amazons, often fought at the time of the Trojan War along with her army of Amazons,[3] who were women, not

1. Ezekiel i, 13–14.
2. Ovid, *Metamorphoses*, 4, 428. Cf. Letter 7, p. 225.
3. Penthesilea is probably known to Peter from Virgil's *Aeneid*.

men, while from God's chosen people the prophetess Deborah is said to have roused Barach, a judge in Israel, against the heathen.[1] Why then should not virtuous women also march to battle against the armed foe, become leaders in the army of the Lord, if Penthesilea could fight the enemy with her own hand, in defiance of convention, and our Deborah roused, armed and spurred on the men of Israel to fight God's wars? Then when Jobin the King was defeated, Sisera his commander lay dead, and the heathen army was destroyed, she sang at once the song she wrote in devout praise of God. For you and yours, after the victory granted by God's grace over a far more formidable foe, there will be a far more glorious song, which you will so rejoice to sing that ever afterwards you will continue to sing it and rejoice. Meanwhile you will be for the handmaids of God, your heavenly army, what Deborah was for the Jewish people; whatever happens, you will never break off the battle for which the reward is so high until victory is yours. And because the name of Deborah, as your learning knows, means 'bee' in the Hebrew tongue, you will be a Deborah in this respect too, that is, a bee. For you will make honey, but not only for yourself; since all the goodness you have gathered here and there in different ways, by your example, word, and every possible means, you will pour out for the sisters in your house and for all other women. In this brief span of our mortal life you will satisfy yourself with the hidden sweetness of the Holy Scriptures, as also your fortunate sisters by your public instruction, until, in the words of the prophet,[2] on that promised day 'the mountains shall run with sweetness and the hills flow with milk'. For though this is said of the time of grace to come, nothing prevents it from being applied to an hour of glory and, indeed, it is pleasanter to take it thus.

It would also be pleasant for me to talk with you like this for longer, both because I am delighted by your renowned learning, and far more because I am drawn to you by what many have told me about your religion. If only our Cluny possessed you, or you were confined in the delightful prison

1. Judges iv, 9 ff. 2. Joel iii, 18.

of Marcigny[1] with the other handmaids of Christ who are there awaiting their freedom in heaven! I would have preferred your wealth of religion and learning to the richest treasures of any kings, and would rejoice to see that noble community of sisters still further illuminated by your presence there. You too would have derived no small benefit from them, and would have marvelled to see the highest nobility and pride of the world trodden underfoot. You would see every kind of worldly luxury exchanged for a wonderful poverty of life, and the former impure vessels of the devil turned into spotless temples for the Holy Spirit. You would observe those young girls of God stolen, as it were, from Satan and the world, building high walls of virtue in the foundation of their innocence, and raising the summit of their blessed edifice to the very threshold of heaven. You would rejoice to see them in the flower of their angelic virginity united with chaste widows, all alike awaiting the glory of that great and blessed Resurrection, their bodies confined within the narrow walls of their house as if buried in a tomb of blessed hope. Yet since you may have all these joys, and perhaps greater things than these in the companions given you by God, it may be that nothing can be added as regards your zeal for holy matters; but our own community would be enriched by no small advantage, I think, from the addition of your own gracious gifts.

But although God's providence which dispenses all things has denied us your presence, we have still been granted that of him who was yours, him, I say, who is often and ever to be named and honoured as the servant and true philosopher of Christ, Master Peter, whom in the last years of his life that same providence sent to Cluny, and by doing so enriched her in his person with a gift more precious than any gold and topaz.[2] The nature and extent of the saintliness, humility and devotion of his life among us, to which Cluny

1. Marcigny was a famous Cluniac nunnery in the diocese of Autun near Semur-en-Brionnais, which Peter's mother Raingard had entered after her husband's death about 1117. Cf. his Letter 53.

2. Cf. Psalm cxix, 127.

can bear witness, cannot briefly be told. I do not remember seeing anyone, I think, who was his equal in conduct and manner: St Germain could not have appeared more lowly nor St Martin himself so poor. And although at my insistence he held superior rank in our large community of brothers, the shabbiness of his attire made him look the humblest of them all. I often marvelled, and when he walked in front of me with the others in the usual processional order, I almost stood still in astonishment that a man who bore so great and distinguished a name could thus humble and abase himself. And because some who profess the religious life want unnecessary extravagance even in the habits they wear, he was completely frugal in such matters, content with a simple garment of each sort, seeking nothing more.

He was the same as regards food and drink and anything for his bodily needs, and condemned by word and by his living example, for himself as well as for others, not merely what was superfluous, but everything except the barest necessities. His reading was continuous, his prayer assiduous, his silence perpetual, except when informal conference amongst the brothers or a public sermon addressed to them in assembly on sacred subjects compelled him to speak. He was present at the holy Sacraments, offering the sacrifice of the immortal Lamb to God whenever he could, and indeed, almost without interruption, after he had been restored to apostolic grace through my letter and efforts on his behalf. What more need I say? His mind, his speech, his work were devoted to meditation, to teaching and to profession of what was always holy, philosophic and scholarly.

In such a way this simple, upright man lived among us, fearing God and shunning evil; and in this way, I repeat, he stayed for some time, dedicating the last days of his life to God, until I sent him to Chalon to give him respite, since he was more troubled than usual from skin-irritation and other physical ailments. I believed this would be a suitable place for him, near the city on the opposite bank of the Saône, because of its mild climate which is about the best in our part of Burgundy.[1] There he renewed his former studies, as far as his ill-health permitted, and was always bent over his books; and as it is said of Gregory the Great, he never let a moment pass without praying, reading, writing or composing.[2]

He was engaged on such holy occupations when the Visitor of the Gospels came to find him, and found him awake, not asleep like so many; found him truly awake, and summoned him to the wedding of eternal life as a wise, not a foolish virgin. For he brought with him a lamp full of oil, that is, a conscience filled with the testimony of his saintly life. As the time came for him to pay the common debt of humanity, the sickness from which he suffered worsened and quickly brought him to his last hour. Then he first professed his faith, afterwards confessed his sins, and indeed in so holy, devout and Christian a manner; with such eagerness of heart he received the viaticum for his journey and the pledge of eternal life, the body of our Lord and Redeemer; to him he commended his body and soul here on earth and for eternity with such true faith: as all his brothers in religion and the whole community of the monastery where the body of St Marcellus the martyr lies can bear witness.

Thus did Master Peter end his days. He who was known nearly all over the world for his unique mastery of knowledge and who won fame everywhere as a disciple of one who said[3] 'Learn from me, for I am gentle and humble-hearted,' steadfast in his own gentleness and humility, thus passed over to him, as we must believe. Him, therefore, venerable and dearest sister in the Lord, him to whom after your union in the

1. This was the Cluniac priory of St Marcel (Marcellus) at Chalon-sur-Saône. Abelard suffered from *scabies*, amongst other things, a term which could apply to various forms of skin disease or irritation accompanying other complaints. The most recent suggestion is that he had been suffering for some time from leukaemia or Hodgkin's disease, that he was having a severe attack when he could not bring himself to face Bernard at the Council of Sens, but afterwards had remission at Cluny.

2. In fact none of Abelard's known works can be dated to the eighteen months he spent at Cluny and St Marcel. See Introduction, p. 42.

3. Matthew xi, 29.

flesh you are joined by the better, and therefore stronger, bond of divine love, with whom and under whom you have long served God: him, I say, in your place, or as another you, God cherishes in his bosom, and keeps him there to be restored to you through his grace at the coming of the Lord, at the voice of the archangel, and the trumpet-note of God descending from heaven. Remember him in the Lord, remember me too, if you are pleased to do so, and duly commend to the prayers of the sisters serving God with you the brothers of our community, and also the sisters throughout the world who, to the best of their ability, serve the same Lord as you.

Heloise: Letter (167) to Peter the Venerable

To Peter, most reverend lord and father and venerable abbot of Cluny, Heloise, God's and his humble servant: the spirit of grace and salvation.

The mercy of God came down to us in the grace of a visit from your Reverence. We are filled with pride and rejoicing, gracious father, because your greatness has descended to our lowliness, for a visitation from you is a matter for great rejoicing even for the great. Others are well aware of the great benefits conferred on them by the presence of your sublimity but, for my own part, I cannot even formulate my thoughts, much less find words for what a benefit and joy your coming was to me. Our abbot and Lord, on the 16th November of the past year[1] you celebrated a Mass here in which you commended us to the Holy Spirit. In Chapter you fed us by preaching the word of God. You gave us the body of our master and so yielded up the privilege which belonged to Cluny. To me too, whom (unworthy as I am to be called your servant) your sublime humility has not disdained to address as sister in writing and speech, you granted a rare privilege in token of your love and sincerity: a trental of masses[2] to be said on my behalf by the abbey of Cluny after my death. You also said that you would confirm this gift in a letter under seal.

Fulfil then, my brother or rather, my lord, what you promised to your sister, or I should say, to your servant. May it please you too to send me also under seal an open document containing the absolution of our master, to be hung on his tomb. Remember also, for the love of God, our Astralabe and yours,[3] so that you may obtain for him some prebend either from the bishop of Paris or in some other diocese. Farewell; may the Lord keep you, and sometimes grant us your presence.

1. i.e. November 1143. See Letter 115, note 2, p. 277.

2. i.e. a series of thirty masses for the repose of a soul.

3. Astralabe was born about 1118 and would now be twenty-six or twenty-seven. What the suggested connection was between him and Peter the Venerable is not clear, but see p. 287.

Peter the Venerable: Letter (168) to Heloise

To our venerable and dearest sister in Christ, the handmaid of God, Heloise, guide and mistress of the handmaids of God, brother Peter, humble abbot of Cluny: the fullness of God's salvation and of our love in Christ.

I was happy, very happy, to read the letter from your Sanctity, where I learned that my visit to you was no transitory call, and which made me realize that I have not only been with you, but in spirit have never really left you. My stay, I see, was not one to be remembered as that of a passing guest for a single night, nor was I treated as 'a stranger and a foreigner among you', but as 'a fellow-citizen of God's people and member of God's household.'[1] Everything I said and did on that fleeting or flying visit of mine has remained so firmly in your holy mind and made such an impression on your gracious spirit that, to say nothing of my carefully-chosen phrases on that occasion, not even a chance, unconsidered word of mine fell to the ground unheeded. You noted all, you committed all to your retentive memory in the warmth of your unbounded sincerity, as if all were the mighty, the heavenly, the sacrosanct words or deeds of Jesus Christ himself. You may have been prompted to remember them in this way by the injunctions on receiving guests in our common Rule, which belongs to us both: 'Let Christ be worshipped in them, who is received in their persons.'[2] Perhaps you were also reminded of the Lord's words concerning those given authority, though I have no authority over you: 'Whoever listens to you listens to me.'[3]

May I ever be granted this grace from you: that you will think me worthy to be remembered, and will pray for the mercy of the Almighty upon me, along with the holy com-

1. Genesis xxiii, 4; Ephesians ii, 19.
2. *Regula*, chapter 53. 3. Luke x, 16.

munity of the flock entrusted to your care. I am repaying you now as far as I can, for long before I saw you, and particularly since I have come to know you, I have kept for you in the innermost depths of my heart a special place of real and true affection. I am therefore sending you, now that I have left you, a ratification of the gift of a trental I made you in person, in writing and under seal, as you wished. I am also sending the absolution for Master Peter you asked for, similarly written on parchment and sealed. As soon as I have an opportunity, I will gladly do my best to obtain a prebend in one of the great churches for your Astralabe, who is also ours for your sake. It will not be easy, for the bishops, as I have often found, are apt to show themselves extremely difficult when occasions have arisen for them to give prebends in their churches. But for your sake I will do what I can as soon as I can.[1]

1. It is not known whether Peter the Venerable was successful on behalf of Astralabe, nor what became of him. He is never mentioned by Heloise in her letters to Abelard, and Abelard's only reference to him (outside the *Historia calamitatum*) is in the verses of advice addressed to him and thought to have been written about 1135. See Introduction, p. 42. His death-day is recorded in the necrology of the Paraclete as 29 or 30 October and he is named there as *Petrus Astralabius magistri nostri Petri filius*, but no year is given. An Astralabe is on record as a canon of the Cathedral of Nantes in the year 1150, and another as abbot of a Cistercian abbey at Hauterive in the Swiss canton of Fribourg, but it is uncertain if either refers to him. See McLeod, op. cit., pp. 253 and 283–4.

The Absolution for Peter Abelard[1]

I, Peter, Abbot of Cluny, who received Peter Abelard as a monk of Cluny, and gave his body, removed in secret, to the Abbess Heloise and the nuns of the Paraclete, by the authority of Almighty God and of all the saints, in virtue of my office, absolve him from all his sins.

1. The text is printed by Cousin, Vol. 1, p. 717, who took it from the notes written by André Duchesne to the edition of the Letters of Peter the Venerable published in Paris in 1614, but it cannot be traced in the records of the Paraclete.

Two Hymns by Abelard

Sabbato ad Vesperas

O quanta qualia
  sunt illa sabbata,
quae semper celebrat
  superna curia
quae fessis requies,
  quae merces fortibus,
cum erit omnia
  deus in omnibus.

Vera Jerusalem
  est illa civitas
cuius pax iugis est
  summa iucunditas:
ubi non praevenit
  rem desiderium,
nec desiderio
  minus est praemium.

Quis Rex, quae curia,
  quale palatium,
quae pax, quae requies,
  quod illud gaudium,
huius participes
  exponant gloriae,
si quantum sentiunt
  possint exprimere.

Nostrum est interim
  mentem erigere
et totis patriam
  votis appetere,
et ad Jerusalem
  a Babylonia
post longa regredi
  tandem exsilia.

Vespers: Saturday Evening

How mighty are the Sabbaths,
  How mighty and how deep,
That the high courts of heaven
  To everlasting keep.
What peace unto the weary,
  What pride unto the strong,
When God in whom are all things
  Shall be all things to men.

Jerusalem is the city
  Of everlasting peace,
A peace that is surpassing
  And utter blessedness;
Where finds the dreamer waking
  Truth beyond dreaming far,
Nor is the heart's possessing
  Less than the heart's desire.

But of the courts of heaven
  And him who is the King,
The rest and the refreshing,
  The joy that is therein,
Let those that know it answer
  Who in that bliss have part,
If any word can utter
  The fullness of the heart.

But ours, with minds uplifted
  Unto the heights of God,
With our whole heart's desiring,
  To take the homeward road,
And the long exile over,
  Captive in Babylon,
Again unto Jerusalem,
  To win at last return.

Illic, molestiis
  finitis omnibus,
securi cantica
  Sion cantabimus,
et iuges gratias
  de donis gratiae
beata referet
  plebs tibi, Domine.

Illic ex Sabbato
  succedit Sabbatum,
perpes laetitia
  sabbatizantium,
nec ineffabiles
  cessabunt iubili,
quos decantabimus
  et nos et angeli.

Perenni Domino
  perpes sit gloria,
ex quo sunt, per quem sunt,
  in quo sunt omnia.
ex quo sunt, Pater est,
  per quem sunt, Filius,
in quo sunt, Patris et
  Filii Spiritus.

Text in P.L. 178, 1786–8; Cousin, Vol. I, p. 306.

There, all vexation ended,
  And from all grieving free,
We sing the song of Zion
  In deep security.
And everlasting praises
  For all thy gifts of grace
Rise from thy happy people,
  Lord of our blessedness.

There Sabbath unto Sabbath
  Succeeds eternally,
The joy that has no ending
  Of souls in holiday.
And never shall the rapture
  Beyond all mortal ken
Cease from the eternal chorus
  That angels sing with men.

Now to the King Eternal
  Be praise eternally,
From whom are all things, by whom
  And in whom all things be.
From whom, as from the Father,
  By whom, as by the Son,
In whom, as in the Spirit,
  Father and Son in one.

Translated by Helen Waddell, *Mediaeval Latin Lyrics*, pp. 175–7.

In Parasceve Domini: III. Nocturno

Solus ad victimam procedis, Domine,
morti te offerens quam venis tollere:
quid nos miserrimi possumus dicere
qui quae commisimus scimus te luere?

Nostra sunt, Domine, nostra sunt crimina:
quid tua criminum facis supplicia?
quibus sic compati fac nostra pectora,
ut vel compassio digna sit venia.

Nox ista flebilis praesensque triduum
quod demorabitur fletus sit vesperum,
donec laetitiae mane gratissimum
surgente Domino sit maestis redditum.

Tu tibi compati sic fac nos, Domine,
tuae participes ut simus gloriae;
sic praesens triduum in luctu ducere,
ut risum tribuas paschalis gratiae.

G. M. Drèves, *Petri Abaelardi Peripatetici Palatini Hymnaris Paraclitensis*, p. 109.

Good Friday: the Third Nocturn

Alone to sacrifice thou goest, Lord,
  Giving thyself to death whom thou hast slain.
For us thy wretched folk is any word,
  Who know that for our sins this is thy pain?

For they are ours, O Lord, our deeds, our deeds,
  Why must thou suffer torture for our sin?
Let our hearts suffer for thy passion, Lord,
  That sheer compassion may thy mercy win.

This is that night of tears, the three days' space,
  Sorrow abiding of the eventide,
Until the day break with the risen Christ,
  And hearts that sorrowed shall be satisfied.

So may our hearts have pity on thee, Lord,
  That they may sharers of thy glory be:
Heavy with weeping may the three days pass,
  To win the laughter of thine Easter Day.

Translation by Helen Waddell, *Mediaeval Latin Lyrics*, p. 179.

Select Bibliography

Christopher Brooke, *The Twelfth Century Renaissance*, Thames & Hudson, London, 1969.

Charlotte Charrier, *Héloïse dans l'histoire et la legende*, Paris, 1933.

M. Chibnall, ed. and trans., John of Salisbury, *Historia pontificalis*, Edinburgh, 1956.

Giles Constable, *The Letters of Peter the Venerable*, 2 vols., Harvard, Cambridge, Massachusetts, 1967.

Victor Cousin, *Petri Abaelardi opera*, 2 vols., Paris, 1849.

E. Gilson, *Heloise and Abelard*, Hollis & Carter, London, 1953.

Leif Grane, *Peter Abelard*, Allen & Unwin, London, 1970.

Elizabeth Hamilton, *Héloïse*, Hodder & Stoughton, London, 1966.

Bruno Scott James, ed. and trans., *The Letters of St Bernard of Clairvaux*, Burns & Oates, London, 1953.

The Jerusalem Bible, Darton, Longman & Todd, London, 1968.

Marcel Jouhandeau, *Lettres d'Héloïse* (ed. French translation by Octave Gréard, 1875), Armand Colin, Paris, 1959.

David Knowles, *The Evolution of Medieval Thought*, Longmans, London, 1962.

From Pachomius to Ignatius, Clarendon Press, Oxford, 1966.

Ronald Knox, *The Holy Bible*: a translation from the Latin Vulgate, Burns & Oates, London, 1955.

Gordon Leff, *Medieval Thought: St Augustine to Ockham*, Penguin Books, London, 1958.

D. E. Luscombe, *Peter Abelard's 'Ethics'*, Oxford University Press, 1971.

The School of Peter Abelard, Cambridge University Press, 1969.

Justin McCann, ed. and trans., *The Rule of St Benedict*, Burns & Oates, London, 1952.

Enid McCleod, *Héloïse*, 2nd edn, Chatto & Windus, London, 1971.

Mary M. McLaughlin, 'Abelard as Autiobiographer: The Motives and Meaning of his *Story of Calamities*', in *Speculum*, Vol XLII (1967), pp. 463–88.

Historia calamitatum and Letters 1–7, ed. J. T. Muckle and T. P. McLaughlin, *Mediaeval Studies*, Vols. XII, XV, XVII, XVIII, Pontifical Institute of Mediaeval Studies, Toronto, 1950, 1953, 1955, 1956.

J. Monfrin, *Historia calamitatum: texte critique avec introduction*, Paris, 1962.

George Moore, *Heloise and Abelard* (a novel), Heinemann, London, 1921.

H. Morten, ed., *The Love Letters of Abelard and Heloise* (John Hughes's paraphrase of 1714), J. M. Dent, London, 1901; 10th edn, 1937.

J. T. Muckle, trans., *The Story of Abelard's Adversities*, Toronto, 1964.

A. Victor Murray, *Abelard and St Bernard*, Manchester University Press, 1967.

The New English Bible, Oxford University Press and Cambridge University Press, 1970.

Zoë Oldenbourg, *Saint Bernard*, Editions Albin Michel, Paris, 1970.

Erwin Panofsky, 'Abbot Suger of St-Denis' in *Meaning in the Visual Arts*, Penguin Books, London, 1970.

Patrologia Latina, Vol. 178 (J. P. Migne), Paris, 1855.

Régine Pernoud, *Héloïse et Abélard*, Paris, 1970.

F. J. E. Raby, ed., *The Oxford Book of Medieval Latin Verse*, 2nd edn, Oxford University Press, 1959.

H. Rashdall, *The Universities of Europe in the Middle Ages*, Vol. I, Oxford University Press, 1895.

H. W. Robbins, ed., and trans., *The Romance of the Rose*, E. P. Dutton, New York, 1962.

J. G. Sikes, *Peter Abailard*, Cambridge University Press, 1932.

C. K. Scott Moncrieff, *The Letters of Abelard and Heloise*, Guy Chapman, London, 1925.

Beryl Smalley, *The Study of the Bible in the Middle Ages*, 2nd edn, Blackwell, Oxford, 1952.

R. W. Southern, *The Making of the Middle Ages*, Hutchinson, London, 1967.

'The Letters of Abelard and Heloise' in *Medieval Humanism and Other Studies*, Blackwell, Oxford, 1970.

Western Society and the Church in the Middle Ages (Vol. 2 of The Pelican History of the Church), Penguin Books, London, 1970.

Helen Waddell, *Mediaeval Latin Lyrics*, 4th edn, Penguin Books, London, 1952.

Peter Abélard (a novel), Constable, London, 1933.

Philippe Wolff, *The Awakening of Europe*, Penguin Books, London, 1968.

Maps

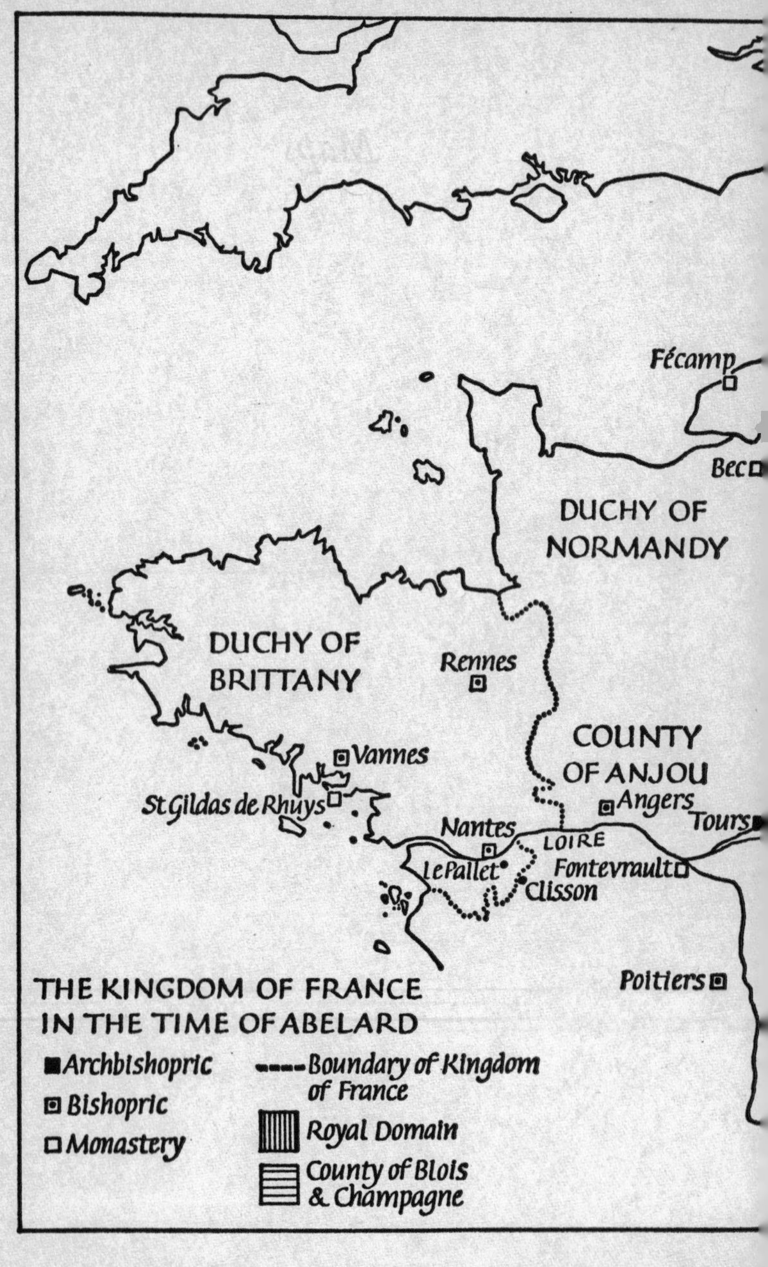
Fécamp
Bec
DUCHY OF NORMANDY
DUCHY OF BRITTANY
Rennes
COUNTY OF ANJOU
Vannes
St Gildas de Rhuys
Angers
Tours
Nantes
LOIRE
Le Pallet
Fontevrault
Clisson
Poitiers
THE KINGDOM OF FRANCE IN THE TIME OF ABELARD
Archbishopric
Bishopric
Monastery
Boundary of Kingdom of France
Royal Domain
County of Blois & Champagne

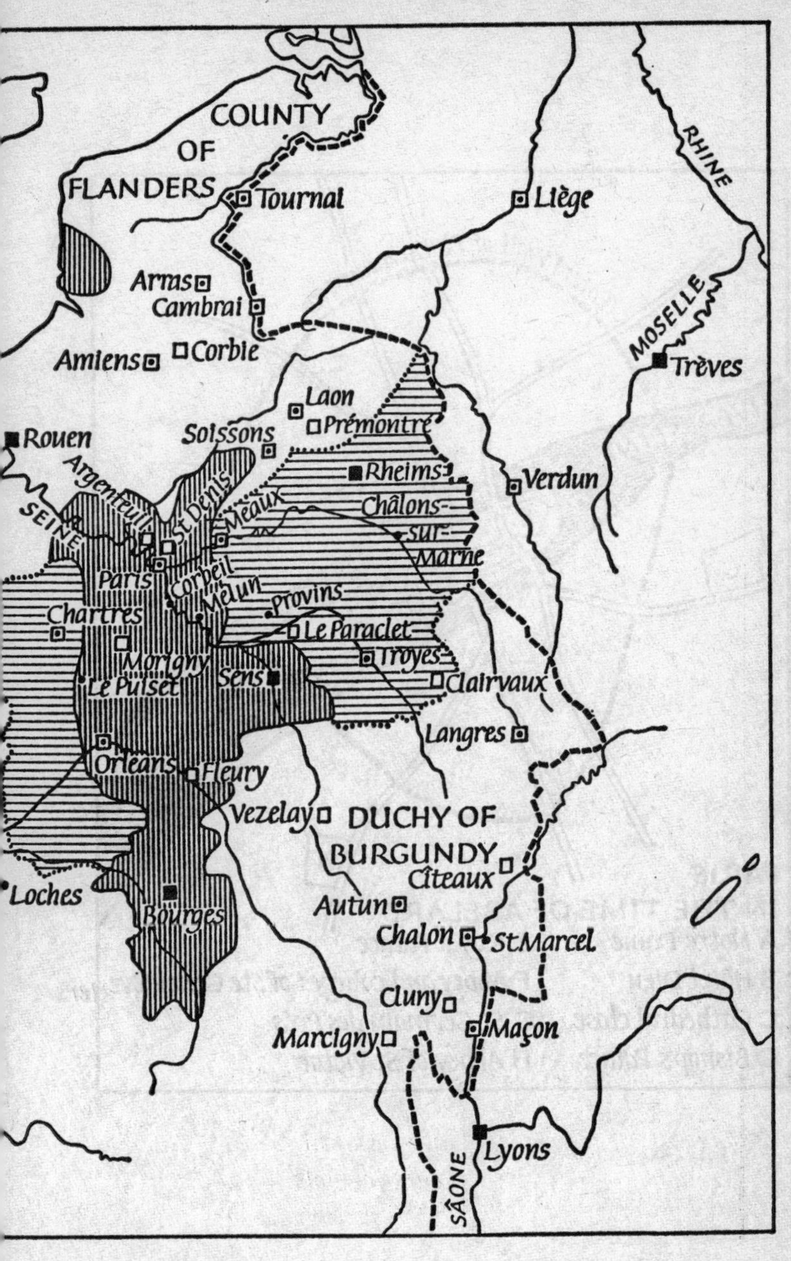
COUNTY OF FLANDERS
Tournai
Liège
RHINE
Arras
Cambrai
MOSELLE
Amiens
Corbie
Trèves
Laon
Prémontré
Rouen
Soissons
Argenteuil
St Denis
Rheims
Verdun
SEINE
Meaux
Châlons-sur-Marne
Paris
Corbeil
Melun
Provins
Chartres
Le Paraclet
Morigny
Troyes
Le Puiset
Sens
Clairvaux
Langres
Orleans
Fleury
Vezelay
DUCHY OF BURGUNDY
Cîteaux
Loches
Autun
Bourges
Chalon
St Marcel
Cluny
Maçon
Marcigny
Lyons
SÂONE

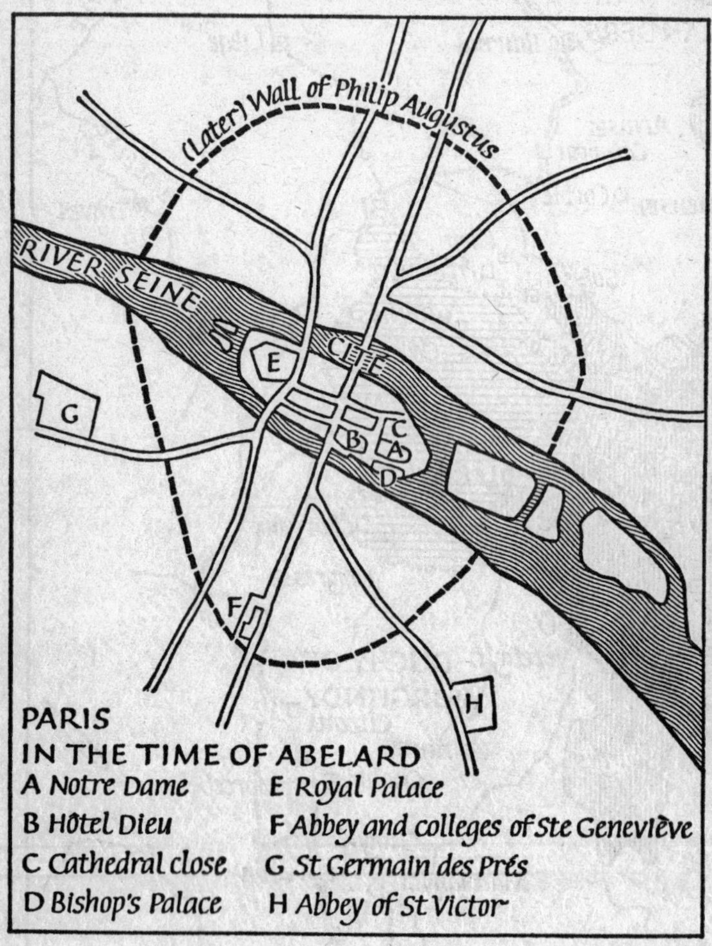
(Later) Wall of Philip Augustus
RIVER SEINE
CITÉ
E
G
C
B
A
D
F
H
PARIS
IN THE TIME OF ABELARD
A Notre Dame
B Hôtel Dieu
C Cathedral close
D Bishop's Palace
E Royal Palace
F Abbey and colleges of Ste Geneviève
G St Germain des Prés
H Abbey of St Victor

Index

FOR THE BEST IN PAPERBACKS, LOOK FOR THE 

Penguin Twentieth-Century Classics offer a selection of the finest works of literature published this century. Spanning the globe from Argentina to America, from France to India, the masters of prose and poetry are represented by the Penguin.

If you would like a catalogue of the Twentieth-Century Classics library, please write to:

Penguin Marketing, 27 Wrights Lane, London W8 5TZ

(Available while stocks last)

PENGUIN CLASSICS

Bashō	**The Narrow Road to the Deep North**
	On Love and Barley
Cao Xueqin	**The Story of the Stone** *also known as* The Dream of the Red Chamber (in five volumes)
Confucius	**The Analects**
Khayyam	**The Ruba'iyat of Omar Khayyam**
Lao Tzu	**Tao Te Ching**
Li Po/Tu Fu	**Li Po and Tu Fu**
Sei Shōnagon	**The Pillow Book of Sei Shōnagon**

ANTHOLOGIES AND ANONYMOUS WORKS

The Bhagavad Gita
Buddhist Scriptures
The Dhammapada
Hindu Myths
The Koran
New Songs from a Jade Terrace
The Rig Veda
Speaking of Śiva
Tales from the Thousand and One Nights
The Upanishads

PENGUIN CLASSICS

Plautus	**The Pot of Gold/The Prisoners/ The Brothers Menaechmus/ The Swaggering Soldier/Pseudolus**
	The Rope/Amphitryo/The Ghost/ A Three-Dollar Day
Pliny	**The Letters of the Younger Pliny**
Plutarch	**The Age of Alexander** (Nine Greek Lives)
	The Fall of the Roman Republic (Six Lives)
	The Makers of Rome (Nine Lives)
	The Rise and Fall of Athens (Nine Greek Lives)
	Plutarch on Sparta
Polybius	**The Rise of the Roman Empire**
Procopius	**The Secret History**
Propertius	**The Poems**
Quintus Curtius Rufus	**The History of Alexander**
Sallust	**The Jugurthine War** and **The Conspiracy of Cataline**
Seneca	**Four Tragedies** and **Octavia**
	Letters from a Stoic
Sophocles	**Electra/Women of Trachis/Philoctetes/Ajax**
	The Theban Plays (King Oedipus/Oedipus at Colonus/Antigone)
Suetonius	**The Twelve Caesars**
Tacitus	**The Agricola** and **The Germania**
	The Annals of Imperial Rome
	The Histories
Terence	**The Comedies (The Girl from Andros/The Self-Tormentor/The Eunuch/Phormio/The Mother-in-Law/The Brothers)**
Thucydides	**The History of the Peloponnesian War**
Virgil	**The Aeneid**
	The Eclogues
	The Georgics
Xenophon	**Conversations of Socrates**
	A History of My Times
	The Persian Expedition

FOR THE BEST IN PAPERBACKS, LOOK FOR THE

PENGUIN CLASSICS

ANTHOLOGIES AND ANONYMOUS WORKS

The Age of Bede
Alfred the Great
Beowulf
A Celtic Miscellany
The Cloud of Unknowing and Other Works
The Death of King Arthur
The Earliest English Poems
Early Irish Myths and Sagas
Egil's Saga
The Letters of Abelard and Heloise
Medieval English Verse
Njal's Saga
Seven Viking Romances
Sir Gawain and the Green Knight
The Song of Roland